Hornbook Series

and

Black Letter Series

of

WEST PUBLISHING COMPANY

P.O. Box 64526

St. Paul, Minnesota 55164

Accounting

FARIS' ACCOUNTING AND LAW IN A NUTSHELL, 377 pages, 1984. Softcover. (Text)

Administrative Law

AMAN AND MAYTON'S HORNBOOK ON ADMINISTRATIVE LAW, Approximately 750 pages, 1993. (Text)

GELLHORN AND LEVIN'S ADMINISTRATIVE LAW AND PROCESS IN A NUTSHELL, Third Edition, 479 pages, 1990. Softcover. (Text)

Admiralty

MARAIST'S ADMIRALTY IN A NUTSHELL, Second Edition, 379 pages, 1988. Softcover. (Text)

SCHOENBAUM'S HORNBOOK ON ADMIRALTY AND MARITIME LAW, Student Edition, 692 pages, 1987 with 1992 pocket part. (Text)

Agency—Partnership

REUSCHLEIN AND GREGORY'S HORNBOOK ON THE LAW OF AGENCY AND PARTNERSHIP, Second Edition, 683 pages, 1990. (Text)

STEFFEN'S AGENCY-PARTNERSHIP IN A NUTSHELL, 364 pages, 1977. Softcover. (Text)

NOLAN–HALEY'S ALTERNATIVE DISPUTE RESOLUTION IN A NUTSHELL, 298 pages, 1992. Softcover. (Text)

RISKIN'S DISPUTE RESOLUTION FOR LAWYERS VIDEO TAPES, 1992. (Available for purchase by schools and libraries.)

American Indian Law

CANBY'S AMERICAN INDIAN LAW IN A NUTSHELL, Second Edition, 336 pages, 1988. Softcover. (Text)

Antitrust—see also Regulated Industries, Trade Regulation

GELLHORN'S ANTITRUST LAW AND ECONOMICS IN A NUTSHELL, Third Edition, 472 pages, 1986. Softcover. (Text)

HOVENKAMP'S BLACK LETTER ON ANTITRUST, Second Edition approximately 325 pages, April 1993 Pub. Softcover. (Review)

HOVENKAMP'S HORNBOOK ON ECONOMICS AND FEDERAL ANTITRUST LAW, Student Edition, 414 pages, 1985. (Text)

SULLIVAN'S HORNBOOK OF THE LAW OF ANTITRUST, 886 pages, 1977. (Text)

Appellate Advocacy—see Trial and Appellate Advocacy

Art Law

DUBOFF'S ART LAW IN A NUTSHELL, Second Edition, approximately 325 pages, 1993. Softcover. (Text)

Banking Law

LOVETT'S BANKING AND FINANCIAL INSTITUTIONS LAW IN A NUTSHELL, Third Edition, 470 pages, 1992. Softcover. (Text)

Civil Procedure—see also Federal Jurisdiction and Procedure

CLERMONT'S BLACK LETTER ON CIVIL PROCEDURE, Third Edition, approximately 350 pages, May, 1993 Pub. Softcover. (Review)

FRIEDENTHAL, KANE AND MILLER'S HORNBOOK ON CIVIL PROCEDURE, Second Edition, approximately 1000 pages, May 1993 Pub. (Text)

KANE'S CIVIL PROCEDURE IN A NUTSHELL, Third Edition, 303 pages, 1991. Softcover. (Text)

KOFFLER AND REPPY'S HORNBOOK ON COMMON LAW PLEADING, 663 pages, 1969. (Text)

SIEGEL'S HORNBOOK ON NEW YORK PRACTICE, Second Edition, Student Edition, 1068 pages, 1991. Softcover. (Text) 1992 Supplemental Pamphlet.

SLOMANSON AND WINGATE'S CALIFORNIA CIVIL PROCEDURE IN A NUTSHELL, 230 pages, 1992. Softcover. (Text)

Commercial Law

BAILEY AND HAGEDORN'S SECURED TRANSACTIONS IN A NUTSHELL, Third Edition, 390 pages, 1988. Softcover. (Text)

HENSON'S HORNBOOK ON SECURED TRANSACTIONS UNDER THE U.C.C., Second Edition, 504

Commercial Law—Continued

pages, 1979, with 1979 pocket part. (Text)

MEYER AND SPEIDEL'S BLACK LETTER ON SALES AND LEASES OF GOODS, Approximately 300 pages, 1993. Softcover. (Review)

NICKLES' BLACK LETTER ON COMMERCIAL PAPER, 450 pages, 1988. Softcover. (Review)

STOCKTON AND MILLER'S SALES AND LEASES OF GOODS IN A NUTSHELL, Third Edition, 441 pages, 1992. Softcover. (Text)

STONE'S UNIFORM COMMERCIAL CODE IN A NUTSHELL, Third Edition, 580 pages, 1989. Softcover. (Text)

WEBER AND SPEIDEL'S COMMERCIAL PAPER IN A NUTSHELL, Third Edition, 404 pages, 1982. Softcover. (Text)

WHITE AND SUMMERS' HORNBOOK ON THE UNIFORM COMMERCIAL CODE, Third Edition, Student Edition, 1386 pages, 1988. (Text)

Community Property

MENNELL AND BOYKOFF'S COMMUNITY PROPERTY IN A NUTSHELL, Second Edition, 432 pages, 1988. Softcover. (Text)

Comparative Law

FOLSOM, MINAN AND OTTO'S LAW AND POLITICS IN THE PEOPLE'S REPUBLIC OF CHINA IN A NUTSHELL, 451 pages, 1992. Softcover. (Text)

GLENDON, GORDON AND OSAKWE'S COMPARATIVE LEGAL TRADITIONS IN A NUTSHELL. 402 pages, 1982. Softcover. (Text)

Conflict of Laws

HAY'S BLACK LETTER ON CONFLICT OF LAWS, 330 pages, 1989. Softcover. (Review)

SCOLES AND HAY'S HORNBOOK ON CONFLICT OF LAWS, Student Edition, 1160 pages, 1992. (Text)

SIEGEL'S CONFLICTS IN A NUTSHELL, 470 pages, 1982. Softcover. (Text)

Constitutional Law—Civil Rights

BARRON AND DIENES' BLACK LETTER ON CONSTITUTIONAL LAW, Third Edition, 440 pages, 1991. Softcover. (Review)

BARRON AND DIENES' CONSTITUTIONAL LAW IN A NUTSHELL, Second Edition, 483 pages, 1991. Softcover. (Text)

ENGDAHL'S CONSTITUTIONAL FEDERALISM IN A NUTSHELL, Second Edition, 411 pages, 1987. Softcover. (Text)

MARKS AND COOPER'S STATE CON-

Constitutional Law—Civil Rights—Continued

STITUTIONAL LAW IN A NUTSHELL, 329 pages, 1988. Softcover. (Text)

NOWAK AND ROTUNDA'S HORNBOOK ON CONSTITUTIONAL LAW, Fourth Edition, 1357 pages, 1991. (Text)

VIEIRA'S CONSTITUTIONAL CIVIL RIGHTS IN A NUTSHELL, Second Edition, 322 pages, 1990. Softcover. (Text)

WILLIAMS' CONSTITUTIONAL ANALYSIS IN A NUTSHELL, 388 pages, 1979. Softcover. (Text)

Consumer Law—see also Commercial Law

EPSTEIN AND NICKLES' CONSUMER LAW IN A NUTSHELL, Second Edition, 418 pages, 1981. Softcover. (Text)

Contracts

CALAMARI AND PERILLO'S BLACK LETTER ON CONTRACTS, Second Edition, 462 pages, 1990. Softcover. (Review)

CALAMARI AND PERILLO'S HORNBOOK ON CONTRACTS, Third Edition, 1049 pages, 1987. (Text)

CORBIN'S TEXT ON CONTRACTS, One Volume Student Edition, 1224 pages, 1952. (Text)

FRIEDMAN'S CONTRACT REMEDIES IN A NUTSHELL, 323 pages, 1981. Softcover. (Text)

KEYES' GOVERNMENT CONTRACTS IN A NUTSHELL, Second Edition, 557 pages, 1990. Softcover. (Text)

SCHABER AND ROHWER'S CONTRACTS IN A NUTSHELL, Third Edition, 457 pages, 1990. Softcover. (Text)

Copyright—see Patent and Copyright Law

Corporations

HAMILTON'S BLACK LETTER ON CORPORATIONS, Third Edition, 732 pages, 1992. Softcover. (Review)

HAMILTON'S THE LAW OF CORPORATIONS IN A NUTSHELL, Third Edition, 518 pages, 1991. Softcover. (Text)

HENN AND ALEXANDER'S HORNBOOK ON LAWS OF CORPORATIONS, Third Edition, Student Edition, 1371 pages, 1983, with 1986 pocket part. (Text)

Corrections

KRANTZ' THE LAW OF CORRECTIONS AND PRISONERS' RIGHTS IN A NUTSHELL, Third Edition, 407 pages, 1988. Softcover. (Text)

Creditors' Rights

EPSTEIN'S DEBTOR-CREDITOR LAW IN A NUTSHELL, Fourth Edition,

Creditors' Rights—Continued
401 pages, 1991. Softcover. (Text)

EPSTEIN, NICKLES AND WHITE'S HORNBOOK ON BANKRUPTCY, Approximately 1000 pages, January, 1992 Pub. (Text)

NICKLES AND EPSTEIN'S BLACK LETTER ON CREDITORS' RIGHTS AND BANKRUPTCY, 576 pages, 1989. (Review)

Criminal Law and Criminal Procedure—see also Corrections, Juvenile Justice

ISRAEL AND LAFAVE'S CRIMINAL PROCEDURE—CONSTITUTIONAL LIMITATIONS IN A NUTSHELL, Fourth Edition, 461 pages, 1988. Softcover. (Text)

LAFAVE AND ISRAEL'S HORNBOOK ON CRIMINAL PROCEDURE, Second Edition, 1309 pages, 1992 with 1992 pocket part. (Text)

LAFAVE AND SCOTT'S HORNBOOK ON CRIMINAL LAW, Second Edition, 918 pages, 1986. (Text)

LOEWY'S CRIMINAL LAW IN A NUTSHELL, Second Edition, 321 pages, 1987. Softcover. (Text)

LOW'S BLACK LETTER ON CRIMINAL LAW, Revised First Edition, 443 pages, 1990. Softcover. (Review)

SUBIN, MIRSKY AND WEINSTEIN'S

THE CRIMINAL PROCESS: PROSECUTION AND DEFENSE FUNCTIONS, Approximately 450 pages, February, 1993 Pub. Softcover. Teacher's Manual available. (Text)

Domestic Relations

CLARK'S HORNBOOK ON DOMESTIC RELATIONS, Second Edition, Student Edition, 1050 pages, 1988. (Text)

KRAUSE'S BLACK LETTER ON FAMILY LAW, 314 pages, 1988. Softcover. (Review)

KRAUSE'S FAMILY LAW IN A NUTSHELL, Second Edition, 444 pages, 1986. Softcover. (Text)

MALLOY'S LAW AND ECONOMICS: A COMPARATIVE APPROACH TO THEORY AND PRACTICE, 166 pages, 1990. Softcover. (Text)

Education Law

ALEXANDER AND ALEXANDER'S THE LAW OF SCHOOLS, STUDENTS AND TEACHERS IN A NUTSHELL, 409 pages, 1984. Softcover. (Text)

Employment Discrimination—see also Gender Discrimination

PLAYER'S FEDERAL LAW OF EMPLOYMENT DISCRIMINATION IN A NUTSHELL, Third Edition, 338 pages, 1992. Softcover. (Text)

Judicial Process—Continued
Approximately 350 pages, 1993.
Softcover. (Text)

Juvenile Justice

FOX'S JUVENILE COURTS IN A
NUTSHELL, Third Edition, 291
pages, 1984. Softcover. (Text)

Labor and Employment Law—
see also Employment Dis-
crimination, Workers' Compensation

LESLIE'S LABOR LAW IN A NUT-
SHELL, Third Edition, 388 pages,
1992. Softcover. (Text)

NOLAN'S LABOR ARBITRATION
LAW AND PRACTICE IN A NUT-
SHELL, 358 pages, 1979. Soft-
cover. (Text)

**Land Finance—Property Securi-
ty**—see Real Estate Transactions

Land Use

HAGMAN AND JUERGENSMEYER'S
HORNBOOK ON URBAN PLANNING
AND LAND DEVELOPMENT CON-
TROL LAW, Second Edition, Stu-
dent Edition, 680 pages, 1986.
(Text)

WRIGHT AND WRIGHT'S LAND USE
IN A NUTSHELL, Second Edition,
356 pages, 1985. Softcover.
(Text)

**Legal Method and Legal Sys-
tem**—see also Legal Re-
search, Legal Writing

KEMPIN'S HISTORICAL INTRODUC-
TION TO ANGLO-AMERICAN LAW IN
A NUTSHELL, Third Edition, 323
pages, 1990. Softcover. (Text)

REYNOLDS' JUDICIAL PROCESS IN
A NUTSHELL, Second Edition,
308 pages, 1991. Softcover.
(Text)

Legal Research

COHEN AND OLSON'S LEGAL RE-
SEARCH IN A NUTSHELL, Fifth
Edition, 370 pages, 1992. Soft-
cover. (Text)

COHEN, BERRING AND OLSON'S
HOW TO FIND THE LAW, Ninth
Edition, 716 pages, 1989.
(Text)

Legal Writing and Drafting

MELLINKOFF'S DICTIONARY OF
AMERICAN LEGAL USAGE, 703
pages, 1992. Softcover. (Text)

SQUIRES AND ROMBAUER'S LEGAL
WRITING IN A NUTSHELL, 294
pages, 1982. Softcover. (Text)

**Legislation—see also Legal
Writing and Drafting**

DAVIES' LEGISLATIVE LAW AND
PROCESS IN A NUTSHELL, Second
Edition, 346 pages, 1986. Soft-
cover. (Text)

Local Government

MCCARTHY'S LOCAL GOVERNMENT LAW IN A NUTSHELL, Third Edition, 435 pages, 1990. Softcover. (Text)

REYNOLDS' HORNBOOK ON LOCAL GOVERNMENT LAW, 860 pages, 1982 with 1990 pocket part. (Text)

Mass Communication Law

ZUCKMAN, GAYNES, CARTER AND DEE'S MASS COMMUNICATIONS LAW IN A NUTSHELL, Third Edition, 538 pages, 1988. Softcover. (Text)

Medicine, Law and

HALL AND ELLMAN'S HEALTH CARE LAW AND ETHICS IN A NUTSHELL, 401 pages, 1990. Softcover (Text)

JARVIS, CLOSEN, HERMANN AND LEONARD'S AIDS LAW IN A NUTSHELL, 349 pages, 1991. Softcover. (Text)

KING'S THE LAW OF MEDICAL MALPRACTICE IN A NUTSHELL, Second Edition, 342 pages, 1986. Softcover. (Text)

Military Law

SHANOR AND TERRELL'S MILITARY LAW IN A NUTSHELL, 378 pages, 1980. Softcover. (Text)

Mining Law—see Energy and Natural Resources Law

Mortgages—see Real Estate Transactions

Natural Resources Law—see Energy and Natural Resources Law, Environmental Law

TEPLY'S LEGAL NEGOTIATION IN A NUTSHELL, 282 pages, 1992. Softcover. (Text)

Office Practice—see also Computers and Law, Interviewing and Counseling, Negotiation

HEGLAND'S TRIAL AND PRACTICE SKILLS IN A NUTSHELL, 346 pages, 1978. Softcover (Text)

Oil and Gas—see also Energy and Natural Resources Law

HEMINGWAY'S HORNBOOK ON THE LAW OF OIL AND GAS, Third Edition, Student Edition, 711 pages, 1992. (Text)

LOWE'S OIL AND GAS LAW IN A NUTSHELL, Second Edition, 465 pages, 1988. Softcover. (Text)

Partnership—see Agency—Partnership

Patent and Copyright Law

MILLER AND DAVIS' INTELLECTUAL PROPERTY—PATENTS, TRADEMARKS AND COPYRIGHT IN A NUTSHELL, Second Edition, 437 pages, 1990. Softcover. (Text)

Products Liability

PHILLIPS' PRODUCTS LIABILITY IN

Products Liability—Continued
A NUTSHELL, Third Edition, 307 pages, 1988. Softcover. (Text)

Professional Responsibility
ARONSON AND WECKSTEIN'S PROFESSIONAL RESPONSIBILITY IN A NUTSHELL, Second Edition, 514 pages, 1991. Softcover. (Text)

LESNICK'S BEING A LAWYER: INDIVIDUAL CHOICE AND RESPONSIBILITY IN THE PRACTICE OF LAW, 422 pages, 1992. Softcover. Teacher's Manual available. (Coursebook)

ROTUNDA'S BLACK LETTER ON PROFESSIONAL RESPONSIBILITY, Third Edition, 492 pages, 1992. Softcover. (Review)

WOLFRAM'S HORNBOOK ON MODERN LEGAL ETHICS, Student Edition, 1120 pages, 1986. (Text)

WYDICK AND PERSCHBACHER'S CALIFORNIA LEGAL ETHICS, 439 pages, 1992. Softcover. (Coursebook)

Property—see also Real Estate Transactions, Land Use, Trusts and Estates
BERNHARDT'S BLACK LETTER ON PROPERTY, Second Edition, 388 pages, 1991. Softcover. (Review)

BERNHARDT'S REAL PROPERTY IN A NUTSHELL, Second Edition, 448 pages, 1981. Softcover. (Text)

BOYER, HOVENKAMP AND KURTZ' THE LAW OF PROPERTY, AN INTRODUCTORY SURVEY, Fourth Edition, 696 pages, 1991. (Text)

BURKE'S PERSONAL PROPERTY IN A NUTSHELL, Second Edition, approximately 400 pages, May, 1993 Pub. Softcover. (Text)

CUNNINGHAM, STOEBUCK AND WHITMAN'S HORNBOOK ON THE LAW OF PROPERTY, Second Edition, approximately 900 pages, May, 1993 Pub. (Text)

HILL'S LANDLORD AND TENANT LAW IN A NUTSHELL, Second Edition, 311 pages, 1986. Softcover. (Text)

Real Estate Transactions
BRUCE'S REAL ESTATE FINANCE IN A NUTSHELL, Third Edition, 287 pages, 1991. Softcover. (Text)

NELSON AND WHITMAN'S BLACK LETTER ON LAND TRANSACTIONS AND FINANCE, Second Edition, 466 pages, 1988. Softcover. (Review)

NELSON AND WHITMAN'S HORNBOOK ON REAL ESTATE FINANCE LAW, Second Edition, 941 pages, 1985 with 1989 pocket part. (Text)

Regulated Industries—see also Mass Communication Law, Banking Law

GELLHORN AND PIERCE'S REGULATED INDUSTRIES IN A NUTSHELL, Second Edition, 389 pages, 1987. Softcover. (Text)

Remedies

DOBBS' HORNBOOK ON REMEDIES, Second Edition, approximately 1000 pages, April, 1993 Pub. (Text)

DOBBYN'S INJUNCTIONS IN A NUTSHELL, 264 pages, 1974. Softcover. (Text)

FRIEDMAN'S CONTRACT REMEDIES IN A NUTSHELL, 323 pages, 1981. Softcover. (Text)

O'CONNELL'S REMEDIES IN A NUTSHELL, Second Edition, 320 pages, 1985. Softcover. (Text)

Sea, Law of

SOHN AND GUSTAFSON'S THE LAW OF THE SEA IN A NUTSHELL, 264 pages, 1984. Softcover. (Text)

Securities Regulation

HAZEN'S HORNBOOK ON THE LAW OF SECURITIES REGULATION, Second Edition, Student Edition, 1082 pages, 1990. (Text)

RATNER'S SECURITIES REGULATION IN A NUTSHELL, Fourth Edition, 320 pages, 1992. Softcover. (Text)

Sports Law

CHAMPION'S SPORTS LAW IN A NUTSHELL. Approximately 300 pages, January, 1993 Pub. Softcover. (Text)

SCHUBERT, SMITH AND TRENTADUE'S SPORTS LAW, 395 pages, 1986. (Text)

Tax Practice and Procedure

MORGAN'S TAX PROCEDURE AND TAX FRAUD IN A NUTSHELL, 400 pages, 1990. Softcover. (Text)

Taxation—Corporate

SCHWARZ AND LATHROPE'S BLACK LETTER ON CORPORATE AND PARTNERSHIP TAXATION, 537 pages, 1991. Softcover. (Review)

WEIDENBRUCH AND BURKE'S FEDERAL INCOME TAXATION OF CORPORATIONS AND STOCKHOLDERS IN A NUTSHELL, Third Edition, 309 pages, 1989. Softcover. (Text)

Taxation—Estate & Gift—see also Estate Planning, Trusts and Estates

MCNULTY'S FEDERAL ESTATE AND GIFT TAXATION IN A NUTSHELL, Fourth Edition, 496 pages, 1989. Softcover. (Text)

PEAT AND WILLBANKS' FEDERAL ESTATE AND GIFT TAXATION: AN ANALYSIS AND CRITIQUE, 265 pages, 1991. Softcover. (Text)

Taxation—Individual

DODGE'S THE LOGIC OF TAX, 343 pages, 1989. Softcover. (Text)

HUDSON AND LIND'S BLACK LETTER ON FEDERAL INCOME TAXATION, Fourth Edition, 410 pages, 1992. Softcover. (Review)

MCNULTY'S FEDERAL INCOME TAXATION OF INDIVIDUALS IN A NUTSHELL, Fourth Edition, 503 pages, 1988. Softcover. (Text)

POSIN'S FEDERAL INCOME TAXATION, Second Edition, approximately 650 pages, May, 1993 Pub. Softcover. (Text)

ROSE AND CHOMMIE'S HORNBOOK ON FEDERAL INCOME TAXATION, Third Edition, 923 pages, 1988, with 1991 pocket part. (Text)

Taxation—International

DOERNBERG'S INTERNATIONAL TAXATION IN A NUTSHELL, 325 pages, 1989. Softcover. (Text)

BISHOP AND BROOKS' FEDERAL PARTNERSHIP TAXATION: A GUIDE TO THE LEADING CASES, STATUTES, AND REGULATIONS, 545 pages, 1990. Softcover. (Text)

BURKE'S FEDERAL INCOME TAXATION OF PARTNERSHIPS IN A NUTSHELL, 356 pages, 1992. Softcover. (Text)

SCHWARZ AND LATHROPE'S BLACK

LETTER ON CORPORATE AND PARTNERSHIP TAXATION, 537 pages, 1991. Softcover. (Review)

Taxation—State & Local

GELFAND AND SALSICH'S STATE AND LOCAL TAXATION AND FINANCE IN A NUTSHELL, 309 pages, 1986. Softcover. (Text)

Torts—see also Products Liability

KIONKA'S BLACK LETTER ON TORTS, 339 pages, 1988. Softcover. (Review)

KIONKA'S TORTS IN A NUTSHELL, Second Edition, 449 pages, 1992. Softcover. (Text)

PROSSER AND KEETON'S HORNBOOK ON TORTS, Fifth Edition, Student Edition, 1286 pages, 1984 with 1988 pocket part. (Text)

Trade Regulation—see also Antitrust, Regulated Industries

MCMANIS' UNFAIR TRADE PRACTICES IN A NUTSHELL, Third Edition, approximately 450 pages, 1993. Softcover. (Text)

SCHECHTER'S BLACK LETTER ON UNFAIR TRADE PRACTICES, 272 pages, 1986. Softcover. (Review)

Trial and Appellate Advocacy—see also Civil Procedure

BERGMAN'S TRIAL ADVOCACY IN A

Trial and Appellate Advocacy— Continued

NUTSHELL, Second Edition, 354 pages, 1989. Softcover. (Text)

CLARY'S PRIMER ON THE ANALYSIS AND PRESENTATION OF LEGAL ARGUMENT, 106 pages, 1992. Softcover. (Text)

DESSEM'S PRETRIAL LITIGATION IN A NUTSHELL, 382 pages, 1992. Softcover. (Text)

GOLDBERG'S THE FIRST TRIAL (WHERE DO I SIT? WHAT DO I SAY?) IN A NUTSHELL, 396 pages, 1982. Softcover. (Text)

HEGLAND'S TRIAL AND PRACTICE SKILLS IN A NUTSHELL, 346 pages, 1978. Softcover. (Text)

HORNSTEIN'S APPELLATE ADVOCACY IN A NUTSHELL, 325 pages, 1984. Softcover. (Text)

JEANS' HANDBOOK ON TRIAL ADVOCACY, Student Edition, 473 pages, 1975. Softcover. (Text)

Trusts and Estates

ATKINSON'S HORNBOOK ON WILLS, Second Edition, 975 pages, 1953. (Text)

AVERILL'S UNIFORM PROBATE CODE IN A NUTSHELL, Second Edition, 454 pages, 1987. Softcover. (Text)

BOGERT'S HORNBOOK ON TRUSTS, Sixth Edition, Student Edition, 794 pages, 1987. (Text)

MCGOVERN, KURTZ AND REIN'S HORNBOOK ON WILLS, TRUSTS AND ESTATES–INCLUDING TAXATION AND FUTURE INTERESTS, 996 pages, 1988. (Text)

MENNELL'S WILLS AND TRUSTS IN A NUTSHELL, 392 pages, 1979. Softcover. (Text)

SIMES' HORNBOOK ON FUTURE INTERESTS, Second Edition, 355 pages, 1966. (Text)

TURANO AND RADIGAN'S HORNBOOK ON NEW YORK ESTATE ADMINISTRATION, 676 pages, 1986 with 1991 pocket part. (Text)

WAGGONER'S FUTURE INTERESTS IN A NUTSHELL, 361 pages, 1981. Softcover. (Text)

Water Law—see also Environmental Law

GETCHES' WATER LAW IN A NUTSHELL, Second Edition, 459 pages, 1990. Softcover. (Text)

Wills—see Trusts and Estates

Workers' Compensation

HOOD, HARDY AND LEWIS' WORKERS' COMPENSATION AND EMPLOYEE PROTECTION LAWS IN A NUTSHELL, Second Edition, 361 pages, 1990. Softcover. (Text)

Advisory Board

[XIV]

SEX DISCRIMINATION
IN A NUTSHELL
SECOND EDITION

By

CLAIRE SHERMAN THOMAS

Lecturer, University of Washington, Seattle

ST. PAUL, MINN.

WEST PUBLISHING CO.

1991

Nutshell Series, In a Nutshell, the Nutshell Logo and the WP symbol are registered trademarks of West Publishing Co. Registered in the U.S. Patent and Trademark Office.

COPYRIGHT © 1982 WEST PUBLISHING CO.
COPYRIGHT © 1991 By WEST PUBLISHING CO.
                              610 Opperman Drive
                              P.O. Box 64526
                              St. Paul, MN 55164–0526

Library of Congress Cataloging-in-Publication Data

Thomas, Claire Sherman.
    Sex discrimination in a nutshell / by Claire Sherman Thomas. —
2nd ed.
        p.   cm. — (Nutshell series)
    Includes index.
    ISBN 0–314–89418–7
    1. Sex discrimination against women—Law and legislation—United
States. I. Title. II. Series.
KF4758.Z9T48   1991
342.73'0878—dc20
[347.302878]
                                                              91–22447
                                                              CIP

ISBN 0–314–89418–7

Thomas, Sex Discrim. 2d Ed. NS
1st Reprint—1993

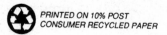

PRINTED ON 10% POST
CONSUMER RECYCLED PAPER

**To our anonymous ancestors
who bequeathed us
the alphabet**

*

III

FOREWORD

EQUAL JUSTICE UNDER LAW

These words are carved in stone over the portal to the United States Supreme Court. They echo the words of Hammurabi sounding across four thousand years: I shall make justice to shine in the language of the land, that the strong shall not oppress the weak. This is the promise of self government under written constitution. Whether, and to what degree, this promise is fulfilled depends on We the People, who in each generation ratify anew the United States Constitution by our willing obedience to it.

Language is the mass art of the world. The United States Constitution is the collective art of the citizens of the United States. As a collective art, the words of the Constitution abound with dual and flexible meanings. These meanings adapt to change, one of law's two major functions, without which the federal Constitution would have demised long ago. Ability of constitutional language to adapt to change is a necessary balance to law's other function, the logical mode which seeks precision and consistent application of unambiguous rules.

Words are more than a collective art; they are simultaneously a collective cage. Unconscious and unquestioned obedience to established meanings binds humankind with steel bands to both the good and the bad of yesterday. Law is called upon to serve goals other than predictability and certainty, which, logic being what it is, walk backwards. The paramount obligation of law is to secure, to make safe, equal rights and justice under law. This is the daunting task of the remarkably few words which comprise the United States Constitution.

Constitutional law under judicial review is the unique contribution of the United States to the world. The particular contribution to constitutional law arising from litigation of sex discrimination is chronicled in this book.

Sex discrimination law makes a distinctly effective subject for legal study. Most importantly, sex discrimination law affects everyone. A legal principle that impacts one half of the male/female relationship inevitably impacts the other. Some topic in this book will be of particular import to every reader. Another aspect is that all major fields of law are touched, providing a perspective of the legal forest that is lacking when the focus is more specialized.

The material presented is popular and informative for undergraduate as well as graduate students. Male readers will be surprised at the number of cases where discrimination against men is at issue. Litigation by men has been significant in shaping sex discrimination law.

Sex or Gender?

Selecting a title for this nutshell presented difficulties. The word "gender" is preferred by some to the word "sex". But gender won't do. It is discrimination because of sex that is prohibited by Congressional legislation and addressed in litigation under the Fourteenth Amendment and state equal rights amendments. Gender does not mean the same thing as sex; gender is a neutral, objective term, and sex discrimination is not neutral and not objective.

Rather it is precisely the invisible discrimination rooted in sex bias that most needs to be eradicated from law. The word sex needs to be elevated to the point of issue before its undesirable connotations, the connotations that are not present in the word gender, can be eliminated. Change of attitude is essential to elimination of discrimination because of sex in United States law. The remedy to avert the evil is not substitution of a word that camouflages the reality of discrimination against both men and women because of their sex.

Rights and Remedies

Mention is frequently made of rights. Some argue that there is no right where there is no legal remedy; that a right without a remedy is no right at all. I disagree. A right without a remedy is just that—a right without a remedy. It is no less a right. The resolution is to secure the right under law.

Rights and remedies are analytically distinct. The cause of equal rights for men and women is best served by maintaining the intellectual distinction between right and remedy while seeking their union in practice. To distinguish is not to divorce. Legal history teaches that cognition of the idea of a right precedes the change in fact that makes the right a reality. Awareness of the cognitive distinction may be equally necessary to secure continued existence of both right and remedy for future generations.

As this second edition is written, controversy over abortion remains central to the question of women's rights, with Supreme Court decisions restricting Roe v. Wade and forcing public debate into state courts and legislatures. The intense and continuing focus on abortion has eclipsed two major developments in women's legal rights in the past decade.

First, women have greatly extended personal experience in self government through involvement in legislative, executive and judicial processes at local, state and national levels. In the last analysis, self government is shaped by those most active in the political process.

Second, statutory remedies at state and federal level have vastly increased each woman's rights to equal opportunities in education and employment.

The extent of embedded discrimination against women is evident in their quick response to an expanded opportunity for education. The promise to women of Title VII in 1964 for equal opportunity in employment was vacuous without equal opportunity for education. Only since 1972 have federally supported vocational and professional schools been required to admit women students.

This legal mandate of improved educational opportunity has changed participation of women in myriad fields of employment, from carpenters and welders to train conductors, surgeons and pilots. Older women have enrolled in droves at community colleges, where for years female students, many over 30, have exceeded male students. This is also true in many universities. Female enrollment in both medical and law schools is approaching 50 percent; enrollment in vocational schools, engineering and science is improving.

Unwelcome verbal or physical sexual overtures in the workplace are actionable in employment under Title VII and in schools under Title IX. The philosophy of these statutory remedies has spilled over into state common law, eroding the strictures of at-will employment and supporting causes of action for sexual harassment as a violation of public policy. Women working in previously all male domains are successfully challenging pornographic pictures in the workplace as unlawful sexual harassment.

Finally, the doors of quasi-public business associations which opened yesterday only to males now open for women as well. These changes, the long term effects of which are incalculable but surely profound, are here to stay.

* * *

Contributions of many people are incorporated in this nutshell. I take the opportunity to acknowledge my indebtedness to Owen Barfield. Without his works, this book would not have been written, although I may well have written a different book with the same title. Barfield's writings expose the relationship between metaphor, logic and law. For those who ponder this question and are unfamiliar with his thought, I recommend two books published by Wesleyan University Press: POETIC DICTION: A STUDY IN MEANING (3d Ed. 1973) and REDISCOVERY OF MEANING AND OTHER ESSAYS (1977), particularly the essays entitled "Poetic Diction and Legal Fiction" and "Participation and Isolation". The latter essay addresses the topic of this book, equality under law of representative government. Barfield writes:

> The practical question is then, Is it possible to retain the kind of participation that makes human society possible without abandoning the relatively new principle

* * * of social equality? There are few more important questions, because the plain truth is that if it is *not* possible, democracy as an experiment has failed.

A particularly helpful reference is SEX–BASED DISCRIMINATION, 3d Ed., by Herma Hill Kay, American Casebook Series, West Publishing Co. (1988). Kay's book includes texts of federal legislation prohibiting sex discrimination as well as opinions of lead cases mentioned in this nutshell. Articles and case development in various law journals devoted to gender discrimination, including the Rutgers Law School *Women's Rights Law Reporter*, the Harvard *Women's Law Journal* and Golden Gate University Law Review *Women's Law Forum* are invaluable.

The nutshell FEDERAL LAW OF EMPLOYMENT DISCRIMINATION by Mack A. Player is complementary. For the quotation from Ruth Bader Ginsburg, Judge, District of Columbia Court of Appeals, introducing Chapter 1, see 4 WRLR 143 (1978); for that from Shirley Hufstedler, formerly judge, Ninth Circuit, introducing Part VI, see University of Michigan 24 *Law Quadrangle Notes* 15 (1979).

Personal thanks are extended to my students, both male and female. Their perceptive questions have sharpened the focus of this book. Joan Young and Sherri Homer helped with research, and Elaine Thomas with critical review. Julie Pan and Natasha Fleschig have given invaluable assistance in preparing the manuscript.

* * *

Judicial review, the focus of this book, is the "last refuge of the wronged" in the words of McGeorge Bundy. It would not be possible without the alphabet; hence the dedication of this book. Judicial review attempts to impose the constraint of reason, of articulated ends and means, on the will of state and federal governments. Through judicial review, individuals can initiate the negation of legislative and executive actions which exceed constitutional grants of power. Representative government under written constitution, subject to judicial review expressed in written and published opinions so that every citizen may examine the logic, remains our best defense against rule by brute strength, majoritarian tyranny and arbitrary power.

CLAIRE SHERMAN THOMAS

Seattle, Washington
June, 1991

OUTLINE

PART IV. REMEDIAL LEGISLATION AND CASE DEVELOPMENT

APPENDICES

*

TABLE OF CASES

References are to Pages

TABLE OF CASES

TABLE OF CASES

TABLE OF CASES

TABLE OF CASES

TABLE OF CASES

TABLE OF CASES

TABLE OF CASES

SEX DISCRIMINATION
IN A NUTSHELL

SECOND EDITION

*

CHAPTER 1

EQUAL JUSTICE UNDER LAW

The classification independent man/dependent woman is the prototypical sex line in the law and has all the earmarks of self-fulfilling prophecy

Judge Ruth Bader Ginsburg (1978)

Discrimination in law against women is pervasive and of long tradition. It touches civil as well as criminal law, in such diverse areas as employment, education, domestic rights and civic obligations.

As recently as 1970, state legislatures and Congress passed statutes which classified on the basis of sex. Most of these statutes, reflecting unexamined cultural assumptions, disadvantaged women.

Women could constitutionally be denied equal rights (taken for granted by men): to attend publicly supported schools, to work in state or federal offices, to receive equal pay if hired, to serve on juries, to be tried by a jury of their peers, to secure prosecution for violent assault, to choose their own domicile, to decide their own name. This book traces the Supreme Court's sporadic and piecemeal extension of constitutionally protected rights to women.

1

Sex discrimination in private sector employment, education, finance and public accommodations, has been equally pervasive. Because private action is outside the protection of federal and most state constitutions, elimination of discriminatory private action requires specific remedial statutes. That male dominated legislatures have enacted remedial statutes prohibiting discrimination on the basis of sex is tribute to the women's movement and changing societal attitudes.

The search by women for equal justice under law is not a recent phenomenon. In 1776 Abigail Adams admonished her husband John to "remember the ladies" in drafting a legal code for the new nation. She insisted that "we * * * will not hold ourselves bound by any laws in which we have no voice or representation." Collective effort to achieve equal rights for women can be dated from the convention of 1848 in Seneca Falls, N.Y. Three hundred women adopted a Declaration of Sentiments, seeking "immediate admission to all the rights and privileges which belong to [women] as citizens of the United States." Listed in the declaration were the rights to vote, to attend college, and to participate in civic government.

Nineteenth century common law to which the declaration was addressed is a basis for American constitutional and case law. Classification by sex was not at all unusual. Discrimination was permissible in any form—civil, public, economic, political—whether the bias was expressed in statute, case precedent, or was embedded in the Constitution itself.

Change of law that discriminates between men and women has been effected through legislation, constitutional amendment and individual litigation. Statutes specifically override prior law, providing a remedy or a right where none existed before.

Law accommodates contemporary needs at the constitutional level, where the highest law of the land is linked to the people through constitutional amendment. Constitutional amendment to guarantee women the right to vote, the sine qua non of self determination, was not achieved until 1920, after a century of bitter struggle.

The Constitution also molds to contemporary life through reinterpretation of constitutional language. This occurs only when individuals initiate challenge to the law in a trial court and pursue the issue to the appellate level. Litigation similarly shapes the contours of state constitutions, which can provide greater, but not less, protection to civil rights than the federal constitution. Protection provided by state constitutions is particularly important under restrictive interpretation of the United States Constitution by federal courts.

Collision of concrete fact and abstract legal principle in the trial court is basic to development of the common law itself. In the process of litigation, the common law examines, distinguishes, discards, ignores or even forgets its own precedent. When appealed to the Supreme Court, the individual litigant shares in creating constitutional law.

Successful individual challenge to sex discrimination under the Constitution dates from 1971 when the Supreme Court for the first time interpreted the Fourteenth Amendment as prohibiting arbitrary statutory classification by sex. Both women and men have litigated numerous cases under this new constitutional protection to eliminate sex discrimination in federal and state statutes and regulations.

Reproductive rights, the topic of Part I, provides the focus for recognition of the constitutional right of privacy. These cases are particularly apt examples of the unique characteristic of United States law by which private citizens can effect major change in constitutional law.

The direction ahead cannot be anticipated without understanding the past. Part II traces constitutional challenges to sex discrimination from the Civil War to 1976, when the Supreme Court articulated a standard of review for gender based classification. Part III traces the wavering application of the gender standard of review under the federal constitution and protection of women's rights through equal rights amendments and gender neutral clauses of state constitutions from 1976 to the present.

Specific legislation to eliminate common law precedent and cultural assumptions that operate to limit equality between the sexes, primarily in employment, is the focus of Part IV. A subtle irony invades case law development under remedial statutes. These statutes were enacted to end longstanding preferential treatment condoned by the Constitution for white males by white males. The remedial statutes are interpreted by some justices, in total denial of their spirit, to preclude any modicum of temporary preferential treatment for minorities and women because to do so would interfere with rights under the same Constitution of white males because they are innocent victims. The women and minorities previously denied equal, let alone preferential treatment, were similarly innocent, but the Constitution did not avail them. Discrepancy of treatment on the basis of sex under the criminal justice system is discussed in Part V.

*

PART I

REPRODUCTIVE RIGHTS AND HEALTH CARE

When elected leaders cower before public pressure, this Court, more than ever, must not shirk its duty to enforce the Constitution for the poor and powerless

Justice Marshall, dissenting, Beal v. Doe

(S.Ct.1977)

CHAPTER 2

CONTRACEPTION AND ABORTION

2.01 Perspectives

A grasp of the difference between criminal and civil law is essential to understanding United States law regarding reproductive rights.

The most controversial Supreme Court decision in recent history removed abortion before viability from criminal prosecution by ruling that the decision whether to bear a child is constitutionally protected within the fundamental right of privacy. Roe v. Wade.

Because law concerning reproductive rights is highly controversial and marks a boundary between criminal and civil law, it provides a central perspective for introduction to the law of sex discrimination.

The law regarding reproductive rights covers contraception, abortion, sterilization, fertility, artificial insemination, in vitro fertilization, fetal testing and treatment, pregnancy and surrogate gestation. Availability and quality of medical care and product liability are also included. Reproductive rights of teens and pre-teens have been subjected to particular scrutiny. For women employed out-

8

side the home, employment conditions and practices which impact pregnant workers are critical.

Reproductive concerns are not limited to women. Men are affected as to their right of privacy and economic responsibilities when means of family planning are prohibited or restricted. Hazardous workplace or environmental conditions may affect the reproductive integrity of men as well as women. The interests of both men and women in parenthood are affected when the woman dies or becomes paralyzed or sterile as a result of the use of contraceptives.

The spectre of AIDS (Acquired Immune Deficiency Syndrome) hovers over contemporary health issues. Women, like men, contract AIDS primarily through sexual activity with infected partners or through sharing contaminated drug needles. AIDS is presently the leading cause of death for black women of child bearing age, 15 to 44, in New York and New Jersey, and the third leading cause of death in these states for all women of this age. One in three babies born to a human immuno-deficiency virus (HIV) positive mother contracts the virus in utero or during birth.

2.02 Contraception

A. MARRIED COUPLES

Before 1965 a state could prohibit sale or use of contraceptives with criminal penalties for violation. A Connecticut statute enacted in the 19th century provided that use of any drug or instrument to prevent conception was a crime. Since it was illegal to use contraceptives, any person who advised another about the use of contraceptives would be guilty as an accessory.

Two officials of a Planned Parenthood clinic were arrested for dispensing information about contraceptives to married persons. Each was convicted as an accessory to the crime of using contraceptives and was fined $100. The Supreme Court overturned the conviction on the grounds that the statute invaded the constitutionally protected right of privacy. Griswold v. Connecticut. The opinion of the Court articulates the constitutional basis for the right of privacy which underlies much litigation involving women's reproductive rights.

Nowhere does the Constitution use the word "privacy." The Fourteenth Amendment provides that "No State shall * * * deprive any person of life, liberty, or property, without due process of law; nor deny to any person within its jurisdiction the equal protection of the laws." Privacy is not mentioned here nor in the Bill of Rights, the first ten amendments to the Constitution.

The federal government is a government of written law. Rights protected by the federal Constitution must be found in the federal Constitution. A right that is not grounded in the Constitution cannot be protected by the federal courts against interference with that right by a state.

Seven of the nine justices in *Griswold* found language in the Constitution to support a right of privacy which prohibits states from enforcing legislation making use of contraceptives by married persons a crime.

Justice Douglas, writing for the Court, discussed the specific rights listed in the First, Third, Fourth, and Fifth Amendments. A right of privacy emanates from the protections explicitly enumerated in the Bill of Rights, forming a penumbra that protects rights not specifically mentioned, creating a zone of privacy which the government may not force a citizen to surrender.

The concept of a fundamental right in the context of procreation was first given constitutional recognition in 1942 when the Court declared unconstitutional a statute ordering sterilization of habitual criminals because the right to have offspring is fundamental. Skinner v. Oklahoma. To unjustifiably sterilize the defendant would forever deprive him of a basic liberty. The focus in *Skinner* is the right to have children; *Griswold* poses the opposite question—the right not to have children.

B. SINGLE PERSONS

Seven years later the Court ruled that the right of privacy protects the right of single persons as well as married persons to use contraceptives. Eisenstadt v. Baird (S.Ct.1972).

The significant language in *Eisenstadt* builds on the right of privacy enunciated first in *Griswold.*

In *Eisenstadt* the Court paved the way for Roe v. Wade by saying, "If the right of privacy means anything, it is the right of the *individual,* married or single, to be free from unwarranted governmental intrusion into matters so fundamentally affecting a person as the decision whether to bear or beget a child."

C. TEENS

Statutes prohibiting selling or dispensing non-prescription contraceptives to minors are unconstitutional. Carey v. Population Services Intern. (S.Ct.1977). A regulation under Title X of the Public Health Service Act requiring notice to parents when contraceptive drugs or devices were distributed to unemancipated minors by a grantee was ruled inconsistent with legislative intent. Planned Parenthood Federation of America, Inc. v. Schweiker (D.D.C.1983). Parental opposition to distribution of condoms through public school health clinics has materially lessened since the advent of AIDS.

2.03 Abortion

A. PERSPECTIVES

A state cannot impose criminal penalties for an abortion before viability under Roe v. Wade (S.Ct. 1973). This basic ruling was left undisturbed in a major challenge to Roe v. Wade by the Rehnquist Court in Webster v. Reproductive Health Services (S.Ct.1989).

The Constitution prohibits governmental interference with exercise of fundamental rights, but the government need not make the fundamental right to choose an abortion effective by financing it. Harris v. McRae (S.Ct.1980). Funding of abortion with tax dollars is a civil benefit and legislative option, not a constitutional requirement.

Legislation is a product of political activity, and the political activity regarding abortion has been intense in the past three decades. In the 1960s abortion supporters were seeking removal of criminal penalties against abortion by political and judicial activity that culminated in Roe v. Wade. Following *Roe,* anti-abortion supporters sought to narrow the scope of permissible abortions through every possible means. This activity is evidenced in legislation imposing procedural and funding obstacles to abortion. The Missouri statute upheld in *Webster* is one example. The political activity continues. Anti-abortion supporters seek federal legislation or a constitutional amendment to prohibit abortion. They have engaged in numerous acts of civil disobedience in defiance of *Roe,* incurring criminal and civil sanctions for doing so. Pro-choice supporters work for repeal of procedural and funding restrictions, and simultaneously seek enactment of federal and state statutes codifying *Roe.* They are also looking more closely to state constitutions for judicial protection of privacy rights. In states that have strong home rule, the abortion dispute conceivably can move to cities and counties.

The majority and minority reports issued by the First National Women's Conference summarize the positions of the opposing United States views. The minority report recommends that Congress enact and the states ratify a mandatory human life amendment that constitutional protection begins at the moment of conception. The minority report also recommends that no federal or state tax money be used for abortion.

The majority report states that every woman, regardless of her age, economic condition, race, ethnic origin, education, marital status, rural or metropolitan residence, is entitled as a fundamental human right to have readily available safe means of controlling reproduction. It opposes exclusion of reproductive care from federal, state, local, or privately financed medical services. Those who support a woman's right to choose abortion do not recommend abortion as a vehicle for reproductive control, but insist that safe, legal abortion remain an option for all women, not just for those able to afford it.

B. LEGALIZATION

1. State Legislation and Judicial Action

The years preceding Roe v. Wade were marked by direct efforts at legislative reform and judicial review to have criminal sanctions removed from abortions.

Most state codes allowed abortion only to save the mother's life. Legislative battles were intense and by 1970 resulted in legalization in four states: New York, Washington, Alaska, and Hawaii.

While some women were active in the legislative arena, others were pursuing remedies through judicial intervention. A principle argument relied upon the right of privacy as developed in *Griswold* and *Eisenstadt*. By 1972 statutes prohibiting abortion had been held unconstitutional in eight states: New Jersey, Florida, Illinois, Connecticut, Wisconsin, California, Texas, and Georgia. The decisions in the Texas and Georgia cases were reviewed by the United States Supreme Court in Roe v. Wade and Doe v. Bolton.

2. Supreme Court Intervention

The Woman and the State

The Texas abortion statute in effect in 1970 permitted abortion only "for the purpose of saving the life of the mother." Numerous procedural requirements in the Georgia abortion statute severely restricted access to abortion. Jane Roe of Texas and Mary Doe of Georgia each challenged the validity of the applicable statute. Decisions in both cases were handed down on the same day in 1973.

Justice Blackmun wrote the opinion for the Court. The right of privacy enunciated in *Griswold* and *Eisenstadt* involves the basic "right of the *individual,* married or single, to be free from unwarranted governmental intrusion into matters so fundamentally affecting a person as the decision whether to bear or beget a child." The right of privacy is "broad enough to encompass a woman's decision whether or not to terminate her pregnancy."

Roe holds that the State may proscribe abortion after viability. The parameters of this provision have not been delineated. The issue can be anticipated to arise in connection with a fetus suffering from severe genetic, metabolic, teratogenic, or other malformation that is not discovered until after viability.

The protections of the Fourteenth Amendment are guaranteed to all persons. The Court found that the word "person" in the Fourteenth Amendment has postnatal application only and does not include the unborn.

Three stages of pregnancy were recognized, although the differentiation between them is necessarily indistinct. As a pregnancy proceeds to term, the woman's right to an abortion may be subjected to increasingly restrictive state regulations and even prohibited. The Court summarized permissible state regulations as follows:

(a) For the stage prior to approximately the end of the first trimester, the abortion decision and its effectuation must be left to the medical judgment of the pregnant woman's attending physician.

(b) For the stage subsequent to approximately the end of the first trimester, the State, in promoting its interest in the health of the mother, may, if it chooses, regulate the abortion procedure in ways that are reasonably related to maternal health.

(c) For the stage subsequent to viability, the State in promoting its interest in the potentiality of human life, may, if it chooses, regulate, and even proscribe, abortion except where it is necessary, in appropriate medical judgment, for the preservation of the life or health of the mother.

The term "health" includes mental health. United States v. Vuitch (S.Ct.1971).

Federal and state legislation following Roe sought to limit its scope. Challenges were easily turned back by the pre-Rehnquist court.

Viability

Several cases since *Roe* have addressed the concept of viability. In two early cases, the Court reaffirmed that viability is not a specifically determinable time and cannot be fixed by a single criterion, whether it be weeks of gestation or fetal weight. Rather, viability is a matter of medical judgment to be determined by the attending physician. Planned Parenthood of Central Missouri v. Danforth. The statute challenged in Colautti v. Franklin (S.Ct.1979) conditioned potential criminal liability on confusing and ambiguous criteria regarding viability and therefore was unconstitutionally vague. It was little more than " 'a trap for those who act in good faith.' " United States v. Ragen (S.Ct.1942).

Justice O'Connor addressed viability in City of Akron v. Akron Center for Reproductive Health, Inc. (S.Ct.1983), where she voted with the two *Roe* dissenters, then Justice Rehnquist and Justice White. Justice O'Connor said the concept of viability is on "collision course" with itself. Emerging medical technologies on the one hand make late abortions less dangerous to maternal health, and on the other enhance the survival rate of late second trimester fetuses outside the womb.

The Webster Decision. When Webster v. Reproductive Health Services reached the Court, Justices Kennedy and Scalia were seated, providing a 5–4 plurality to uphold Missouri's public funding and viability testing restrictions on abortion. Justice Scalia castigated the Justices for not overruling Roe v. Wade.

The *Webster* Court rejected several challenges to the Missouri statute. The preamble states that life begins at conception, defined as the fertilization of the ovum of a female by a sperm of a male. Chief Justice Rehnquist said this language expresses a value judgment, not a substantive restriction on abortion before viability. The preamble and the statute leave the core holding of *Roe* undisturbed.

Only Justices Kennedy and White joined with Justice Rehnquist's opinion regarding fetal testing for viability before performing an abortion after 20 weeks. Justice Rehnquist used this provision as a vehicle to challenge the *Roe* trimester and viability framework. Justice O'Connor, concurring in the *Webster* judgment, found the fetal testing provisions consistent with *Roe* and thus saw no need to re-examine the rationale of *Roe.*

Right of Privacy. Justice Stevens, dissenting in part, found the statute unconstitutional in so far as it interferes with contraceptive choices. By defining life as beginning at fertilization, the preamble implies regulation not only of previability abortions, but also of common modes of contraception such as the IUD and morning-after pill. He could find no secular purpose for the preamble, which he regards as a theological position that violates the establishment and free exercise clauses of the First Amendment.

Justice Blackmun, dissenting, criticized the plurality for not addressing the central issue of abortion. "The true jurisprudential debate underlying this case [is] whether the Constitution includes an 'unenumerated' general right to privacy * * * and, more specifically, whether and to what extent such a right of privacy extends to matters of childbearing and family life, including abortion."

Post–Webster. Even though *Webster* did not overrule *Roe,* legislatures acted quickly. Statutes codifying Roe were introduced to Congress and enacted in several states. Maryland enacted a statute granting adult women unrestricted access to abortions up to the time a fetus is able to survive outside the womb. Subsequently, an abortion may be performed if the fetus is deformed or if necessary to save the mother's life.

Other states enacted laws restricting or prohibiting abortion, depending upon the legislative clout of the opposing views. Provisions in a Pennsylvania statute banning abortion performed after 24 weeks or to select a baby's sex were not legally challenged, but a federal district court ruled other restrictions unconstitutional. The court observed that protection of "a woman's privacy rights and individual autonomy may soon be subjected to the vicissitudes of the legislative process". The nature of the protection, "if any," would primarily "depend on the ballot box" and "could vary from term-to-term, depending on the composition of the legislature." Planned Parenthood of Southeastern Pennsylvania v. Casey (E.D.Pa.1990).

The Territory of Guam enacted a statute that prohibits most abortions, including those resulting from rape or incest, or involving fetal abnormality. It permitted abortion only if a pregnancy would "endanger the life of the mother" or "gravely impair" her health, when approved by two independent physicians, whose decisions would be reviewed by a medical committee. The abortion procedure would constitute a felony for the provider and a misdemeanor for the woman. The statute was ruled unconstitutional in Guam Society of Obstetricians and Gynecologists v. Ada (D.C.Guam 1990). The *Guam* court said *Webster* leaves *Roe* "undisturbed," and *Roe* applies "with equal force" in Guam as in the states.

CHAPTER 3

RESTRICTIONS ON REPRODUCTIVE RIGHTS

3.01 Abortion Restrictions

A. PROCEDURAL RESTRICTIONS

Preliminary Requirements

A woman's right to an abortion as articulated by the Supreme Court is not absolute. The state may place procedural restrictions upon this right. Procedural restrictions include regulation of the facilities, the medical procedure chosen, and the personnel involved. Certain time constraints regarding the interval between dissemination of information about the abortion procedure to the woman and its actual performance also apply.

In *Roe* and *Bolton* the Court said the state may require a licensed physician to perform the abortion. But the state may not require accreditation by the Joint Commission on Accreditation of Hospitals, approval by a hospital staff abortion committee, concurrence of the performing physician's judgment by two independent physicians, or state residency of the woman.

The Court has recognized the right of a state to require reasonable record keeping and written consent of the woman. But a state cannot require consent of the woman's husband, nor prohibit abortion by saline amniocentesis after the twelfth week. Planned Parenthood of Central Missouri v. Danforth (S.Ct.1976). Nor can a state require spousal notification; the risk to future pregnancies is "de minimus." Scheinberg v. Smith (S.D.Fla. 1982).

Akron v. Akron Center for Reproductive Health, Inc. (S.Ct.1983) reaffirmed that the state's interest in protecting maternal health becomes compelling at approximately the end of the first trimester, but the challenged legislation was not reasonably designed to serve this interest. The Court ruled unconstitutional restrictions on abortion relating to "truly informed consent", a 24 hour waiting period, mandatory hospitalization for abortions after the first trimester and "humane and sanitary" disposal of fetal remains. Similarly, Thornburgh v. American College of Obstetricians and Gynecologists (S.Ct.1986), where Justice Blackmun commented that states are not free "to intimidate women into continuing pregnancies."

Two companion cases with *Akron* addressed different facts and reached different results. Justice Burger, Justice Powell and the three *Akron* dissenters voted to uphold a Missouri statute which required that a second physician be in attendance for abortions of a viable fetus, and that tissue removed during all abortions be examined by a pathologist. Planned Parenthood Assn. of Kansas City, Mo.,

Inc. v. Ashcroft (S.Ct.1983). The Court also upheld the conviction of a licensed obstetrician-gynecologist for performing a second trimester abortion outside of a licensed facility. Simopolous v. Virginia (S.Ct.1983).

The restrictions ruled unconstitutional by the federal district court in Pennsylvania's post-*Webster* statute included parental consent for minors, spousal notification, state-prepared informed consent and a 24 hour waiting period. Every section employing the statutory definition of "medical emergency" was enjoined because the definition interferes with the attending physician's judgment. Planned Parenthood of Southeastern Pennsylvania v. Casey (E.D.Pa.1990).

Parental Consent. A requirement of parental consent for abortions for minors under 18 was also prohibited in *Planned Parenthood*. Minors as well as adults possess constitutional rights.

The statute in Bellotti v. Baird (S.Ct.1979) attempted to circumvent the prohibition upon parental veto by allowing the minor to petition a court for overrule of the veto. This statute was struck on the narrow ground that the court had discretion to deny authorization for abortion to a mature, informed minor who was capable of making her own decision.

A Michigan statute which establishes a judicial bypass to parental consent requires public school officials to inform all students in grades six through 12 that they can seek an abortion without

their parents' knowledge or permission by petition-
ing a probate court for a waiver of the consent
requirements.

A private hospital may refuse to perform second
trimester abortions on minors in absence of parental consent even if no other hospitals in the area
provide such abortions. Simopoulos v. Virginia
(Va.S.Ct.1981).

Parental Notification. In general, carefully
drafted statutes which call for notification to parents and include a judicial bypass for mature or
emancipated minors will survive. See two post-
Webster cases, Ohio v. Akron Center for Reproductive Health, upholding a one-parent notification
statute with a judicial bypass and Hodgson v.
Minnesota (S.Ct.1990) striking a two-parent notification statute without a judicial bypass. *Hodgson*
said a state may require the minors to prove to the
court by clear and convincing evidence that they
are mature enough to make the abortion decision
without parental involvement. Parental notice
can be required where a minor is not emancipated
and does not demonstrate she is mature. H.L. v.
Matheson (S.Ct.1981). A pregnant student has a
cause of action under 42 U.S.C. § 1983 where she is
coerced into obtaining an abortion. Arnold v.
Board of Education of Escambia Co. (11th Cir.
1989).

Privacy and State Constitutions. Some states
provide constitutional protection for a minor's
right to abortion. Florida ruled unconstitutional a

parental consent statute which provided for appointment of a guardian ad litem for the fetus and a judicial bypass for parental consent. The right of a woman to choose abortion is a fundamental constitutional right, and "this right extends to minors." In re T.W., A Minor (Fla.S.Ct.1989). Similarly, Washington v. Koome (Wn.S.Ct.1975). The state's asserted interests in parental authority and support of the family unit do not justify this interference with the minor's right of privacy.

Fetal Tissue. Medical research on aborted fetal tissue is banned by the Department of Health and Human Services on grounds such research encourages abortions and would foster a "fetal-tissue" industry. A Minnesota statute providing for "dignified" burial or cremation of all aborted or miscarried fetuses was ruled not unconstitutionally vague; it was not an unconstitutional burden on the abortion choice, and neither over- nor under-inclusive. Planned Parenthood v. Minnesota (8th Cir.1990).

Regulation of Facilities

Availability of clinics and hospitals at which abortions are performed directly affects a woman's right to abortion. Most abortion facilities are located in metropolitan centers. Access to abortion is limited for women who live in rural areas.

Licensing of "freestanding surgical outpatient facilities" which in operation applies primarily to abortion clinics, was held constitutional in Birth Control Centers, Inc. v. Reizen. Conversely, a city ordinance regulating location, physical conditions, staff qualifications, and types of service and equipment required for abortion was held unconstitutional on the grounds of discriminatory and unnecessary conditions. Mahoning Women's Center v. Hunter (6th Cir.1979). Prohibition of advertising of abortions is not permissible. Bigelow v. Virginia.

B. FUNDING RESTRICTIONS

Congressional prohibitions against use of public funds for abortions for indigent women have severely limited their access to abortion. Riders restricting abortion have been attached to appropriations bills, defense bills, District of Columbia bills, international aid bills and Medicaid bills. Some states have also passed stringent funding restrictions.

1. Federal Funding

Medical care to the needy is largely made available through Medicaid, Title XIX of the Social Security Act. Medicaid funding is provided primarily by the federal government and administered by participating states. Participation is optional, but states that do take part must abide by the provisions of the federal legislation.

Hyde Amendment

A vote taken in 1976 attached the Hyde Amendment as a rider to an omnibus appropriations bill severely restricting funding of medically necessary abortions under Medicaid. Before passage of the Hyde Amendment, Medicaid paid for three of every ten abortions.

A federal district court ruled the Hyde Amendment unconstitutional, supporting the decision with a 213 page opinion documented with studies and statistics on the adverse effects of carrying to term pregnancies for which abortion is medically necessary. McRae v. Califano. Two arguments were emphasized. First, the amendment invades the constitutionally protected right of privacy of indigent women by precluding their right to an abortion. Second, indigent women are denied equal protection of the law since medically necessary procedures other than abortions are funded, including sterilization procedures such as vasectomies and tubal ligations.

The Supreme Court rejected these arguments and ruled the Hyde Amendment constitutional. Harris v. McRae. The Court expressly directed its analysis to the most restrictive version of the Hyde Amendment, allowing funding only to save the mother's life, although that amendment was not directly before the Court. The Court argued that pregnant women who are also poor still have a choice to have an abortion. The governmental objective to protect potential life is a legitimate objective, and unequal subsidization of necessary medical treatment is a rationally related means to achieve this objective.

First Amendment Concerns. *Harris* also rejected claims that the Hyde Amendment violates the establishment and free exercise clauses of the First Amendment. Any similarity to official church positions is coincidence. The same reasoning justifies the Adolescent Family Life Act, providing for chastity counseling of teens. Kendrick v. Bowen (S.Ct.1988).

Pro-choice supporters lack standing under Article III to challenge the tax exempt status granted to religious organizations as constituting government involvement in religion in violation of the establishment clause. No nexus exists between the taxpayers' allegations and Congressional exercise of taxing and spending powers. Abortion Rights Mobilization Inc. v. Baker (2d Cir.1989).

NGO Grants. Federal agencies frequently insert clauses in grants to nongovernmental organizations (NGOs) that preclude their performing or promoting abortions, even with separate funds. First Amendment rights of free speech and freedom of information are directly implicated in prohibitions against use of public funds for abortion counseling.

Title X, The Family Planning Services and Population Act of 1970, is the largest source of federal financial support for family planning. Regulations prohibit Title X grantees from referring or counseling about abortion, and from promoting abortion through such activities as preparing or disseminating educational information. They affirmatively mandate that grantees separate physical plant and financial records between prohibited and permitted Title X activities, and distribute to every pregnant client "a list of available providers that promote the welfare of the mother and the unborn child." The Supreme Court upheld these regulations in Rust v. Sullivan (U.S.1991) against challenge that the regulations exceed the scope of the statute and violate the First and Fifth Amendments. Chief Justice Rehnquist, writing for the Court, said "This is not the case of the Government 'suppressing a dangerous idea'"; rather, it is "simply insisting that public funds be spent for the purpose for which they were authorized." Similarly, Planned Parenthood Federation of America, Inc. v. AID, Agency for International Development (2d Cir. 1990).

2. State Funding

As a consequence of *Harris,* funding of abortions is determined by state government.

Webster, a logical extension of *Harris,* allows a state to prohibit performance of an abortion by any public employee or in any public facility unless necessary to save the mother's life. Some states have elected not to fund abortions; some have elected to fund abortions. Both positions have been subjected to judicial review.

Election Not to Fund. Election not to fund abortions has been overturned as a violation of state constitutions in some states, on either privacy or equal protection grounds.

Privacy Rights. The Michigan Court of Appeals ruled that a ban on Medicaid-financed abortions except to save the woman's life violates women's rights to privacy and equal protection of the laws under the state constitution. Doe v. Director of Mich. Dept. of Social Services (Mich.App.1991). Doe, a 15 year old girl, was impregnated by a rapist. An abortion was medically necessary, but her life was not at risk.

California and Connecticut similarly stress the right of privacy under their state constitutions in striking bans on abortion funding. Committee to Defend Reproductive Rights v. Myers, (Cal.S.Ct. 1981), and Doe v. Maher (Conn.Super.1986). The Connecticut court said that the state's asserted compelling interest in protecting the potentiality of human life does not outweigh the health of the woman at any stage of pregnancy.

Equal Protection Rights. Oregon refused to recognize a special privacy right under the state constitution, but the privileges and immunities clause requires striking a regulation which restricts funding for medically necessary abortions while allowing funding for some elective abortions. Planned Parenthood Ass'n, Inc. v. Department of Human Resources (Or.App.1983). Similarly, Massachusetts, Moe v. Secretary of Administration and Finance (Mass.S.Ct.1981).

Election to Fund. Challenges to election of local governmental units to fund abortions have arisen under capacity of taxpayers to bring suit. Denial of standing blocked an action which claimed that funding was in excess of county authority. Stam v. State. Taxpayers were granted standing in two Maryland counties but failed to persuade the court that a program of "comprehensive medical and other care" allows exclusion of funding of abortions that a woman and her physician determine are in her best interest. Kindley v. Governor of Maryland.

3.02 Third Party Interference

Interference with abortion rights by private entities and individuals takes myriad forms.

Direct Interference. Operation Rescue stages dramatic nationwide protests by blocking access and egress from abortion clinics, often resulting in arrests and jail terms for the protestors, and imposition of hundreds of thousands of dollars in fines. Private conspiracy claims against the protestors under 42 U.S.C. § 1985(3) have been successful in some jurisdictions and disallowed in others.

Permanent injunctions issued against Operation Rescue and individual protestors were upheld in National Organization for Women v. Operation Rescue (4th Cir.1990). The court said that women qualify as a protected class under the conspiracy statute. The permanent injunctions prohibiting Operation Rescue and its members from trespassing on, blockading, impeding or obstructing access to or egress from the medical clinics at which abortions are performed are not abuse of discretion. Fines totalling more than $450,000 in New York alone were imposed for violation of injunctions imposed against the protestors in New York State National Organization for Women v. Terry (2d Cir.1989).

The Fifth Circuit disallowed a private conspiracy action under Section 1985(3) on grounds the abortion context does not create an identifiable class within the statute, which was enacted to protect blacks against the Ku Klux Klan. Roe v. Abortion Abolition (5th Cir.1987). Similarly, for denial of abortion insurance, which failed on remand in Life Ins. Co. of North America v. Reichardt (9th Cir. 1979). For a private conspiracy action against a mock abortion clinic, see Lewis v. Pearson Foundation Inc. (8th Cir.1990).

Circuit courts disagree whether RICO liability may be imposed where defendants' actions lack a profit motive. A successful RICO suit was brought against abortion protestors in Northeast Women's Center, Inc. v. McMonagle (3d Cir. 1989), and Feminist Women's Health Center v. Roberts (W.D. Wash.1989). RICO actions absent a profit motive were disallowed in United States v. Ivic (2d Cir. 1983) and United States v. Flynn (8th Cir.1988).

The Supreme Court upheld the right of communities to ban picketing aimed specifically at an individual's home, in this case, an abortion provider. Frisby v. Schultz (S.Ct.1988). Justice O'Connor said such bans do not necessarily violate free speech rights; "there simply is no right to force speech into the home of an unwilling listener". A woman's health facility parking lot is not public property such that state and federal free speech guarantees preclude prosecution of abortion protestors. Fardig v. Municipality of Anchorage (Alaska App.1990).

Hospital Refusal. For a hospital's refusal to perform a first trimester abortion on a comatose woman at her husband's request without a court order, see Matter of Klein (N.Y.A.D.1989). The hospital acted in response to outsiders who petitioned for guardianship. The court ruled a nonviable fetus is not a "person" for whom a guardian could be appointed. Further, the strangers failed to demonstrate sufficient adverse interest between husband and wife to preclude a nonstatutory preference for appointment of the husband.

Private hospitals may claim a right to prohibit abortions in their facilities. New Jersey disallowed such a claim in Doe v. Bridgeton Hospital Ass'n, Inc. (N.J.S.Ct.1976) for private, nonprofit, nonsectarian hospitals which hold themselves open to the general public.

Physician Refusal. Physicians are generally free to refuse to perform abortions. Some women who test positive for the AIDS virus have been unable to secure abortions for this reason alone.

Other physicians, willing to perform abortions, may not do so because of difficulty in securing insurance for abortion related expenses. See Bauman v. Roberts (Or.S.Ct.1990), and Teamsters, Local No. 59 v. Chatham (Mass.S.Ct.1989).

3.03 Sterilization and Caesarean Abuse

Sterilization. Unlike abortion, sterilization is a procedure which permanently prevents conception. Coercive abuse occurs when sterilization is required tacitly or explicitly as a condition for welfare or child care allotments.

In Walker v. Pierce (4th Cir.1977), plaintiffs alleged that as Medicaid recipients the attending obstetrician at a county hospital required them "to consent to undergo a tubal ligation if they were delivering a third living child." The court reversed a verdict against the obstetrician. Nothing precludes a physician from pursuing a "personal economic philosophy" that has been publicly and freely announced.

Compulsory sterilization relates to sterilization directed against selected groups of people and effected through governmental action. Sterilization of institutionalized mental patients and sterilization of prison inmates has received different treatment by the Supreme Court.

The Court ruled that compulsory sterilization of an institutionalized woman does not violate her due process rights to bodily integrity when the procedure is in "the best interests of the patients and society." Buck v. Bell (S.Ct.1927).

Compulsory sterilization of an habitual criminal, however, would forever deny him of his fundamental right to have children. Skinner v. Oklahoma (S.Ct.1942). The Court distinguished *Buck* because her sterilization enabled "those who otherwise must be kept confined to be returned to the world."

Sterilization abuse also occurs when the procedure is performed without fully informed consent, particularly when the woman or man is unaware of the permanence of the procedure. For absence of fully informed consent, see Relf v. Weinberger (D.C.Cir.1977). Two girls, 12 and 14, were sterilized with federal funds, upon their mother's signed X. The mother later alleged she did not know the permanent consequences of the surgery. The case was declared moot when HEW withdrew the objectionable regulations.

Sterilization of mentally incompetent persons on petition of parents or guardians is generally permitted upon appointment of a guardian ad litem and other conditions. Matter of Guardianship of Hayes. Similarly, Matter of Grady. For abusive sterilization by parents, see Stump v. Sparkman (S.Ct.1978). The Supreme Court ruled that a judge has absolute immunity against action by a 15 year old girl whose mother secured an order for her sterilization without a hearing or notice to the girl. She was told the procedure was an appendectomy.

Caesarean Sections. A woman's right to control her own pregnancy has also been contested in the context of mandatory caesarean sections. A hospital secured a court order without notice to the family and performed a caesarean section on a woman dying of cancer in an unsuccessful attempt to save the life of the fetus. On appeal after the woman's death, the District of Columbia's highest court overturned the order because "the right of bodily integrity is not extinguished simply because someone is ill, or even at death's door." Nor can a fetus "have rights in this respect superior to those of a person already born." In re A.C. (D.C.App. 1990). Similarly, Curran v. Bosze (Ill.S.Ct.1990), rejecting bone marrow transplant to a half-brother.

In settlement of a civil action by A.C.'s family, George Washington University Medical Center developed a policy to inform pregnant patients of their right to determine the treatment for themselves and their fetus, and to authorize a family member or other person to make decisions on their behalf if necessary.

Compare Jefferson v. Griffin Spaulding County Hospital Authority (Ga.S.Ct.1981), upholding a similar order mandating a caesarean section where both the woman's life and the life of the fetus were in danger. The state may infringe on the right of the mother to the extent necessary to give a full term fetus a right to live.

3.04 Employment: Workplace Hazards

The workplace has been a major locale of discrimination against women because of their reproductive capacities. The likelihood that working conditions will be hazardous to fertility or dangerous for pregnant women cannot be used to exclude women from certain positions, or, conversely, to require sterilization or nonpregnancy as a condition of employment. International Union, United Automobile, Aerospace and Agricultural Implement Workers of America, UAW v. Johnson Controls, Inc. (S.Ct.1991).

Neutral plans designed to protect all employees are permissible. Lead, hormones, pesticides and herbicides are among the substances implicated in infertility and genetic damage for male workers. Dibromochloropropane is an example. Numerous factory and agricultural workers suffered testicular damage, sterility and chromosomal mutations before the chemical was banned by the Environmental Protection Agency. See Burdine v. Dow Chemical Company (8th Cir.1991). Members of the armed services have alleged reproductive disorders arising from spraying herbicides and participating in nuclear testing.

CHAPTER 4

HEALTH CARE

4.01 Liability: Theories of Recovery

Nature dictates that women bear the burdens of pregnancy and childbirth. Culture dictates that women bear the burden of contraception. In consequence of these natural and cultural dictates, women face critical health care risks that men do not. Women are the major consumers of health care largely because of medical treatment connected with their reproductive capacity.

Principles of tort and contract law have been shaped over the centuries from litigation between males arising in a laissez-faire buyer-beware relationship. It is not surprising that tort and sales law is strained to redress injuries caused by drugs and devices used exclusively by millions of women. Products have been marketed with minimum testing for short term adverse effects, and less for long term. Recovery in different states for resultant injuries is not uniform.

Some legal scholars recommend strict liability for redress of injury from female birth control methods. Because population control is of national concern and birth control is critical to population control, it is argued that women should not be legally required to bear the financial as well as the physical consequences of serious injury resulting from unavoidably unsafe birth control products.

Intensified research at public expense for safe, effective male contraceptives, such as a male pill or reversible vasectomy, has been recommended. Some doctors propose a simpler, more immediate solution: a return to the safe, easily used, inexpensive, readily available, gonorrhea protective, 97 percent effective (when properly used) condom.

Use of condoms has increased notably in the last decade, but not because of risk to women from ingestion of The Pill or insertion of an IUD. Fear of AIDS is the motivating factor.

A. RECOVERY UNDER TORT

Lawsuits against physicians for improper treatment are generally grounded in negligence and require fault for liability. Recovery requires proof of defendant's failure to conform to acknowledged professional standards of performance. Only rarely in medical malpractice is the defendant physician strictly liable without fault.

Suits for product liability often name the prescribing physician, the assisting facility, the dispensing pharmacy, and the manufacturing drug company. These actions may be grounded in either tort or contract. Each avenue has disadvantages for the plaintiff. Tort theory in recent years has mitigated the requirement of negligence in drug product liability. However, this move toward strict liability has been countered by adoption of the tort doctrine of unavoidably unsafe products in states that have adopted § 402(A) comment k of the Restatement, Second, Torts. Use of an unavoidably unsafe product with a high degree of social utility provides the drug company with an affirmative defense of assumption of risk by the patient.

B. RECOVERY UNDER UCC

The patient-consumer may seek the easier proof of strict liability by suing under the Uniform Commercial Code (UCC). This theory of action for product liability has specific limitations. The UCC covers only contracts of sale. Products secured under circumstances not constituting a sale, such as contraceptives dispensed free of charge by a public agency or sample drugs distributed free by the physician, are not covered. Second, the UCC does not generally cover services, which may include insertion of an intra-uterine device. If a prescription is filled at the same clinic at which it was prescribed, the UCC may be inapplicable because filling of a prescription under these circumstances constitutes a service.

Sales carry an express or implied warranty that the product is safe and effective for the claimed purpose. A third limitation of the UCC is that the warranty is inoperative if the patient has been informed of potential adverse side effects. The company can negate an implied warranty by providing information of side effects through clear, written notice to the physician or patient.

This defense is particularly effective for injuries resulting from prescription drugs or devices where a "learned intermediary", usually a physician, has been informed by the company of possible adverse side effects from use of the product or device. The learned intermediary theoretically at least passes this information to the patient along with the prescription. The patient, by using the product after notification, has consented to the possibility that injury may result and thus is barred from recovery.

C. LEGAL INADEQUACY

Note that tort and UCC suits are resolved in favor of the defendant at the same point of legal inquiry. Use of an unavoidably unsafe product with high social utility constitutes assumption of risk at tort law. Use of a product about which the patient has been warned of adverse side effects constitutes agreement to potential injury under the UCC.

Where a government agency is involved, an otherwise valid claim may fail. A county planning clinic providing free medication is an expansion of traditional governmental functions; sovereign immunity shields the county from liability for negligent insertion of an IUD. Casey v. Wake County Health Dept. (N.C.App.1980).

4.02 Product Liability

A. CONTRACEPTION

The early 1960s marked introduction of two methods of contraception that have revolutionized birth control. The first was the birth control pill, used by 150 million women world-wide. The impact of the birth control pill is so profound that to say simply "the pill" is to exclude reference to all other pills. By 1965, the pill accounted for one-third of all contraceptive procedures in use. The IUD was the second contraceptive devise widely adopted in the 1960s. The intra-uterine device interferes with implantation of the fertilized egg on the uterine wall.

Both the pill and the IUD were widely heralded as safe and sure methods of contraception. The unquestioning confidence of women in the pill and the IUD was misplaced.

Injuries from the pill and IUDs have spawned litigation in state and federal courts across the country. When women have been informed of potential risks, their use of the product is legally treated as acceptance of the risks. To recover for any injury suffered, the plaintiff must prove that the defendant was somehow negligent in producing or marketing the product.

The Pill

An estimated 10,000,000 women in the United States and 89,000,000 world-wide, take the pill.

The most serious side effect is blood clotting, which can cause permanently disabling and fatal strokes.

Women have had mixed success in litigation to recover for injuries from the pill. Planned Parenthood was liable to plaintiff under warranty of sale in Berry v. G.D. Searle & Co. A woman who was given free pills was not so fortunate. She was hospitalized with blood clots nine days after she began taking the pill. There was no consideration, therefore, no code warranty, therefore no recovery. Allen v. Ortho Pharmaceutical Corp.

However, where the patient is not warned that birth control pills create a risk of stroke, a judgment for defendant notwithstanding the verdict will be reversed. MacDonald v. Ortho Pharmaceutical Corporation (Mass.S.Ct.1985). Compliance with FDA guidelines does not provide the company with an automatic shield from liability. Justice Ruth Abrams wrote for the court that oral contraceptives differ from other prescription drugs. These "particular characteristics warrant the imposition of a common law duty on the manufacturer to warn users directly of associated risks".

Women consumers of the pill are not the only ones injured by them. Workers in a manufacturing facility for estrogen pills in Puerto Rico were covered under workmen's compensation for physiological disorders arising from exposure to the hormones. Santiago–Hodge v. Parke Davis & Co. (1st Cir.1988, 1990).

The IUD

Intra-uterine devices (IUDs) to prevent pregnancy were heralded as far less invasive than ingesting a little but powerful pill. Because IUDs are devices, stringent Federal Drug Administration pre-market testing required for drugs were not applicable. A.H. Robins Co. placed the IUD known as the Dalkon Shield on the market in 1971 with minimal testing. Adverse complications were immediately experienced and reported by physicians to Robins. Among the complications were damage to the fetus if pregnancy occurred, perforation of the uterus, pelvic inflammatory disease (PID), sterility, and death.

The Dalkon Shield was removed from the market in 1974. By this time 2.2 million had been sold. Ultimately, more than 190,000 women claimed damages from Robins for complications resulting from use of the device. Nearly 6,000 lawsuits were pending when Robins filed for bankruptcy. Theories of recovery against Robins were negligence, strict liability, express warranty, and fraud. In re A.H. Robins Co., Inc. "Dalkon Shield," (Multidistrict Litigation).

A punitive award of $7.5 million was upheld against Robins by the Kansas Supreme Court. The defendant argued that never before had such a high award been approved. The court responded that never before had it handled a case that demonstrated "corporate misconduct of such gravity and duration." The punitive award was justified "to punish Robins for its conduct and to discourage others from committing like wrongs in the future". Tetuan v. A.H. Robins Co. (Kan.S.Ct.1987). Dalkon Shield litigation to the fall of 1984 is ably outlined in Palmer v. A.H. Robins Co. (Colo.S.Ct.1984), which affirmed punitive damages of $6,200,000. Awards of punitive damages in civil cases do not fall under the Eighth Amendment's prohibition of excessive fines. Browning–Ferris Industries of Vermont, Inc. v. Kelco Disposal, Inc. (S.Ct.1989), or violate due process rights. Pacific Mutual Life Insurance Co. v. Haslip (S.Ct.1991).

Class actions operated to the benefit of Robins, since the issue of fault is kept separate from the issue of compensation. Statutes of limitations left many women without a remedy. Although the statute runs from date of infection, not insertion, Lindsey v. A.H. Robins Co. (N.Y.A.D.1983), if no cause of action accrues within 8 years, the claim is barred, Dortch v. A.H. Robins Co. (Or.App.1982).

Litigation finally ended when the Supreme Court declined to review cases which raised objections to a complex bankruptcy settlement. Denial of review cleared the way for payment of $2.5 billion dollars to more than 100,000 Dalkon Shield claimants. Menard–Sanford v. Mabey (4th Cir.1989) and In re A.H. Robins Co., (4th Cir.1989). The bankruptcy settlement bars future lawsuits against senior Robins officials, including members of the Robins family, and Aetna, the Robins insurance carrier.

IUDs manufactured by companies other than Robins have also caused injuries. The learned intermediary defense protected the drug company in Lacy v. G.D. Searle & Co. (Del.S.Ct.1989). Warning of risk "in precisely the manner" in which plaintiff was injured barred recovery in Collins v. Ortho Pharmaceutical Corp. (Cal.App.1986).

B.   DIETHYLSTILBESTROL

The drug diethylstilbestrol (DES), a synthetic estrogen, was widely used a generation ago to prevent miscarriage. Vaginal cancer and sterility in the daughters and granddaughters of the estimated 3,000,000 women who took DES have been linked to the drug. Thousands of DES claims have been filed. Some plaintiffs suffer from the rare clear cell adenocarcinoma cancer found almost exclusively in DES daughters. The signature cancer has appeared in a granddaughter, who died of the cancer at age 13, born to the wife of a DES son. DES daughters also suffer a marked increase in infertility, miscarriages, premature births and ectopic pregnancies. DES was manufactured under a common formula; a substantial amount was produced collectively. It was marketed generically and pharmacists often substituted one brand for another. As a consequence it is impossible for a plaintiff in a tort action to identify precisely the manufacturer of the drug that her mother or grandmother used in order to establish cause in fact. Conventional tort principles are inadequate to apportion risk sharing for the injuries caused by generic drugs produced by 300 companies. Different jurisdictions have come up with novel theories to accommodate the "inordinately difficult problems of proof caused by contemporary products and marketing techniques", in the words of New York State's highest court. Hymowitz v. Eli Lilly & Co. (N.Y.Ct.App.1989).

Recognizing that it is generally impossible for a DES plaintiff to identify which manufacturer supplied the drug used by her mother, *Hymowitz* held that liability could be imposed on the manufacturers in accordance with their share of the national DES market.

However, market share liability is several only. Recovery against any one company cannot be inflated to provide 100% compensation to the plaintiff when all companies are not before the court.

Class actions will lie where a substantial number of DES firms have been joined. A company will be liable for its market share unless it shows that it could not have produced the drug that injured a particular plaintiff. Sindell v. Abbott Laboratories.

Several states have adopted a "risk contribution" theory. The plaintiff need sue only one company, and that company need not constitute a substantial share of the market. If no other company is impleaded, the defendant company is liable for all damages from which it cannot exculpate itself. Collins v. Eli Lilly Co. (Wis.S.Ct.1984).

Illinois has adhered to conventional tort principles, and rejected market share liability where the manufacturer of the specific drug that caused the injury cannot be identified. The court said it is a fundamental principle of both negligence and strict liability law that the plaintiff must prove by a preponderance of the evidence that the defendant caused the plaintiff's injury. Smith v. Eli Lilly & Co. (Ill.App.1990). Accord, Mulcahy v. Eli Lilly & Co. (Iowa S.Ct.1986).

Third Generation. Granddaughters cannot recover unless the jurisdiction recognizes a pre-conception tort. New York rejected a third generation preconception tort on behalf of DES granddaughters in Enright v. Eli Lilly & Co. (N.Y.Ct.App.1991). The court quoted Albala v. City of New York (N.Y.Ct.App.1981), " 'the law cannot provide a remedy for every injury incurred.' " Several courts have found a preconception tort outside the DES context. See Bergstreser v. Mitchell (8th Cir.1978), Renslow v. Mennonite Hospital (Ill.S.Ct.1977), and Jorgensen v. Meade Johnson Laboratories, Inc. (10th Cir.1973).

Injury in utero to male children of DES mothers is uncertain but not ruled out. Further research is being conducted after a pilot test indicated that DES exposed men were infertile in higher proportion than the non-exposed control group.

The anti-nausea drug Bendectin allegedly has also caused in utero injury. Proof of causation, however, has been difficult. See Brock v. Merrell

Dow Pharmaceuticals, Inc. (5th Cir.1989). For jury rejection of claims of more than 800 youngsters in a class action see In Re Bendectin Litigation (6th Cir.1988).

4.03　Medical Malpractice

Actions against abortion providers for negligently performed abortions generally are not successful where the negligence results in the birth of a healthy child. Nanke v. Napier (Iowa S.Ct.1984). Similarly, for a failed sterilization. Macomber v. Dillman (Maine Sup.Ct.1986). But where the sterilization was sought for financial considerations, parents may recover the cost of rearing a normal, healthy but unwanted child. Burke v. Rivo (Mass. S.Ct.1990).

Costs of rearing a child with orthopedic disabilities born from a negligent sterilization are actionable. Ochs v. Borrelli (Conn.S.Ct.1982). Similarly, parents can receive extraordinary costs incurred raising a child born with severe genetic defect, following erroneous advice from a genetic counselor. The child, however, does not have a cause of action for wrongful life, grounded in a preconception tort. Viccaro v. Milunsky (Mass.S.Ct.1990).

Servicewomen who suffer injuries from negligent reproductive care in government facilities are faced with the *Feres* doctrine, which bars recovery against the government for injuries incidental to service. Feres v. United States (S.Ct.1950). However, recovery was allowed where Army doctors

failed to diagnose a neural tube defect during pregnancy. The woman would have undergone an
abortion had she known. Arche v. United States
Dept. of Army (Kan.S.Ct.1990).

4.04   Legislative Reform

In addition to pursuing personal injury judgments, women are utilizing other avenues to im-
prove their health care. A major legislative effort
is directed to reform of restrictive midwifery statutes under which the practice of midwifery has
been treated as the equivalent of practicing medicine without a license. See Bowland v. Municipal
Court (Cal.S.Ct.1976) and People v. Rosburg (Colo.
S.Ct.1991). In Massachusetts, an unusual statute
was upheld which has no restrictions on lay mid-
wives, who do not use obstetrical instruments or
prescribe drugs, but prohibits nurses from practicing midwifery without proper authorization.
Leigh v. Board of Registration in Nursing (Mass.S.
Ct.1985).

Traditionally, federally funded medical research
has neglected topics of concern to women, including osteoporosis and hormone therapy after meno-
pause. Research that is of importance to both
sexes, such as dietary changes or use of aspirin to
prevent heart attacks, has been conducted primarily with male subjects. Results with women subjects could vary significantly. There is a major
exception. Dollars spent to research contraceptives for females far exceeds that spent to research

contraceptives for males. Pressure by women's groups has resulted in National Institute of Health guidelines calling for increased attention to women's health concerns and use of female subjects in federally funded medical research projects.

4.05 Teenage Pregnancy

Each year approximately 400,000 girls between the ages of 10 and 17 become pregnant, including one in four who has been involved in an incestuous relationship. These young girls have a higher than average maternal mortality and deliver a higher than average percentage of babies with birth defects. McRae v. Califano (E.D.N.Y.1980).

The teenage girl, like the adult woman, bears the responsibility of preventing conception. Contraceptives are available to the young women and their partners; minors under 16 have a constitutional right to information about and access to contraceptives. Carey v. Population Services International (S.Ct.1977).

Educational Concerns. Pregnancy is the principal reason girls drop out of school. Compulsory exclusion of a pregnant girl from attendance in high school was barred as violation of personal right and liberty in Ordway v. Hargraves. Federal law now requires that pregnant students be allowed to remain in any school receiving federal funding. A more difficult problem for a pregnant teenage student is continuing her education if she

decides to keep the baby and has child care responsibilities. Many never return to school.

* * *

Part I has addressed legal aspects of reproductive rights and health care particularly affecting
women. Part II turns to rights at civil law, beginning with an historical perspective.

PART II

HISTORICAL DEVELOPMENT CONSTITUTIONAL AND CASE LAW TO CRAIG v. BOREN

[A]rbitrary power is like most other things which are very hard, very liable to be broken

Abigail Adams to John Adams (1776)

CHAPTER 5

CONSTITUTIONAL RIGHTS

5.01 The Constitution and State Autonomy

A. STATE AUTONOMY

The relationship between federal and state governments is closely linked to equal civil rights before the law. The federal government is one of delegated powers only. States have plenary power, sometimes called general police power.

Most laws that affect day to day activities are state laws, whether statutes or common law developed by the judiciary. Before the Civil War, the federal government had little power to interfere with the plenary power of states over individuals living in the state. States could pass just about any legislation they pleased, regardless of how restrictive of personal rights. Women's freedom of action was particularly restricted.

At the outbreak of the Civil War, state laws decreed that women, married or single, could not vote, serve on government boards, be elected to political office, attend college, or practice a profession. Married women could not sue or be sued, take out credit in their own names, own personal property, manage real property or enter into contracts.

The Civil War was fought to limit the plenary power of the states. Victory by the North established the supremacy of the federal government over the states, supremacy constitutionalized in the Civil War Amendments. The three Civil War Amendments—the 13th, prohibiting slavery; the 15th, protecting the right to vote; and the 14th, addressing due process and equal protection of the laws—were deliberately designed as counter majoritarian safeguards against arbitrary exercise of power by the states against individual rights. The purpose of the Civil War Amendments is parallel to that of the Bill of Rights, designed as counter majoritarian control against arbitrary interference with individual rights by the federal government.

Women sought unsuccessfully to be included in the protections of the Civil War Amendments. Their efforts were instead rewarded with inclusion of the word "male" in the Constitution for the first time, in the Fourteenth Amendment clause limiting Congressional representation of states which arbitrarily restrict the voting rights of "male citizens."

The Operative Clauses

The Fourteenth Amendment contains three clauses to protect individuals from unwarranted state interference with their rights. The amendment provides that "No State shall make or enforce any law which shall abridge the privileges or immunities of citizens of the United States * * * deprive any person of life, liberty, or property, without due process of law; nor deny to any person within its jurisdiction the equal protection of the laws." The Fourteenth Amendment also defines who are citizens: "All persons born or naturalized in the United States * * * are * * * citizens of the United States and of the State wherein they reside."

Before women could secure protection of the federal judiciary against invasion of their rights by the states, the Fourteenth Amendment must first have sufficient meaning to warrant federal judicial interference with state law, and second, must be interpreted to prohibit sex as well as race discrimination.

B. WOMEN AND THE FOURTEENTH AMENDMENT

The language that all persons born or naturalized in the United States are citizens of both the United States and the state in which they reside would seem broad enough to require that any rights protected by the states for men under the Fourteenth Amendment should also be protected for women. In two early sex discrimination challenges, the Court decided to the contrary: women as well as men enjoy the rights of national citizenship, but national citizenship does not include either the right to vote or the right to practice a profession, both of which may be restricted by the state to men.

1. Right to Practice Law

Myra Bradwell successfully completed the study of law, but was denied admission to the Illinois state bar. She claimed that the privileges and immunities clause of the Fourteenth Amendment protected her right as a citizen to practice the profession for which she had qualified. The Supreme Court disagreed. The privilege of practicing law is a privilege of the states, and "in no sense depends on citizenship of the United States." Bradwell v. Illinois. (S.Ct.1873).

Justice Bradley's concurring opinion observed that "The natural and proper timidity and delicacy which belongs to the female sex evidently unfits it for many of the occupations of civil life." Because a married woman had no legal existence separate from her husband and could not make binding contracts without his consent, she was "incompetent" to perform the duties of an attorney. Removal of the legal disability of married women to contract appears not to have occurred to the Court.

2. Right to Vote

Two years after *Bradwell* the Court had opportunity to decide whether the Fourteenth Amendment granted women the right to vote. At that time, no state granted women suffrage, although women could vote in the territories of Utah and Wyoming.

Virginia Minor, a citizen of the United States and of the State of Missouri as defined by the

Fourteenth Amendment, sought to enter her name on Missouri's voting records. The registrar refused. Because Virginia Minor was a woman, she could not sue on her own behalf, and her husband pressed a civil suit as joint plaintiff to compel the registrar to register his wife. The Supreme Court in an unanimous decision rejected her claim. Minor v. Happersett.

The Court acknowledged that "[t]here is no doubt that women may be citizens [and they] are persons * * *. But * * * it did not need this amendment to give them that position." Rather, the Court discussed the privileges and obligations of national citizenship, saying "Each one of the persons * * * becomes a member of the nation * * *. He owes it allegiance and is entitled to its protection. * * * The object is to designate by a title the person and the relation he bears to the nation." (Emphasis added). Since the Fourteenth Amendment relates only to federal citizenship and not to state citizenship, it did not require that the states allow women to vote.

Following Minor v. Happersett, campaigns were renewed to have Congress submit to the states a constitutional amendment granting suffrage to women. This did not occur until 1919, following years of intense effort, including picketing of the White House, arrests for obstructing the side walk, and hunger strikes by incarcerated suffragettes. When the amendment was submitted to the states for ratification, male voters were ready to accept women as voting associates. The Nineteenth Amendment was ratified in fifteen months.

Although women have acquired the right to vote, the decision in *Minor* is viable precedent today. In holding that at large election of city commissioners does not unconstitutionally dilute the voting strength of Blacks, the Court in Mobile v. Bolden (S.Ct.1980) borrowed these words from *Minor:* "More than 100 years ago the Court unanimously held that 'the Constitution of the United States does not confer the right of suffrage upon any one' * * *."

5.02 Expanding Federal Jurisdiction

A. SUBSTANTIVE DUE PROCESS

In the years following the turn of the century, the due process clause was selected as the vehicle for attempts to invalidate state statutes. The right to contract was a right included in the protection of the Fourteenth Amendment's prohibition to the states to deprive any person of "life, liberty, or property without due process of law." For due process clause interpretation, the Court used alternative approaches in challenges to social welfare legislation depending upon whether men or women were the focus of the legislation.

Men and Social Welfare

Where men were involved, the right to contract freely took dominance and led to the doctrine historically known as "substantive due process." The

principal case involving substantive due process is
Lochner v. New York (S.Ct.1905). In *Lochner,* a
New York statute that set a 60 hour limit on the
work week of bakers was held unconstitutional
because interference with an individual's right to
contract exceeded the state's police powers.

Women and Social Welfare

Where social welfare legislation involved women,
the Supreme Court took a different stance. In
Muller v. Oregon (S.Ct.1908) the Court said that
maximum weekly hours worked by women could
be regulated as reasonable exercise of the state
police power. Although under Oregon law women
did have power to contract equal to that of men,
the precedent of *Lochner* was not binding because
such a position would assume that "the difference
between the sexes does not justify a different rule
respecting a restriction of the hours of labor."

Justice Brewer, writing for the Court, said that a
woman "is not an equal competitor with her brother. * * * [L]egislation designed for her protection
may be sustained * * *. [H]er physical structure
and a proper discharge of her maternal functions—
having in view not merely her own health, but the
well-being of the race—justify legislation to protect
her from the greed as well as the passion of man."

In West Coast Hotel Co. v. Parrish, the Court
upheld a statute that regulated wages and hours
for women and children. A shift in the Court's
perspective for the proper scope of state police
power to address economic concerns of all workers

undergirds the 1937 decision in *West Coast*. The substantive due process concept of *Lochner* was rejected as inappropriate interference with social welfare legislation at both state and federal levels. Judicial approval of federal wages and hours regulations for men followed shortly. United States v. Darby (S.Ct.1941).

B. EQUALITY VIA SUFFRAGE

The Nineteenth Amendment prohibited the United States and any state from denying or abridging the right of citizens to vote on account of sex. This is the only place the word "sex" occurs in the Constitution. But equal political representation or appointment to public office did not automatically follow. Nor did an equal right to vote.

1. Procedural Differences

Procedural prerequisites to voting included payment of poll taxes. A Georgia law required men to pay poll taxes whether or not they voted; "females who do not register for voting" were exempt. The Supreme Court unanimously ruled that "[i]n view of burdens necessarily borne by [women] for the preservation of the race, the State reasonably may exempt them from poll taxes." Breedlove v. Suttles. The challenged statute was not repugnant to the Nineteenth Amendment.

Procedural restrictions upon voting that have been imposed only upon married women include

re-registering in the husband's name, and requiring them to vote in the husband's legal domicile.

2. Substantive Influences

The extent to which the Nineteenth Amendment
carried with it the right of women to participate in
other civic activities also was not clear. Common
law did not allow women to hold elective or appointive public office, including the judiciary, or to
serve on juries.

Jury Duty. Many states continued to exclude
women from jury duty although this position was
inconsistent with the Supreme Court's interpretation of the Fifteenth Amendment, which grants
suffrage to Blacks, and, by extension, the right to
serve on juries as well. Neal v. Delaware.

Women did not acquire the constitutional right
and obligation to have their names automatically
included in jury pools until 1975, when Billy Taylor challenged the absence of women from his jury
in Taylor v. Louisiana.

Elective and Appointive Office. Several courts
decided in the affirmative that the Nineteenth
Amendment entitles women to hold elective and
appointive offices. As a matter of practice, however, few women ran for office or sought appointment, and even fewer were elected or appointed.

Mandatory Equality. Participation by women in
politics was addressed in some states by requiring
that women have equal representation with men

on the governing bodies of state political parties. Washington state legislation enacted in 1927 was typical. The statute was unsuccessfully challenged 50 years later as an impermissible classification on the basis of sex in violation of the state equal rights amendment. Marchioro v. Chaney.

C. INCORPORATION

As has been seen, the substantive due process theory of *Lochner* was challenged during the depression years as inappropriate federal judicial interference with state welfare legislation. The federal judicial activism that characterized economic substantive due process has been replaced by activism pertaining to fundamental civil rights with which the states may not interfere.

State Action and Civil Rights

Before development of the doctrine of incorporation, citizens had no recourse to federal courts for protection against state interference with civil righs such as freedom of speech and press, and criminal rights such as right of counsel, and freedom from unreasonable search and seizure. State constitutions also include bills of rights, but the protections afforded citizens by state courts against invasion of these rights may be either more or less than that provided by the federal constitution.

Conversely, the language of the Fourteenth Amendment that prohibits states from denying any person equal protection of the law has no parallel language in the Bill of Rights applicable to the federal government. Congress could pass laws that treated people unequally subject only to the traditional standard of review for constitutionality of legislation known as the rational basis test.

Since 1965, the Supreme Court has recognized a right of privacy that is protected by the federal constitution against some state and federal interference.

Articulation of the right of privacy in the Bill of Rights and emergence of the legal principle of incorporation were necessary before the federal judiciary could protect the right against federal or state invasion. Incorporation came first.

The Logical Link

Identical language in the Fifth and Fourteenth Amendments that no person shall be deprived "of life, liberty, or property, without due process of law," provides logical support for the doctrine of incorporation. Beginning with First Amendment rights of freedom of speech, press, religion, and assembly fifty years ago and burgeoning in the civil rights litigation during the 1950s, the protections of the Bill of Rights have been selectively incorporated into the due process clause of the Fourteenth Amendment. See Gitlow v. New York (S.Ct.1925). By 1965 the principle was at hand by which the right of privacy, emanating from the penumbra of the Bill of Rights, was incorporated into the protections of the Fourteenth Amendment. Today most of the individual rights which are protected against federal invasion can be redressed in federal courts against state interference.

In like manner, the due process clause of the Fifth Amendment has been infused with an equal protection component through the Supreme Court decision in Bolling v. Sharpe (S.Ct.1954), a racial segregation case. As a consequence, federal laws are bound to treat equally all persons who are similarly situated. The link of the Bill of Rights to the Fourteenth Amendment and the equal protection clause of the Fourteenth Amendment to the Fifth Amendment of the Bill of Rights has significantly expanded the jurisdiction of the federal judiciary.

Incorporation enables federal courts to adjudicate the constitutionality of state statutes that infringe on the fundamental right of privacy, as occurred in *Griswold* and *Roe,* and of federal statutes that are alleged to treat men and women unequally, as occurred in challenge to the male only registration under the Military Selective Service Act. Rostker v. Goldberg (S.Ct.1981).

D. STANDARDS OF REVIEW

The Supreme Court has the power of judicial review through which it determines whether actions of the other two branches conform to the Constitution. It has formulated three standards of review to assist them in this task. Each standard has an ends and a means test, both of which must be satisfied if legislation and implementing executive action are to survive constitutional challenge.

The standard of review selected by the Court is critical to the decision ultimately reached. When the Court applies the lenient "rational basis" standard, most statutes survive challenge. Under the "heightened", or "intermediate", or "gender" standard, some legislation survives and some legislation falls. Where governmental classification invokes the "strict scrutiny" standard, the Court usually finds the challenged statute unconstitutional. The rational basis test is the default standard, used when the statutory or executive classification does not invoke either the gender standard or strict scrutiny.

In every Supreme Court case which addresses a constitutional issue, a standard of review is explicitly or implicitly at work, testing constitutional requirements of ends and means.

1. Rational Basis Test

The rational basis test is phrased as requiring that the purpose, the end for which a statute is enacted, must be constitutionally legitimate, and the means selected must be rationally related to accomplishing this end.

The prongs of the rational basis test are set forth in two early opinions written by Chief Justice John Marshall. Marbury v. Madison (S.Ct.1803) establishes the principle of judicial review by ruling

unconstitutional an act of Congress which was not
authorized by the Constitution.

"To what purpose," Marshall asks, "are powers
limited, and to what purpose is that limitation
committed to writing; if these limits may, at any
time, be passed by those intended to be restrained?
The distinction between a government with limited
and unlimited powers is abolished, if those limits
do not confine the persons on whom they are
imposed." Only statutes which seek to accomplish
purposes entrusted by the people to the Congress
through the Constitution are legitimate.

Nor is it enough that the statutory purpose be
legitimate. The means adapted to carry out a
legitimate purpose must be "plainly adapted" to
this end, and "consist with the letter and the spirit
of the constitution" or it will fail. McCulloch v.
Maryland (S.Ct.1819).

Development of standards of review alternative
to the rational basis test depending upon the subject matter with which the statute deals, has further expanded the federal judiciary's jurisdiction.
Articulation of differing standards accompanied development of the doctrine of incorporation.

2. Strict Scrutiny

If a statute classifies on the basis of a fundamental right or a suspect group of persons, the Court
sets aside the rational basis test and applies the
"strict scrutiny" standard.

A statute subject to strict scrutiny must serve a compelling government interest and the specific provisions of the statute must be "strictly tailored" to the achievement of the compelling purpose, with no less invasive means available. Under strict scrutiny, a statute that serves only a legitimate governmental purpose or is only rationally related to achievement of its purpose will not support selective imposition of a burden on, or denial of a benefit to, a suspect class of people. Nor will it legitimatize invasion of a fundamental right.

a. Fundamental Right

Justice Cardozo defined a fundamental right as one " 'so rooted in the traditions and conscience of our people as to be ranked as fundamental,' " a right "implicit in the concept of ordered liberty." Palko v. Connecticut.

Invasion of the fundamental right of privacy was the constitutional ground for striking the statute prohibiting use of contraceptives in Griswold v. Connecticut and the statute prohibiting abortion before viability in Roe v. Wade. In neither case was a compelling state purpose established that warranted invasion of the personal rights of individuals.

b. Suspect Classification

Suspect classifications are those made on the basis of race or national origin. They are classifications of "discrete and insular minorities" in the

words of Justice Stone's famous footnote four in
United States v. Carolene Products Co. Where a
criminal statute prohibited racially mixed couples
from "habitually" occupying "in the nighttime the
same room," the Court applied strict scrutiny and
ruled the statute unconstitutional. McLaughlin v.
Florida. The state's alleged objective "to prevent
breaches of the basic concepts of sexual decency"
was not sufficiently compelling to justify subjecting
only interracial couples to criminal punishment for
the assumed promiscuous behavior. Although the
Court analyzed *McLaughlin* in terms of equal protection and discrimination against interracial couples compared to couples of the same race, it is
noteworthy that the right of privacy, articulated
just the year before in *Griswold,* was also involved.

3. A Gender Standard?

Under federal constitutional review, gender
based classifications are not subjected to strict
scrutiny. Nonetheless, a more stringent standard
of review than the traditional rational basis test
has developed in the Court's adjudication of gender
based statutes. Before discussing the gender standard of review, a look at the historical application
of the rational basis test to sex based classifications
is warranted.

a. Perspectives

Statutes that impinge a fundamental right invoke strict scrutiny under either equal protection

or due process analysis. An issue of the appropriate standard of review to apply occurs in challenge to statutes that classify de jure by sex but are interpreted by the Court not to touch a fundamental right. The Supreme Court in the 1970s reviewed several federal and state statutes which expressly classified on the basis of sex. The Court applied the traditional rational basis test, but analyzed much more critically both the importance of the claimed statutory purpose, and the means by which the statute proposed to accomplish this purpose. In some of the cases, the statutes survived; in others, they fell.

These cases culminated in Craig v. Boren (S.Ct. 1976), which articulated an intermediate, or gender standard of review. The gender standard is applied primarily to de jure sex based classifications that implicate the equal protection clause of the Fourteenth Amendment and its Fifth Amendment due process counterpart.

Selection of a standard of review for analysis of statutes involving women's rights and sex based discrimination must initially distinguish cases involving denial of fundamental rights under due process claims from those involving gender based classification under equal protection claims. The Supreme Court does not always agree whether due process or equal protection analysis is appropriate for alleged gender based discrimination. Cleveland Board of Education v. LaFleur (S.Ct.1974).

When claims of discrimination are made that laws do not treat equally men and women who are similarly situated, the equal protection clause of the constitution is implicated. The concept of equal protection of the law is potentially weaker than that of due process protection of fundamental rights because equality before the law is relative. Equal protection ostensibly does not address the content of the laws, which may be either a gratuitous benefit or an odious burden. The equal protection clause requires only that the benefit or burden be imposed equally upon every person.

Historically, the Court applied the rational basis test to evaluate statutes classifying on the basis of gender. A survey of Supreme Court cases dating from 1948 reveals the range of gender based classifications held constitutional under the rational basis test. Many are grounded in the common law principle that the husband and wife constitute a legal unity, in which the wife's status before the law is merged with that of her husband.

The *Commentaries* of Sir William Blackstone, an eighteenth century English jurist, were reference for lawyers and judges during the formative years of American law. His language delineating the legal consequences of matrimony became the basis for United States marriage law. Blackstone wrote, "By marriage, the husband and wife are one person in law; the very being of legal existence of the woman is suspended during the marriage, or at least is incorporated and consolidated into that of the husband; under whose wing, protection and cover, she performs everything." The legal term for this relationship is coverture.

When legal submersion in coverture did not apply, women were classified in statutes with infants and incompetents. Married or single, women did not fare well under constitutional law, common law or statutory law until the recent past.

b. The Recent Past

Between 1940 and 1971, a number of determined women brought suit to challenge state and federal statutes that classified by sex and pursued them to the Supreme Court. Equally important, the Supreme Court granted review. The plaintiffs were not successful, but the cases heightened public debate that women are entitled under the federal constitution to be treated equally with men. Before 1971, the Court consistently applied the rational basis test and in every instance the de jure sex based classification was found not to violate women's rights under the federal constitution.

States could systematically exclude women from serving on juries, Hoyt v. Florida (S.Ct.1961); deny married women the right to make contracts, even if taxpayers ultimately foot the bill, Yazell v. United States (S.Ct.1966); establish as a matter of law that a wife's domicile is that of her husband, Riley v. New York Trust Co. (S.Ct.1940); exclude women from specified employment, Goesaert v. Cleary

(S.Ct.1948); establish separate but seldom equal single sex schools, Williams v. McNair. (S.Ct. 1971).

State courts and lower federal courts ruled that states could set an earlier age of majority for females, so that daughters did not receive financial support for as long as sons, Jacobson v. Lenhart (Ill.S.Ct.1964); bar women from suing penurious husbands for support as having tacitly accepted the conditions under which they live, McGuire v. McGuire (Neb.S.Ct.1953); provide working women with fewer benefits for paid employment under workmen's compensation laws, Duley v. Caterpillar Tractor Co. (Ill.S.Ct.1969); and restrict hours for women students but not for men students, Robinson v. Board of Regents (6th Cir.1973).

Separate and unequal public schools for males and females were not at all unusual. Many cities had a separate high school for boys which specialized in rigorous academic study, particularly in the sciences and mathematics. Girls wanting a stiffer education were shuffled off to a smaller girls' academic school with poorer facilities, less qualified teachers and less challenging class offerings. State vocational and professional schools prohibited females altogether or limited enrollment to as low as 2%. Sports offerings for girls at all educational levels were nonexistent or nominal compared to those for boys.

c. A New Approach

But a change was in the wind. A federal district court in 1970 found unconstitutional the exclusion of women from a New York pub that had served males exclusively for 115 years. Seidenberg v. McSorleys' Old Ale House, Inc. (S.D.N.Y.1970). Two women who were denied service brought suit pursuant to 42 U.S.C. § 1983, claiming that defendant's refusal to serve women at its bar constituted a denial of rights secured by the equal protection clause of the Fourteenth Amendment. The court applied the rational basis test and granted judgment on the pleadings for the female plaintiffs. Discrimination based on sex will be tolerated only if the exclusion of women bears a rational relationship to the permissible purpose of the exclusion, and no rational basis for serving men but not women was offered. The court rejected argument that customer preference, avoidance of moral problems, or need to modify sanitary facilities justified the ban against women. *Seidenberg* is the sole case applying the rational basis test before 1971 that resulted in a finding of unconstitutional gender based classification.

While *Seidenberg* was being litigated in a New York federal court, a statute similar to that upheld in Goesaert v. Cleary was challenged in California. The court unanimously invalidated the statute prohibiting all women except female bar owners and wives of bar owners from tending bar. Sail'er Inn, Inc. v. Kirby. The California supreme court stated

that sex, like race and lineage, "is an immutable
trait, a status into which the class members are
locked by the accident of birth." Sex is differentiated from nonsuspect classes in that the sex of an
individual frequently bears no relation to ability to
perform or contribute to society. A further characteristic underlying suspect classifications is the associated stigma of inferiority and second class citizenship. The court therefore concluded that "sexual classifications are properly treated as suspect"
and ruled the statute in violation of the California
constitution, the United States constitution, and
Title VII of the Civil Rights Act of 1964.

Another challenge to sex classification was taking place in a federal court, this time to regulations providing that men be given priority over
women for acceptance to the federally funded WIN
work training program. The male preference was
ruled a violation of the Fifth and Fourteenth
Amendments, and also of rights secured by Title
VII. Thorn v. Richardson.

Seidenberg, Sail'er Inn and *Thorn* were decided
within months of Reed v. Reed, in which the Supreme Court for the first time struck a statute that
classified on the basis of sex as violating the equal
protection clause of the federal constitution. The
Reed Court utilized the rational basis test and did
not address argument that a statute that classifies
by gender should be subjected to strict scrutiny.

Reed ushered in a decade of intense judicial
activity concerning sex discrimination, culminating

in numerous Supreme Court decisions interpreting the constitutional guarantee of equal protection in face of de jure and de facto gender based classifications. The standard of review evolved by the Court in deciding de jure classifications—a standard midway between the rational basis test and strict scrutiny—is the focus of the next chapter.

CHAPTER 6

THE GENDER STANDARD

6.01 Reed v. Reed

The Idaho statute in Reed v. Reed provided that between husband and wife, both of whom file applications to administer a deceased child's estate, the husband has absolute preference to be administrator. The Supreme Court once again applied the rational basis test, but this time the Court took a closer look at the ends and means of the statute. The Court struck the statute because the gender classification was not substantially related to the statutory purpose of administrative convenience. Reed v. Reed. Chief Justice Burger, speaking for the Court, recognized that the equal protection clause does not deny to states the power to treat different classes of persons differently. The question, however, is whether "a difference in the sex of competing applicants for letters of administration bears a rational relationship to a state objective" that the statutory classification seeks to serve.

To give a mandatory preference to either sex merely to eliminate a hearing on the merits is to make the very kind of arbitrary legislative choice that the equal protection clause prohibits. Nor does the purpose of avoiding intrafamily controversy suffice in this context.

Challenges to other gender based classifications followed *Reed* in rapid succession. The widely divergent fact patterns of these cases helped to focus the Court's analysis of gender based statutes and to expose embedded discrimination against women, and not infrequently against men, solely because of their sex. In consequence, an appropriate standard of review for gender based classifications was formulated.

The increasing momentum of the women's movement was a major factor influencing judicial development of a gender standard of review. Some courts, as California in *Sail'er Inn,* applied strict scrutiny to statutory classifications by sex. Four justices of the Supreme Court wanted to establish sex as a class protected by strict scrutiny under federal constitutional analysis. Frontiero v. Richardson (S.Ct.1973).

Equal Rights Amendments. Between 1968 and 1976, fifteen states adopted equal rights amendments, and Congress submitted a federal equal rights amendment to the states for ratification. The close failure of the federal ERA to be ratified, just shy of the necessary number of states, reflects in large measure the male composition of state legislatures and the imbalance between allotting an equal vote for sparsely populated and heavily populated states. Of the 12 states with the largest populations, nine voted to ratify, including the four most highly populated: California, New York, Texas and Pennsylvania.

The quest and the need for a constitutional guarantee of equal rights for women arise from the same ideological and pragmatic factors that drove the founding fathers to establish the Constitution itself and insist upon inclusion of the Bill of Rights: to secure themselves against unwarranted governmental interference with their lives.

6.02 An Emerging Standard

A. EARLY CASES

The significant element of gender based challenges following *Reed* is not the Court's uncertainty as to analysis and outcome. It is judicial recognition that sex discrimination arising from unconscious acceptance of sexual assumptions has been codified into law, and that gender based classifications are entitled to a closer scrutiny than the traditional rational basis test provides.

Two significant cases in addition to Reed v. Reed were addressed by the Court in 1971. The traditional rational basis test was sufficient to uphold the challenged statute against an equal protection challenge in Williams v. McNair, in which male plaintiffs were denied admission to a public college for women. A constitutional issue was avoided in United States v. Vuitch when the Court interpreted "health" in an abortion statute to include "mental health," a critical definition in subsequent adjudication of Roe v. Wade. The right of privacy and pregnancy were also involved in Struck v. Secretary of Defense, in which a lieutenant plaintiff challenged the Air Force policy under which she was terminated upon becoming pregnant. The Court declared the case moot after the Air Force abandoned its policy.

B. DISCRIMINATION AGAINST MEN

1. Unwed Fathers

Shortly after *Reed,* the Court addressed the first of many cases involving discrimination against men. The right of parenting, one of the "basic civil rights of man" was at issue in Stanley v. Illinois. Stanley was an unwed father of three children, with whom he had lived intermittently and supported. Upon their mother's death, two of the children were declared wards of the state under a statute which conclusively presumed that unwed fathers are unfit parents. The Court struck the statute as a violation of due process because Stanley was entitled to a hearing to determine whether in fact he was an unfit parent. Denial of the hearing also denied him equal protection of the laws since unwed mothers were presumed fit and entitled to a hearing before losing custody.

2. Spousal Benefits

Housing and Medical Benefits. Discrimination against women in the military, and indirectly against their spouses, was at issue in Frontiero v.

Richardson (S.Ct.1973). A female member of the armed services was required to prove that her spouse was financially dependent upon her before spousal housing and medical benefits were awarded. A married male serviceman received spousal benefits automatically; his wife's financial status was irrelevant. Because a Congressional statute was at issue, the equal protection component of the due process clause of the Fifth Amendment was invoked. The Court ruled the statute unconstitutional. Concerns for administrative convenience were not sufficiently important to override the right of women to equal treatment before the law.

Justice Brennan, announcing the judgment of the Court, observed that *Reed* made a "departure from 'traditional' rational basis analysis with respect to sex-based classifications", a departure which is clearly justified. Justice Brennan argued that strict scrutiny should be applied to classifications on the basis of sex. He noted that the United States has had a "long and unfortunate" history of sex discrimination. The paternalistic attitude was "so firmly rooted in our national consciousness" that the condition of the nineteenth century woman was comparable to that of the slave before the Civil War. Justice Rehnquist dissented on the grounds that the rational basis test is the proper standard of review for gender based classifications.

Survivors' Benefits. A provision of the Social Security Act that denied benefits to surviving husbands with dependent children that were automatically awarded to surviving wives with dependent children was struck in Weinberger v. Wiesenfeld. As in *Frontiero,* the discrimination against men was derivative from discrimination against women. Wiesenfeld's wife, who had worked full time in covered employment and was the principal support of her husband, died in childbirth. Although men are more likely to be the primary support of their wives and children, a "gender-based generalization cannot suffice to justify the denigration of the efforts of women who do work and whose earnings contribute significantly to their families' support."

3.   Compensatory Statutes

Statutes providing economic advantages to women to compensate for past discrimination were upheld in Kahn v. Shevin and Schlesinger v. Ballard although in both instances discrimination against men resulted.

Tax Exemption. In *Kahn,* a Florida statute provided property tax exemptions to widows, but not to widowers. The Court agreed that the classification between widows and widowers was a "fair and substantial relation" to the state objective of reducing "the disparity between the economic capabilities of a man and a woman." Justice Brennan, dissenting, argued that gender classifications are suspect and must be subjected to close judicial scrutiny because classification by sex has "too often * * * been inexcusably utilized to stereotype and stigmatize politically powerless segments of society." Justice White, dissenting, observed that many rich widows do not need largess from the state, and many widowers do.

Promotion Advantage. The *Schlesinger* Court upheld a naval regulation that women line officers may have a minimum of thirteen years of officer service duty before being discharged for nonpromotion, whereas male line officers were discharged in the year of their second failure to be promoted. The Court's 5–4 decision did not clarify the Court's position on gender based discrimination. Justice Stewart, speaking for the majority, said the statutory preference given women is rationally related to the goal of providing women officers with "fair and equitable career advancement programs." The preference reflects "demonstrable fact that male and female line officers in the Navy are *not* similarly situated with respect to opportunities for professional service."

C. EMPLOYMENT AND PREGNANCY

Three key cases interpreting the rights of pregnant employed women were decided during the period the Court was seeking to establish a consistent standard of review for gender based classification. Two cases analyzed pregnancy under the due process concept of the fundamental right of procreation and familial privacy. The strict scrutiny standard applied, and the women plaintiffs prevailed. The third case analyzed pregnancy from the standpoint of classification under the equal protection clause. The court decided pregnancy is not gender based and therefore the rational basis test applies. The challenge failed.

1. Fundamental Right

Mandatory Leave. Mandatory unpaid leave for pregnant school teachers constitutes unwarranted interference with their freedom of personal choice in matters of family life and violates their right of privacy. Cleveland Board of Education v. LaFleur. Arguments that mandatory leave was necessary to maintain continuity of instruction and to protect the health of the mother and unborn child were rejected by the Court. No rational relationship was established between asking the pregnant teacher to leave in mid-December rather than at the end of the semester in January, as she requested. Nor were concerns for physical capacity justified since they established an irrebuttable presumption of physical incompetency. Justice Rehnquist, dissenting, rejected reliance on the due process clause and a trend toward individualized treatment of cases. He argued that the Court's "disenchantment with 'irrebuttable presumptions,' and its preference for 'individualized determination,' is in the last analysis nothing less than an attack upon the very notion of lawmaking itself."

Unemployment Compensation. The right of familial privacy supported a brief per curiam opinion in which the Court invalidated Utah's denial of unemployment compensation to women in the last three months of pregnancy and the first six weeks after childbirth on the conclusive presumption that they are unfit for gainful employment. Turner v. Department of Employment Security.

The Utah supreme court framed the issue in terms of whether the statute "denies to her rights which are given to males," and said, "We do not think so." The court reasoned, "Should a man be unable to work because he was pregnant, the statute would apply to him equally as it does to her. What she should do is to work for the repeal of the biological law of nature. She should get it amended so that men shared equally with women in bearing children. If she could prevail upon the Great Creator to so order things, she would be guilty of violating the equal protection of the law unless she saw to it that man could also share in the thrill and glory of Motherhood."

2. Gender Neutral Classification

For discrimination claims arising under a state employment medical program that excluded pregnancy coverage, the Court applied the rational basis test and found the state program rationally served a legitimate state purpose. Geduldig v. Aiello. The purpose was to provide low cost medical and disability protection to employees, and the selected means—exclusion of coverage for medical and disability expenses accompanying normal pregnancy and delivery—was rationally related to the end.

The standard of strict scrutiny required by the fundamental right/due process strand of *Cleveland* and *Turner* was not invoked in *Geduldig* because the disability program was regarded as an economic benefit rather than a state imposed burden on the fundamental right of a woman to be pregnant. The more stringent equal protection standard of review utilized in *Reed, Frontiero* and *Stanley* did not apply because the Court said pregnancy is not a gender based classification.

Justice Stewart, writing for the majority, said "While it is true that only women can become pregnant, it does not follow that every legislative classification concerning pregnancy is a sex-based classification * * *." Rather, the program "divides potential recipients into two groups—pregnant women and nonpregnant persons. While the first group is exclusively female, the second includes members of both sexes." Actuarial benefits therefore accrue to both sexes. It follows that the program is not discriminatory on the basis of sex.

D. AGE DIFFERENTIAL

A state statute setting the age of majority for women at 18 and for men at 21 was challenged in Stanton v. Stanton. Appellee ceased providing support for his daughter at age 18, and continued payments on the son's account. The Court found it unnecessary to decide whether a classification based on sex is inherently suspect. There was nothing rational in the state's claim that girls tend to mature and marry earlier than boys, particularly since by statute the boys gained majority upon marriage. The Court said the female is no longer destined solely for the home and rearing of the family and the male only for the marketplace and the world of ideas. Justice Rehnquist alone dissented.

E. JURY DUTY

Gwendolyn Hoyt, convicted of second degree murder of her husband by an all male jury, appealed her conviction to the Supreme Court in 1961 on grounds that a Florida statute which required women to make a trip to the court house and register before being called for jury duty denied her equal protection of the laws.

Hoyt argued that women jurors would have been "more understanding or compassionate than men" in assessing the quality of her act and her defense of temporary insanity. In rejecting her challenge, the Court said a defendant is not entitled to "a jury tailored to the circumstances of the particular case."

A similar statute insulating women from jury duty was addressed again in 1975 in Taylor v. Louisiana (S.Ct.1975). Taylor, charged with aggravated kidnapping and rape, was male. This time the Court ruled the statute unconstitutional. The Court obliquely said that *Taylor* overruled *Hoyt* to the extent they were inconsistent. Other than the time frame, the factual difference between the two cases is difficult to identify. The two defendants were similarly situated. Both were criminal defendants; each was charged with violent assault against a member of the opposite sex.

A right to an impartial jury and equal protection of the laws were clearly implicated in both cases. As Justice Rehnquist pointed out in dissent in *Taylor,* the male defendant had less claim to unconstitutional treatment than did the female defendant in *Hoyt.*

There is, however, a significant legal difference. Taylor relied on his fundamental right to a trial by jury guaranteed by the Sixth Amendment; Hoyt relied on her right to equal protection of the laws under the Fourteenth Amendment. Taylor is tacit evidence that the judiciary gives less protection to rights analyzed under the equal protection strand, to which women's rights are often funneled, than under the fundamental rights strand, where men's rights tend to land.

6.03 Craig v. Boren

By 1976 only scattered remnants remained in the laws of the fifty states that differentiated between the age of majority for males and females. An Oklahoma statute prohibited the sale but not the consumption of 3.2 beer to males under age 21, and prohibited sale to females under 18, setting a criminal penalty against both buyer and seller upon violation. Thus the young men's female companions over age 18 could buy the beer, and both

could drink it. Men under 21 out on the town
without female companions could not buy any
beer. This discrimination against men provided
the vehicle for a suit seeking declaratory and injunctive relief against enforcement of the statute.
On these facts the Supreme Court articulated a
standard of review for gender based classifications
in Craig v. Boren.

A. ARTICULATING THE STANDARD

In writing the *Craig* opinion for the Court, Justice Brennan drew on the principle that he developed in *Frontiero, Wiesenfeld* and *Stanton* that the
equal protection clause commands that classifications based solely upon sex must be subjected to
more stringent review than is provided by the
rational basis test. Justices Blackmun, Powell and
Stevens wrote concurring opinions for a total of six
justices agreeing on the standard of review for sex
based classifications articulated by Justice Brennan. Justice Powell observed that the Court has
had difficulty in agreeing upon a standard, but said
that "candor compels" recognition that the relatively deferential rational basis standard takes on
a sharper focus when the Court reviews gender
based classifications.

Craig is of particular significance as the vehicle
for articulation of a gender based standard of review because it does not involve a fundamental
right, as was true in Stanley v. Illinois; nor protection of a widower parent, as was true in Wein-

berger v. Wiesenfeld; nor compensatory remedial preference, as was true in Kahn v. Shevin and Schlesinger v. Ballard. In *Craig,* as in *Reed,* the issue of sex discrimination was raised without undue coloring by other factors.

"Fair and Substantial"

Key language of the gender based standard can be traced to F.S. Royster Guano Co. v. Virginia, which was quoted in *Reed* as requiring that a classification "must be reasonable, not arbitrary, and must rest upon some ground of difference having a fair and substantial relation to the object of the legislation, so that all persons similarly circumstanced shall be treated alike." Justice Brennan began his analysis by stating that *Reed* and subsequent cases establish that "[t]o withstand constitutional challenge classifications by gender must serve important governmental objectives and must be substantially related to achievement of those objectives."

Craig interprets *Reed* and its successors as holding that there is no place in gender based classification for deferential scrutiny of the rational basis test under which the Court may imagine a legitimate objective and accept any nexus linking statutory classification to achievement of the statutory purpose. Adopted in its place is a more stringent standard which, nonetheless, is not so strict as that commanded by suspect classifications of race and national origin.

In short, the language of the gender based standard suggests that some statutes classifying by sex will be sustained and others will be invalidated. This expectation comports with Court decisions in gender based classifications both before and after *Craig.*

B. APPLYING THE CRAIG STANDARD

In applying the standard articulated to the facts of *Craig* itself, Justice Brennan concluded that the statute "invidiously discriminates against males 18–20 years of age." Justice Brennan agreed that the proffered state objective of furthering traffic safety was important. However, statistics offered by the state did not establish that prohibition of sale of 3.2 beer to males under 21 substantially contributed to a reduction in automobile accidents.

Justice Rehnquist, dissenting, claimed that the Court has pulled the new standard of review "out of thin air." The words "important" and "substantially" are "so diaphanous and elastic as to invite subjective judicial preferences * * * masquerading as judgments * * *."

6.04 Paradigm Cases

On analysis, *Reed* and *Craig* constitute clear examples of the two prongs of the gender standard of review. The statute in *Reed* was unconstitutional because the state objective of administrative convenience was not sufficiently important to override women's right to equal protection of the laws.

The statute in *Craig* was unconstitutional because the connection between the important state objective of traffic safety and sale of 3.2 beer was not substantial.

PART III

CONTEMPORARY ISSUES CONSTITUTIONAL AND CASE LAW SINCE CRAIG v. BOREN

Traditionally, [sex] discrimination was rationalized by an attitude of romantic paternalism which, in practical effect, put women not on a pedestal, but in a cage

Justice Brennan, Frontiero v. Richardson (1973)

Perspectives

The Supreme Court is not in complete agreement that a three tiered level of review—rational scrutiny, gender scrutiny and strict scrutiny—is an appropriate mode of constitutional analysis. Nor are the Justices in accord that the gender standard should be applied to classifications that discriminate against men with the same tenor in which it is applied to classifications that discriminate against women. These differences are not resolved. They surface repeatedly in Supreme Court analysis of cases challenging sex discrimination and will continue to be refined in future litigation.

Nonetheless, since *Craig* the gender standard has usually been acknowledged as a point of departure for addressing challenges to prima facie, de jure classifications by sex that discriminate against women. Application of the *Craig* standard to de jure classifications that discriminate against men is less clear.

Gender Neutral Statutes. Statutes that classify by gender neutral terms and have an admitted disparate impact against one sex are nonetheless subject only to the rational basis test. To establish a claim of sex discrimination for such statutes, plaintiffs must prove that the legislative body enacted the statute with invidious discriminatory purpose. Classification by pregnancy for insurance purposes is an extreme example of what the Supreme Court treats as gender neutral. Geduldig v. Aiello (S.Ct.1974).

Reserved Rights. The core meaning of equal rights between the sexes is not that men and women are the same, which clearly they are not, but that women and men are entitled as a matter of right to equal justice under law. Equal justice includes both equal protection of the laws, a relative concept, and equal possession and enjoyment of rights, which is absolute. The right to equal protection of the laws is itself a fundamental right.

Constitutions, in the United States at least, are not a grant of rights from the government to the people. Rather, We the People institute constitutions to secure, to make safe, our innate, reserved rights. These reserved rights existed before creation of and are superior to the government. The Constitution cannot, and does not attempt to, list all of these reserved rights. This is the significance of the Bill of Rights, and particularly of the Ninth Amendment. Historically, women have enjoyed neither equal protection of the laws protected by the Fourteenth Amendment nor equal innate, reserved, fundamental rights protected by the Bill of Rights.

Constitutional Guarantee. Federal and state legislation prohibiting sex discrimination in selected areas does not fill the absence of a constitutional prohibition of discrimination on the basis of sex. Under the federal constitution and most state constitutions, women have not yet been raised to the status of constitutional protection enjoyed by males.

Words in a constitution provide stronger protection against sex discrimination than words in a statute. This single cogent fact is sufficient reason for ratification of an equal rights amendment to the federal constitution and to states which do not have one. Opposition to equal rights amendments in most instances is opposition to equal rights for women. The root of sex discrimination under United States law is as simple, and as profound, as that. This is not to say that equal rights amendments would automatically eliminate sex discrimination. The problem is more invidious and pervasive. They would, however, establish a public concensus of committment to, and constitutional grounds for eradication of, sex discrimination in law.

CHAPTER 7

EQUAL PROTECTION: A FUNDAMENTAL RIGHT?

7.01 Discrimination Against Men

Single sex statutory classifications that disadvantage men have presented the Supreme Court with its most difficult analytic problems since Reed v. Reed first opened gender classification to heightened scrutiny. Two major decisions upholding the constitutionality of male only classifications, one state and one federal, were decided within weeks of each other. Michael M. v. Superior Court of Sonoma County, addressed a male only statutory rape law, and Rostker v. Goldberg, the male only draft registration. The rationale for the two cases is basically the same. The constitutional guarantee of equal protection does not require subjecting women to statutory rape or draft registration statutes because women are not situated similarly to men in either case. A third case, Mississippi University for Women v. Hogan (S.Ct.1982), is contrary, holding that Mississippi must admit males for matriculation to a state professional nursing school for women. Compare United States v. Virginia (W.D.Va.1991), holding that a public male only military college does not deny women equal protection of the laws.

Both *Michael M.* and *Rostker* gave verbal acknowledgment of the gender based standard of review, but there was considerable difference of opinion as to whether and how the standard should be applied. Chief Justice Rehnquist has consistently argued against utilization of a tiered standard of review and for the single rational basis standard, particularly as to gender based classifications that disadvantage men. Justice Rehnquist announced the judgment of the court in *Michael M.* and wrote for the Court in *Rostker.*

7.02 Single Sex Criminal Statutes

Statutory Rape. The California statute at issue in *Michael M.* provided that only males are criminally liable for statutory rape, "an act of sexual intercourse accomplished with a female not the wife of the perpetrator where the female is under the age of 18 years."

Justice Rehnquist began his analysis with the statement that the traditional minimum rationality test takes on a somewhat "sharper focus" when gender based classifications are challenged, citing *Reed* and *Craig.*

Although Justice Rehnquist stated the test of *Craig,* his accommodation of the gender standard of review was oblique. The state's claimed justification for the statute was to prevent illegitimate

teenage pregnancies. Justice Rehnquist was satisfied that the stated objective was at least one of the
state's purposes, and that this constituted a
"strong" state interest.

The harmful consequences of teenage pregnancy
fall on the young female, and the risk of pregnancy
itself is a substantial deterrence to young females.
Justice Rehnquist therefore reasoned that a criminal sanction imposed solely on males "serves to
roughly 'equalize' the deterrents on the sexes."
The relevant question is not whether the statute
might be drawn more precisely but whether "it is
within constitutional limits."

Because the California legislature had specifically considered making the statute gender neutral
and declined to do so, the male only classification
did not constitute unconscious sexual stereotyping;
this circumstance supports judicial deference to
legislative judgment. Finally, Justice Rehnquist
could "find nothing to suggest that men, because of
past discrimination or peculiar disadvantages, are
in need of the special solicitude of the courts."

Justice Brennan in dissent insisted that the gender based standard of *Craig* applies to men as well
as women. The government must prove both the
importance of its asserted objective and the substantial relationship between the classification and
that objective. California has not established that
there are fewer teenage pregnancies under its gender based statutory rape law than there would be if
the law were gender neutral.

Justice Stevens, dissenting, considered it "utterly irrational" to exempt 50% of the potential violators from prosecution, particularly where the criminal penalty runs only against the persons who are not subject to the harm sought to be prevented.

Contrast *Michael M.* with United States v. Green (9th Cir.1977) upholding the federal Mann Act against constitutional challenge on grounds that it criminalized transporting females but not males across state lines. The *Green* court said the statute was sexually neutral because both men and women could be arrested for violating the act.

Numerous other defendants have challenged sex based classifications in criminal statutes. States with equal rights amendments generally extend sex-specific statutes to both sexes. See Finley v. State (Tex.Cr.App.1975), rape; and Plas v. Alaska, (Alaska 1979), prostitution. Illinois overturned a long line of cases when it ruled that the state ERA prohibits a gender based adult offender statute. People v. Ellis (Ill.S.Ct.1974). But Illinois upheld a gender based incest statute, People v. Yocum (Ill.S. Ct.1977), and Colorado, a male only rape statute. People v. Salinas (Colo.S.Ct.1976).

A Florida court of appeals sidestepped a trial court's ruling that statutory rape prosecutions are unconstitutional because an underage victim who can elect to have an abortion can also legally consent to sex. Florida v. Phillips and Williams (Fla.App. 4 Dist.1991). The appellate court said the defendant lacked standing to raise the victim's right of privacy, and thus the court did not address the constitutional issue. Compare, New York v. Gonzales (N.Y.Cty.Ct.1990). See also Ferris v. Santa Clara County (9th Cir.1989).

Prostitution. Prostitution statutes, either expressly or as enforced, select women for prosecution. The adult male customer, like the consenting minor female for statutory rape, is seldom subjected to criminal penalty. Statutory and de facto singling out of female prostitutes for prosecution has survived due process, equal protection, privacy and freedom of expression challenges.

Massachusetts, an equal rights amendment state, upheld a prostitution statute against claims of selective enforcement against women on grounds the record did not establish that male customers were not prosecuted. Commonwealth v. King (Mass.S.Ct.1977). Accord, United States v. Moses (D.C.App.1975). Men arrested as customers of decoy police prostitutes in a sting operation cannot be subjected to prosecution under a state prostitution statute which criminalizes only the actions of the prostitute. The statute does not offend equal protection requirements, however, since it applies to both male and female prostitutes. Washington v. Wilbur (Wn.S.Ct.1988). Similarly, Plas v. Alaska (Alaska S.Ct.1979).

Moses also rejected First Amendment challenges. Prostitution is a straightforward business proposal which may be regulated under the standards applicable to purely commercial advertising.

7.03 Military Service

Male Only Registration. In Rostker v. Goldberg, the Military Selective Service Act was challenged in a class action on behalf of men subject to registration as a violation of the equal protection component of the Fifth Amendment because women are not also subject to registration.

Because of the de jure classification by sex, the district court applied the gender standard and invalidated the male only registration as a denial of equal protection of the laws. The district court stressed that it was not deciding the issue of whether or to what extent women should serve in combat, but only the issue of registration. The district court examined the evidence and concluded that "military opinion, backed by extensive study, is that the availability of women registrants would materially increase flexibility, not hamper it."

The Supreme Court reversed. Justice Rehnquist, writing for the Court, side-stepped the issue of the appropriate standard of review. He said that levels of scrutiny used by the Court "may all too readily become facile abstractions used to justify a result." Rather, the issue is whether Congress has transgressed an explicit guarantee of individual rights which limits military authority conferred on Congress by the Constitution. The government's interest in raising and supporting armies is clearly an important objective. Furthermore, in no area has the Court accorded Congress "greater deference" to legislate than in the area of national defense and military affairs.

The Court found that the purpose of Congress in limiting registration to men only was to focus on military need of combat ready troops rather than equity between the sexes. Men are not discriminated against because it is reasonable for Congress to conclude that the requirement of combat readiness precludes registration of women. Women are not discriminated against because they may volunteer for military service.

Justice Marshall, dissenting, said the pool of diversified talents is maximized when women as well as men are registered. He challenged Justice Rehnquist's insistence that because Congress had consciously considered whether women should be registered for the draft that the classification was permissible. Rather, conscious deliberation cannot negate the constitutional requirement of equal protection of the laws. The issue is not whether Congress acted intentionally in excluding women, but whether the Constitution prohibits the gender based classification. The question is not whether the goal of military preparedness can be achieved by a male only registration, but whether the gender based classification will substantially advance the goal of military preparedness. Justice Marshall suggests that the Court is doing precisely what it disclaims doing: reaching its conclusion by using an announced degree of deference to legislative judgment as a "facile abstraction" to "justify a particular result".

Civic Obligation. The issue of women's active participation in war has been before the Court before. Rosika Schwimmer, a noted scholar 49 years old, was denied United States citizenship because she refused to consent to take up arms personally in defense of the nation. United States v. Schwimmer. She unsuccessfully pleaded for status of conscientious objector, asserting " 'I am an uncompromising pacifist * * *. I am not willing to bear arms. In every other single way I am ready to follow the law * * *.' "

An obligation of women to share the duty of military service for one's country was not addressed by *Rostker.* This civic obligation is critical to Justice Marshall. He summarized his dissent by saying, "The Court today places its imprimatur on one of the most potent remaining public expressions of 'ancient canards about the proper role of women.' * * * It upholds a statute that requires males but not females to register for the draft, and * * * thereby categorically excludes women from a fundamental civic obligation."

Draft Resisters. Male only draft registration directly limits the rights of young men compared to young women to equal access to entitlements, such as student loans, and to free speech.

The Supreme Court has ruled that males can be required to declare whether they have registered for the draft to be eligible for student loans. This requirement is not a bill of attainder nor a denial of due process. It is a legitimate vehicle to achieve fair distribution of scarce resources. The adverse impact on students' Fifth Amendment rights not to incriminate themselves is not germane. Selective Service System v. Minnesota Public Interest Research Group (S.Ct.1984). Nor are the students' First Amendment rights of free exercise of religion violated. Alexander v. Trustees of Boston University (1st Cir.1985).

The government has a "passive" policy of prosecuting draft resisters who make themselves known. Such selective criminal prosecution of vocal draft resisters does not infringe the resisters' first amendment rights to make a political statement. Wayte v. United States (S.Ct.1985). To prevail the resister must show that the passive enforcement policy had discriminatory effect and discriminatory motive.

Servicewomen. Thousands of women have volunteered for military duty, and number over 10 percent of active military personnel. One in three servicewomen is black, the highest proportion to the general population for any group in the service. Women, like men, leave some rights behind when they walk in the barracks door. Male or female, one follows military orders at one's own risk in areas other than the front line.

Immunity. A sovereign government enjoys absolute immunity from any liability for acts of its employees or agents, and can be sued only if it so consents. The federal government has waived immunity to many suits under the Federal Tort Claims Act. However, the Supreme Court has read a major exception into the FTCA which Congress has not seen fit to remove. The government is not liable for torts which arise out of or are incident to the service of military personnel. "Incident to service" is a broadly defined concept, and includes malpractice by military doctors. Feres v. United States (S.Ct.1950), reaffirmed in United States v. Johnson (S.Ct.1987).

Thus recovery was barred for severe brain injury to a newborn during delivery to a Navy servicewoman allegedly caused by medical malpractice by Air Force personnel. Graham v. United States (D.Me.1990). Similarly, for injuries allegedly arising from negligent prenatal care, Atkinson v. United States (9th Cir.1987).

Nor can injured persons sue the government employees who commit the torts in the course of their employment. They have absolute immunity from suit under the Federal Employees Liability Reform and Tort Compensation Act. Military medical personnel are specifically protected in the Gonzalez act, which substitutes the government as defendant in such cases. United States v. Smith (S.Ct.1991).

The federal government is similarly insulated from suit for intentional, discretionary actions. A former soldier unsuccessfully sued the government for giving him LSD without his knowledge or consent in a secret chemical warfare test during his military service. To allow recovery, said Justice Scalia, would disrupt "military regimen". United States v. Stanley (S.Ct.1987). Recovery for radiation caused illness arising from participation in nuclear weapons testing is at issue in Walters v. National Association of Radiation Survivors (S.Ct. 1985). To compensate for the harsh consequences arising from federal immunity, Congress sometimes enacts legislation to compensate service personnel for service incurred injuries.

Female Restrictions. The Army, Army Reserve, Air Force and Air Force Reserve prohibit enlistment for single parents with children under 18 years of age. Most of such single parents are women. This policy was unsuccessfully challenged in Mack v. Rumsfeld (W.D.N.Y.1985). The court said that *Rostker* requires a strong presumption of validity of military policies that are "reasonably relevant and necessary to furtherance of our national defense". Compare Owens v. Brown (D.D.C. 1978), holding that the government failed to establish that an important interest is substantially served by a rule barring women from duty on naval vessels.

Regulations that bar benefits following normal pregnancy and childbirth for female veterans do not violate the constitution or any statutes. Kirkhuff v. Nimmo (D.C.Cir.1982).

CHAPTER 8

OPENING THE
CONSTITUTIONAL DOOR

8.01 State Constitutions

Perspectives. This nutshell emphasizes sex discrimination law arising under the federal constitution. Nonetheless, most litigation occurs in state courts. Recognition by the federal judiciary that gender based classifications are subject to heightened scrutiny under the federal constitution reflects in part persistent challenge by both men and women to state as well as federal laws that discriminate on the basis of sex.

The federal constitution constitutes a floor under which a state cannot discriminate. State constitutions are a largely untapped source for challenge to sex discrimination by state actors, and, more rarely, by private actors, that is not reached under the Fourteenth Amendment.

ERA States. Citizens in some states have ratified equal rights amendments that expressly prohibit discrimination on the basis of sex. [See Appendix 1]. In these states, any statute that explicitly classifies by sex is subject to closer analysis; and sometimes, but not always, to strict scrutiny. See, for example, Marchioro v. Cheney (Wn.S.Ct.

107

1978), where the Washington supreme court says that the ERA "swept away" its former approach of treating sex as a suspect class, subject to strict scrutiny. The test used in Washington is taken from the language of the amendment: whether equality has been "denied or abridged" on account of sex. Pennsylvania has prohibited sex based classifications under its ERA, Henderson v. Henderson (Pa.S.Ct.1974); Massachusetts applies strict scrutiny, Lowell v. Kowalski (Mass.S.Ct. 1980).

Application of state equal rights amendments has addressed sex discrimination in two ways. The first, legislative review and reform, is direct and comprehensive. Pennsylvania, a common law state, and Washington, a community property state, made extensive review of their statutes and passed bills eliminating most instances of classification by gender. A significant change in Washington State was extension of management rights for community property to wives on a basis equal to the powers previously exercised only by husbands. The criminal code was revised making sex crimes gender neutral.

Second, state equal rights amendments are strong vehicles for judicial challenge to unconstitutional sex discrimination by state and municipal entities. Elimination of sex bias through constitutional litigation is necessarily piecemeal and specific. Whether the courts should judicially extend a statute that would otherwise be unconstitutional, or simply strike the statute and leave extension to the legislature, is a recurring question, with varying results. The case histories suggest that constitutionally protected rights for women are neither the panacea that some people hope nor the disaster that others predict. The lock of logic is not easily unlatched; this truth of language guarantees that change effected through language, the medium of constitutional law, will be culturally linked to the past.

Non–ERA States. States without ERAs, including New York, California and Oregon, often protect women against sex discrimination by regarding women as "citizens" and "persons" under state constitutional clauses phrased in gender neutral terms. By including sex as a protected class under privileges and immunities, privacy and fundamental rights clauses and interpreting such clauses stringently, these states provide both women and men stronger constitutional protection against discrimination on the basis of sex than is secured by the federal constitution. Some non-ERA states give limited constitutional protection to sex based classifications in specified areas, such as employment and professions (California); public office (Delaware); equal protection and public accommodations (Louisiana). The federal judiciary will invalidate state interpretation of these clauses only when incompatible with the federal constitution.

8.02 Jurisdictional Obstacles

State Action Requirement

Most federal and state constitutional clauses do not operate to limit action of private individuals. The New Jersey constitution, which reaches private action, is an exception. See Peper v. Princeton University Board of Trustees (N.J.S.Ct.1978.)

The Bill of Rights is specifically directed to congressional action: "*Congress* shall make no law...." impacting the prohibited subjects. The Fourteenth Amendment similarly provides: "No *state* shall make or enforce any law" which violates the prohibitions. (emphases added). Most parallel clauses in state constitutions have similar restrictive language, or have been so interpreted. As a consequence, plaintiffs must show "state action" to invoke the jurisdiction of a court before proceeding with discrimination claims based on either the federal or state constitutions.

Direct State Action. State action is clearly present when a statute explicitly classifies by sex, or when a practice or policy of a public official is overtly sex based. A congressman who claims that it is "essential" that a position be filled by a male, can be sued directly under the Constitution. Davis v. Passman (S.Ct.1979). Accord, Lipsett v. University of Puerto Rico (1st Cir.1988), allowing a cause of action by a female surgical resident against a director of a medical program in a public university, and O'Connell v. Chasdi (Mass.S.Ct.1987), allowing a cause of action for sexual harassment under the state ERA. But see Browning v. Clerk, United States House of Representatives (1986) which holds that the speech and debate clause immunity applies to legislative personnel decisions.

Indirect State Action. State action may be indirect, as through rental of publicly owned facilities to commercial enterprises. Ludtke v. Kuhn (S.D. N.Y.1978).

Quasi–Public Entities. Proving state action is an obstacle in suits alleging discrimination by entities with quasi-public status, such as non-profit athletic associations, and educational, professional, financial, trade and service organizations. "State action" does not arise from issuance of a liquor license, Moose Lodge No. 107 v. Irvis (S.Ct.1972); providing fire and police service to a male only yacht club, Dezell v. Day Island Yacht Club (9th Cir.1986); allowing usage of school facilities for a summer basketball camp, D.T. v. Independent School District (10th Cir.1990), leasing public property for $1.00 per year to a white public service group, Solomon v. Miami Woman's Club (S.D.Fla. 1973). The black women were denied civil treatment, but not civil rights.

Insurance. Insurance issued by private companies is subject to regulation in every state. State regulatory action alone is generally insufficient to constitute state action. But see Bartholomew v. Foster (Pa.Cmwlth.1988), which holds that Pennsylvania's equal rights amendment bars sex based private insurance rates, even though they meet gender neutral state insurance regulations as being actuarially sound.

Sovereign Immunity

Governmental entities cannot be sued without their express consent under the doctrine of sovereign immunity, unless waived by specific legislation. States have statutes with varying immunity waivers. State sovereign immunity underlies the Eleventh Amendment, which restricts litigation against states in federal courts.

Ratification of the Fourteenth Amendment following the Civil War eroded state immunity under the Eleventh Amendment by empowering Congress "to enforce, by appropriate legislation, the provisions of this article".

The Reconstruction Congress accordingly enacted the precursor to 42 U.S.C. Section 1983, which provides that "Every person who, under color of any statute, ordinance, regulation, custom, or usage ... subjects, or causes to be subjected, any citizen of the United States or other person within the jurisdiction thereof to the deprivation of any rights, privileges, or immunities secured by the Constitution and laws, shall be liable to the party injured". Section 1983 is the ground for numerous actions against public entities and personnel by individuals allegedly injured by public actions or omissions.

Scope of permissible actions under Section 1983 is determined by Supreme Court interpretation.

Will v. Michigan Dept. of State Police (S.Ct.1989)
provides sweeping protection for states and state
officials. Neither is a "person" within the meaning of the statute, and Eleventh Amendment immunity applies. The Court reasoned that although
an official is obviously a person, an action against
a state official is against the office and not the
individual holding the office. Justice Brennan,
dissenting, termed the Court's interpretation "hy-
pertechnical", defeating congressional purpose in
enacting § 1983.

The *Will* Court notes that a municipal entity
does not share a state's Eleventh Amendment protection, and is a "person" within § 1983. This
interpretation was established in Monell v. Department of Social Services of New York City (S.Ct.
1978), which voided a policy under which pregnant
employees were compelled to take unpaid maternity leaves before such leaves were physically required. Punitive damages are not available. City
of Newport v. Fact Concerts, Inc. (S.Ct.1981).

Deprivation of federal statutory as well as constitutional rights is protected under § 1983 in Maine
v. Thiboutot (S.Ct.1980), where Aid to Families
with Dependent Children beneficiaries successfully
claimed that Maine improperly computed available
AFDC benefits. *Will* distinguished *Thiboutot* as a
suit for injunctive relief, under which suits against
state officials are not treated as suits against the
state, and the state official is a person for § 1983
action.

8.03   Men's Words and Women's Rights

Phrasing the Principles. Use of male terms and pronouns in statements of legal principles until very recently has been universal. This is not surprising, since women were seldom involved in the making of the law, not as successful litigants, nor lawyers, nor judges. The subtle role played in law by use of such terms as "reasonable man", "he" and "his" in influencing attorneys, parties, courts and juries has yet to be fully examined. When the question is raised, the response usually is made that male terms, either in practice or specifically by statute, are used generically to include females. But this does not address the question. The artificially imposed legal meaning of "his" and the influence of "his" on the minds of those in the courtroom are two different matters.

Gender Neutral Terms. Even more subtle is the sex discrimination that may be masked when gender neutral terms are selected. Gender neutral terms do not per se eliminate sex discrimination, but sometimes only insulate the discrimination from legal challenge. Because the statutory classification is no longer overtly labeled as based on sex, the lenient rational basis test is applied and the invidious intent rule of Personnel Adm'r of Massachusetts v. Feeney (S.Ct.1979), invoked.

Justice Marshall, dissenting in Lorance v. AT & T Technologies, Inc. (S.Ct.1989), pointed out the misplaced reliance in allowing gender neutral language to shield illegal discrimination in a covertly sex based seniority system. More lenient legal treatment of gender neutral language compared to gender specific language "serves only to reward those employers ingenious enough to cloak their acts of discrimination in a facially neutral guise, identical though the effects of [a facially neutral seniority] system may be to those of a facially discriminatory one."

The experience of Alaska and New Jersey expose the inadequacy of gender neutral constitutional terms to protect women's rights. The drafters of a new constitution in New Jersey following World War II wanted to provide for equal rights for women, but balked at incorporating the word "sex". They elected instead to change the classifying phrase in their privileges and immunities clause from a sex specific "all men" to a gender neutral "all persons".

But the ambiguous gender neutral term enabled challenge 30 years later to contest the inclusion of women as a constitutionally protected class. The New Jersey Supreme Court was compelled in 1978 to rule judicially that the word "persons" legally includes women. The court said the people of New Jersey in ratifying the new constitution intended to signify that "women were granted rights of employment and property protection equal to those enjoyed by men." Peper v. Princeton University Board of Trustees (N.J.S.Ct.1978). Alaska had a similar experience, and specifically added "sex" to amend the gender neutral language in their original bill of rights when they joined the Union in 1959. See Plas v. Alaska.

Lame Words. Much as the word "sex" has strident connotations that some might prefer to avoid, no other word means quite the same thing. Words are workhorses of law. Right words leap to life. Wrong words limp like a lame horse. They cannot do their job well. *Peper* is contemporary evidence of the strength of positive law: elimination of a specific wrong is best secured by express articulation of the word that most specifically describes the wrong.

Clearly the gender neutral terms of the federal constitution do not protect rights of women to the same extent as they protect rights of men. Recall Minor v. Happersett (S.Ct.1874) and Bradwell v. Illinois (S.Ct.1872) where the Supreme Court recognized that the gender neutral term "citizens" includes women, but nonetheless ruled that citizens (female) do not have rights equal to citizens (male).

Male Pronouns and Due Process. Consider, for example, Little v. Streater (S.Ct.1981) and Lassiter v. Department of Social Services (S.Ct.1981), where due process rights were raised by male and female petitioners. In *Little* the Supreme Court granted male petitioner's request for blood tests at state expense to defend a paternity action. On the same day, the Court in *Lassiter* denied female petitioner's request for counsel at state expense to defend a state action to terminate her parental rights.

The *Little* Court viewed the paternity action in the nature of a quasi-criminal proceeding, calling for analysis as invasion of a fundamental right. Since the petitioner could go to jail for non-payment of child support if found to be the father, the Court held unanimously that due process rights required the state to pay for the blood test.

The mother in *Lassiter* was incarcerated. She had four other children in the care of her mother, and wanted her fifth child to be with the other four. Although she was not represented by counsel at the state proceeding to terminate her parental rights, the Supreme Court held she had not been denied due process. She had not asked for counsel, and the proceeding was not criminal but civil, and thus did not invoke fundamental right analysis.

Justice Potter Stewart, writing for the Court, said "[I]t is the defendant's interest in personal freedom * * * which triggers the right to appointed counsel * * *. Significantly, as a litigant's interest in personal liberty diminishes, so does *his* right to appointed counsel." (emphasis added.) Court precedents are grounded in "the presumption that an indigent litigant has a right to appointed counsel only when, if *he* loses, *he* may be deprived of *his* physical liberty." (emphasis added.)

Justice Blackmun, dissenting, said "I deem it not a little ironic that the Court on this very day *grants,* on due process grounds, an indigent putative father's claim for state-paid blood grouping tests in the interest of according him a meaningful opportunity to disprove his paternity * * * but in the present case rejects, on due process grounds, an indigent mother's claim for state-paid legal assistance when the State seeks to take her own child away from her in a termination proceeding." Justice Blackmun pointed out that loss of her child could be as much a deprivation of liberty and property for the woman as incarceration for a man. The proceeding was criminal in the sense that it affected the fundamental right of parenting, and was irrevocable; once the child was taken from her, she could not regain custody.

Little and *Lassiter* can be further contrasted by the legal efficacy of criminal nonsupport statutes, which are notorious for their lack of enforcement. The Supreme Court has said that an unwed mother, seeking to compel enforcement of a nonsupport statute, lacks standing to contest policies and practices of enforcement personnel "when *he* himself is neither prosecuted nor threatened with prosecution." (emphasis added.) Linda R.S. v. Richard D. Compare V.F. v. Alaska, which ruled that the Alaska constitution guarantees counsel to indigent parents in termination proceedings. (Alaska S.Ct. 1983).

Little ironically provided the basis for one court to deny a putative father a right to state-paid legal counsel. The court reasoned that blood tests are so accurate that error of false assignment of paternity is unlikely, so no counsel is needed. Iowa ex rel. Hamilton v. Snodgrass (Iowa S.Ct.1982).

Reasonable Woman Standard. Use of male-specific nouns and pronouns to express general legal rules, as in *Minor* and *Lassiter,* has been found by both state and federal appellate courts to be prejudicial to female litigants, negatively impacting their due process and equal protection rights. Washington v. Wanrow (Wn.S.Ct.1977), establishing a reasonable woman standard and eschewing use of male pronouns in jury instructions where the woman defendant claims self defense, is addressed in Chapter 20. The Ninth Circuit in Ellison v. Brady (9th Cir.1991), citing *Wanrow,* establishes a "reasonable woman" standard for sexual harassment claims under Title VII.

The *Ellison* court rejected gender neutral terminology because "a sex-blind reasonable person standard tends to be male-biased" and "to systematically ignore" the experiences of women. A "gender-conscious examination of sexual harassment enables women to participate in the workplace on an equal footing with men."

A dissenter in *Ellison* rejected the reasonable woman standard as "ambiguous" and therefore "inadequate." Men as well as women can be subjected to sexual harassment in the workplace. The term "reasonable man" as used in tort law, "traditionally refers to the average adult person, regardless of gender, and the conduct that can reasonably be expected of him or her." The term also presupposes the need for a legal term that can apply to all persons, and the impossibility of a more individually tailored standard. He recommends "victim", or "target", or, apparently, retention of "reasonable man". But not "reasonable woman."

8.04 Rights and Responsibilities

With the notable exception of military duty imposed on men, constitutionally imposed civil obligations are few. The explanation is at hand. Anglo–American law is grounded on securing the rights and freedom of individual citizens against government invasion rather than on enlarging their responsibilities with a corresponding restriction on freedom of action. This is the subtle, but central, legal difference between "equal protection" of the laws guaranteed by the Fourteenth Amendment and "equality of rights" which "shall not be denied or abridged" under equal rights amendments. A guarantee of equal protection of the laws is not the same thing as a prohibition against denial of equal rights.

Equality of Responsibility

The Washington state constitution is unique in providing that "Equality of rights *and responsibility* under the law shall not be denied or abridged on account of sex" (emphasis added).

The phrase "and responsibility" was added shortly before the final legislative vote on the amendment in response to a male legislator's concern that women were seeking equality of rights without a corresponding equality of responsibility. The word "responsibility" does not occur in the federal constitution. The requirement of equality of responsibility controlled interpretation of the Washington equal rights amendment in Marchioro v. Chaney (Wn.S.Ct.1978).

The state supreme court ruled that requiring equal representation of men and women on state political party committees and in the offices of chair and vice chair on state and county committees does not violate the state equal rights amendment. The statutes neither deny nor abridge equality on the basis of sex. The statutory mandate of one woman for one man is permitted, but is neither commanded nor prohibited under the state equal rights amendment.

The reasoning of *Marchioro* is germane to the constitutionality of "balance" statutes adopted in other states directed to equal representation between women and men on civic boards and commissions.

In discussing the mandate of equality of responsibility, neither the majority nor minority opinions observed that males have not had protection of their constitutional rights predicated upon acceptance of responsibility, or more specifically, upon acceptance of equal responsibility with women. Responsible and irresponsible males enjoy constitutional rights. Nor do federal or state constitutions condition enjoyment of constitutional rights on ability or talent. Unless, of course, one is a racial minority or female. Only then do one's talents and abilities become controlling.

Representative self government and the principle of judicial review itself are predicated on the adversarial nature of differing interests rather than on abilities and talents. The differing interests of white males, as reflected in statutes passed by state and federal legislatures, enforced by state and federal executives, and interpreted by state and federal judiciaries for 200 years, have shaped United States law. *Marchioro* recognizes that the interests and abilities of men and women are not in all instances precisely the same. In some contexts, constitutional equality between women and men may be served by mandated numerical equality that maps the real world.

CHAPTER 9

CIVIL RIGHTS

Fundamental rights subjected to classification on the basis of sex that have been litigated since Craig v. Boren include the right to vote, to trial by jury, and First Amendment rights of free speech, free press and association.

9.01 Right to Vote

The right to vote is generally regarded as a fundamental right that is securely protected against discriminatory state action. However, classification by Indian tribes that denies the right of suffrage on the basis of sex is immune from federal challenge under the ruling in Santa Clara Pueblo v. Martinez (S.Ct.1978).

A tribal ordinance adopted in 1939 by the Santa Clara Pueblo provides that children born of marriages between "male members of the Santa Clara Pueblo and non-members shall be members of the Santa Clara Pueblo." However, sons and daughters of Santa Clara women who marry nontribal members "shall not be members of the Santa Clara Pueblo." Exclusion from membership in the tribe entails that when the children grow up they cannot vote in tribal elections, and upon their mother's death, have no right to inherit possessory interests in communal lands or to remain on the reservation.

Julia Martinez, a full-blooded Santa Claran, and her daughter brought a class action on behalf of themselves and other Indians similarly situated seeking declaratory and injunctive relief against the tribe on the basis that the ordinance violated a provision in the Indian Civil Rights Act of 1968 that "[n]o Indian tribe in exercising powers of self-government shall * * * deny to any person within its jurisdiction the equal protection of its laws." In light of the recent enactment of the ordinance and its failure to seek to identify children who were culturally Santa Claran, the tenth circuit applied the gender standard and ruled that the tribe's interest in the ordinance was not substantial enough to justify its discriminatory effect against women.

The Supreme Court reversed. Indian tribes are distinct, independent political communities retaining their original natural rights in matters of local self-government. Congress has not required that tribal governments are bound by restrictions identical to the Bill of Rights or the Fourteenth Amendment. Mrs. Martinez' remedy is through the tribal courts and political process.

Denial of a private cause of action to Julia Martinez is "the only case that deviates from [the] pattern of implying a private cause of action to individuals deprived of a federal right in recent years." Cannon v. University of Chicago (S.Ct. 1979).

Closely related to the right to vote is the right to choose one's legal domicile. Julia Martinez' children could not vote if they lived on the reservation during their mother's life, and at her death, did not have a right to remain on the reservation.

9.02 Right of Domicile

From one's domicile stems the location where one may vote, hold elective or appointive public office, work in civil service and attend public schools at in-state tuition rates. At common law, a married woman's domicile is that of her husband, no matter where she might reside. This rule was enshrined by the U.S. Supreme Court in Pennsylvania v. Ravenel (S.Ct.1858) as a matter of law.

The principle of derivative domicile for married women was successfully challenged as unconstitutional interference with eligibility for civil service employment in Brathol v. Milwaukee Co. (Wis.Cir. 1978). Automatic assignment of a husband's domicile to married women students, thus depriving them of in-state tuition rates, was ruled a violation of the equal protection clause in Samuel v. University of Pittsburgh (W.D.Pa.1974).

9.03 Right to Name

At common law persons could change their names at will. In absence of fraudulent intent, anyone could adopt a new legal name simply by using it. Not infrequently, in the interests of inheritance or continuance of a family name, a husband adopted the surname of his wife. However, by custom a woman normally adopted her husband's surname. Many people, and not a few states, assume that women's names automatically change by law upon marriage.

Where there is no express statute that provides for automatic name change, statutes on other matters such as voting registration, property ownership, drivers' licensing or automobile registration may assume such to be the case. These statutes indicate the extent to which custom dictates law. Business practices, such as granting of credit, also have traditionally assumed that marriage changes a woman's name.

Women seeking to retain legal use of their maiden names have utilized two theories in litigation. A theory proceeding upon assumption that common law does not require name change was successful in Stuart v. Board of Supervisors (Md.S.Ct. 1972). The second theory assumes that the husband's name has been imposed on the wife by operation of law, and seeks to restore the maiden name on an equal protection basis since the husband is not subject to the same rule. The Supreme Court rejected a challenge on this ground in Forbush v. Wallace (M.D.Ala.1971), a few months after deciding Reed v. Reed (S.Ct.1971).

A woman may retain her original surname for life for federal social security purposes, which avoids successive changes of name in the event of marriage and divorce.

Naming the baby may have unexpected legal complications. A Colorado statute requiring that a child born to married parents bear the father's surname was challenged in O'Brien v. Tilson (D.N. C.1981). The court rejected argument that the right to select a child's name is *de minimis* and ruled the statute unconstitutional on privacy and equal protection grounds. Nor can a state require that children born in wedlock be given either of the parents' surnames, or a hyphenated combination. Jech v. Burch (D.Hawaii 1979).

9.04 Right to Trial by Jury

Basic constitutional rights in criminal proceedings include the right to trial by jury. At common law, women were regarded as not qualified for jury service by reason of the *propter defectum sexus,* a "defect of sex." Neither the Fourteenth Amendment nor the suffrage amendment required states to treat women and men equally in establishing the pool from which jurors are drawn. Although women are qualified for jury duty in every state, procedures to select jury panels frequently differentiate between men and women, with the consequence that participation of women on juries is a recurring issue.

Women's Jury Responsibilities. In prohibiting systematic exclusion of women from jury panels in Taylor v. Louisiana, the Supreme Court overruled

Hoyt v. Florida only insofar as the decisions were incompatible. Possibly the Court was referring to the observation in *Hoyt* that women are "still regarded as the center of home and family life". This rationale survives in United States v. Daly (N.D.Tex.1983), where a federal district court ruled as "reasonable" an exemption from federal jury duty of persons responsible for children under 10 or for the aged or infirm. The "persons" impacted under this gender neutral statute are largely female.

Systematic peremptory challenge to venire members on the basis of race is prohibited by Batson v. Kentucky (S.Ct.1986), Holland v. Illinois (S.Ct.1990) and Powers v. Ohio (S.Ct.1991), even when the excluded jurors are not of the defendant's race. While the constitution does not require a representative jury, it does require an impartial one.

The rule extends to civil cases. Edmonson v. Leesville Concrete Co. (S.Ct.1991).

The rationale of *Batson* and its progeny was extended to peremptory challenge of venire members because of their gender in a de novo review by the Ninth Circuit in United States v. De Gross (9th Cir.1990), where an Hispanic female was charged with illegally aiding and abetting transportation of undocumented Mexican aliens into the United States.

The defendant challenged eight male venire members, and did not offer any justification. The prosecutor rejected the sole Hispanic on the venire, who happened to be female, offering as a non-racial justification a desire for a better gender balance on the jury. After a review of case law to date, the court ruled that the equal protection component of the Fifth Amendment prohibits sex based peremptory challenges by either prosecution or defendant in a federal criminal trial.

Similarly in civil cases, Dias v. Sky Chefs (D.Or. 1989).

Hawaii relies on its equal rights amendment to bar gender based discrimination in peremptory challenges. Hawaii v. Levinson (Hawaii 1990). The attorney for the defendant, charged with murdering his wife, used 7 of his peremptory challenges to strike women jurors.

9.05　Rights to Free Speech and Press

First Amendment rights are implicated in prior restraint or penalties imposed on allegedly obscene pictures and language.

Pornography. Rights of free speech and press have derailed most legislative attempts to control pornography, which many people believe directly contributes to the derogation and subjugation of women in all areas of life.

Pornography which falls under the definition of obscenity can be subjected to criminal penalty when it satisfies the standard of Miller v. California (S.Ct.1973) and its progeny. *Miller* evaluates whether a publication lacks serious literary, artistic, political or scientific value as a whole, relative to its appeal to prurient interest and its patently offensive treatment of specified sexual conduct, with reference to community standards. A "hate law" making it a misdemeanor to intimidate people on account of race, color, creed, religion or gender, survived First Amendment challenge in the context of crossburning on the private property of an African American family. In re Welfare of R.A.V. (S.Ct.Minn.1991).

Civil remedies to contain porn, whether criminally obscene or something less, must surmount the legal obstacles of identifiable plaintiffs who have suffered a legally cognizable injury. An Indianapolis ordinance providing women a civil remedy against pornography as defined therein was challenged in American Booksellers Ass'n, Inc. v. Hudnut (7th Cir.1985). The seventh circuit ruled the ordinance unconstitutional on First Amendment grounds as far exceeding the restrictions of *Miller.* The Supreme Court summarily affirmed, without opinion.

The *Booksellers'* court accepted the premises of the ordinance, that pornography affects thoughts of both men and women, that "[w]ords and images act at the level of the subconscious before they persuade at the level of the conscious." Depictions of subordination of women "tend to perpetuate subordination of women," which in turn "leads to affront and lower pay at work, insult and injury at home, battery and rape on the streets." The court noted that "[e]ven the truth has little chance" to be heard, let alone believed, "unless a statement fits within the framework of beliefs that may never have been subjected to rational study."

But pornography is not alone in shaping negative cultural values. "Racial bigotry, anti-semitism, violence on television, reporters' biases— these and many more influence the culture and shape our socialization. * * * Yet all is protected as speech, however insidious." To penalize such speech would leave "the government in control of all of the institutions of culture, the great censor and director of which thoughts are good for us." The court found the ordinance's definition of pornography unconstitutional, and "[n]o amount of struggle with particular words and phrases" can leave any provisions in effect.

The court suggested that a "strong guarantee of freedom of speech" is the most effective right to effect change. To rid society of pornography the remedy is more speech, not a civil remedy for injury from pornography as defined in the ordinance.

The Supreme Court has rejected civil remedies against sexually offensive publications where clearly identifiable plaintiffs have suffered clearly identifiable injuries. See Hustler Magazine v. Falwell (S.Ct.1988) and Pring v. Penthouse International (10th Cir.1982).

To high school students, however, censorship of non-pornographic writing is within the power of a school district. Content based prior restraint of articles in a school newspaper relating to teens from divorced homes and teen pregnancy does not offend students' First Amendment rights so long as the censorship is reasonably related to legitimate pedagogical concerns. Hazelwood School District v. Kuhlmeier (S.Ct.1988). The articles were "inappropriate" for 14–year–old first year high school students, although candor compels one to admit that most 14 year olds can beget and be begotten, and many have divorced parents.

A school may also discipline students for speeches with improper sexual content given at school assemblies. Bethel School District v. Fraser (S.Ct.1986). The power of innocent words to adopt explicit sexual innuendo in selective context by a clever speaker is apparent in *Bethel*. In making a nominating speech before 600 students, a student juxtaposed the words "firm", "point", "pound" and "climax" with admitted intent to communicate a sexual metaphor. Some students responded with hoots, others with disgust, and still others with bewilderment.

CHAPTER 10

RIGHTS OF ASSOCIATION AND PRIVACY

The Constitution protects rights that are not explicitly enumerated. Included among these are rights of association and privacy. The parameters of these rights are less distinct than those of specifically enumerated rights.

10.01 Right of Association

Male Only Groups. Male only organizations have traditionally been an informal locale for important business contacts and negotiations. Exclusion of women from membership has greatly curtailed their potential for advancement in the business world. Early law suits against quasi-public organizations that bar membership on the basis of sex were largely unsuccessful.

The last decade, however, has witnessed the resisted demise of numerous male only business and country clubs and community service organizations. Two legal avenues have been utilized to desegregate these organizations.

Most have opened their doors to women as a result of state public accommodations laws which prohibit discrimination, inter alia, on the basis of sex. Male challenges to these laws on First Amendment right of association grounds have been rejected in a series of decisions. The Supreme Court first examined whether the national Jaycees could revoke charters for two Minnesota chapters which admitted women. Roberts v. United States Jaycees (S.Ct.1984). The Court agreed that the Jaycees were subject to state public accommodations law. Constitutional rights of association do not extend to organizations which have an open invitation to an unscreened, unselected and unlimited number of men from the general public to become members. Similarly, Board of Directors of Rotary International v. Rotary Club of Duarte, Cal. (S.Ct.1987).

The most extensive challenge to male only clubs came in New York State Club Association, Inc. v. City of New York (S.Ct.1988). The term "public accommodation" is broadly defined in New York City's human rights law to cover such places as hotels, retail stores, theatres, laundries, parks and public conveyances.

The City council enacted the ordinance because "the city of New York has a compelling interest in providing its citizens an environment where all persons" have a "fair and equal opportunity to participate in the business and professional life of the city, and may be unfettered in availing themselves of employment opportunities." It exempts "any institution, club or place of accommodation which proves that it is in its nature distinctly private."

However, clubs which have more than 400 members, provide regular meal service and regularly receive payment for dues and services directly or indirectly from nonmembers, do not fall under the "distinctly private" exemption. The Court again rejected right of association challenge. The law does not in any significant way affect the ability of individuals to form associations that will advocate public or private viewpoints.

Following *New York State*, the Supreme Court denied certiorari to Frank v. Ivy Club, Tiger Inn & Trustees of Princeton University (N.J.S.Ct.1990), in which a female student challenged the male only eating clubs at Princeton University. The New Jersey supreme court held that application of the state public accommodations statute did not violate the male students' First Amendment rights of association.

Washington, D.C., has an ordinance similar to that in *New York State*. Within days of the decision, the D.C. all male Cosmos Club, which includes members of Congress and the federal judiciary in its membership, opened its doors to women. Other cities with similar laws include Chicago, Detroit, Los Angeles and San Francisco.

Tax Benefit Challenges. For organizations which discriminate on the basis of sex but are not subject to state accommodation laws, constitutional challenge is possible if the state or federal government has granted the organization a tax exempt status. See Bob Jones University v. Simon (S.Ct. 1974).

In a sequence of lawsuits, an exclusive male only golf club forfeited a state tax benefit rather than accept women as members. Maryland enacted a statute providing tax benefits for organizations that preserve open spaces. The statute was later amended to limit the benefit to organizations which do not discriminate on the basis of sex, but specifically exempted clubs whose "primary purpose" was to serve one sex. The open space benefit coupled with the exemption for primary purpose one sex organizations just happened to fit the circumstances of the Burning Tree Club. This de jure statutory classification by sex was successfully challenged as a violation of the state equal rights amendment in Burning Tree Club, Inc. v. Bainum (Md.S.Ct.1985). Burning Tree nonetheless claimed that its open space benefit status survived *Bainum*. The state court did not agree and the Supreme Court denied review. Maryland v. Burning Tree Club, Inc. (Md.S.Ct.1987).

Political Parties. First Amendment right of association claims were also rejected in a challenge to Washington statutes that mandate equal representation of men and women on specified political party committees. Marchioro v. Chaney. Political parties may choose to equalize female participation at national conventions by mandating delegate selection on the basis of sex. Bachur v. Democratic

National Party (4th Cir.1987). New York State's
constitution expressly allows political parties to
provide for equal representation by sex on committees and at conventions.

10.02 Right to be Pregnant

A right of privacy regarding procreation was
protected against criminal prosecution in Griswold
v. Connecticut and its progeny. But civil rights
regarding procreation are considerably lesser. The
right to reproductive choices without state invasion
has spawned innumerable lawsuits involving employment and education.

Pregnant Minors. A former student alleged she
was dismissed from the National Honor Society
because she was pregnant. The trial court accepted the school district's allegation that premarital
sex, not pregnancy, was the basis for her dismissal.
The third circuit agreed that premarital sex was
sufficient grounds for the expulsion. However,
proffered testimony by a male who had engaged in
premarital sex and was not expelled from the
society raised equal protection rights and should
not have been excluded. Pfeiffer v. Marion Center
Area School District (3d Cir.1990). Pregnant or
not, it is unclear how premarital sex destroys one's
academic achievement that warrants membership
in the National Honor Society.

Pregnant and Unemployed. Because pregnancy
in context of employment benefits or entitlements
is viewed as a non-gender based classification un-

der Geduldig v. Aiello (S.Ct.1974), the rational basis test is applied to equal protection claims against alleged state incursions in these contexts. Conversely, the circumstances often provide a reason other than the pregnancy as an acceptable justification for the discrimination.

A woman does not have a right under the federal constitution to unemployment benefits after requesting, and receiving, a leave of absence to have a baby and then being denied a position three weeks after the baby's birth because she left work "voluntarily". Wimberly v. Labor & Industrial Relations Com'n (S.Ct.1987). The Minnesota Court of Appeals reached a different result where a woman with an excellent work record for ten years was denied unemployment benefits when discharged because she missed work to take care of a sick child. McCourtney v. Imprimis Technology, Inc. (Minn.App.1991). Each of her absences was excused for circumstances beyond her control. A dissenting judge said "Under the majority's analysis, an employer becomes the victim of an employee's personal problems with obtaining child care."

Pregnant and Single. Some courts have been sympathetic to women denied employment because they have borne a child out of wedlock. Equal protection and due process rights were violated when a school district rule barred hiring of unwed parents as teachers' aides. Andrews v. Drew Municipal Separate School District (5th Cir.1975).

10.03   Right of Marital Choice

Right to Marry. The right to marry is a fundamental right. A state cannot impose a criminal penalty on marriage without satisfying strict scrutiny analysis. A Wisconsin statute required that any "person" subject to child support for children not in his custody could not marry without demonstrating financial responsibility. No similar restriction was placed on the custodial parent, usually the mother. The Supreme Court ruled the statute unconstitutional because the classification was not necessary to achieve the statutory objective of counseling parents with child support obligations before they incurred new obligations. Zablocki v. Redhail (S.Ct.1978).

Right Not to Marry. Case law is unsettled as to the constitutionality of statutes which limit civil rights or impose criminal sanctions on sexual relationships between consenting adult women and men outside of the marital relationship. Right of privacy and equal protection claims as between married and single persons are inextricably associated in the legal argument.

As a practical matter, societal practices have rendered criminal statutes desuetude that prohibit cohabitation between unwed adult males and females. Benefits under civil statutes for these couples are less certain. Social security widow's and retirement benefits, for example, may not be available to an unwed partner of a covered worker. Peffley–Warner v. Bowen (Wn.S.Ct.1989). But see

In the Matter of Compensation of Williams (Or.S. Ct.1982), applying strict scrutiny under the state privileges and immunities clause and extending to unwed male parent/partners an Oregon statute which allows workmen's compensation death benefits to unwed female parent/partners.

Some states reject even gender neutral classifications on rational basis analysis where civil benefits of cohabiting couples are involved. A woman cannot be denied certification of good moral character, a prerequisite to taking the state bar examination, solely because she jointly owns and lives in a home with a man to whom she is not married. Cord v. Gibb (Va.S.Ct.1979). The state failed to establish a rational link between the applicant's fitness to practice law and cohabitation, the basis for denying the certificate.

10.04 Rights of Single Sex Partners

Single sex partners do not fare so well. In most jurisdictions, lesbians and gays are denied civil benefits and remain subject to criminal penalties.

Criminal Sanctions. The Supreme Court upheld Georgia's sodomy statute in Bowers v. Hardwick (S.Ct.1986). Respondent had been charged with sodomy with another adult male, but the case was set aside unless further evidence developed. Respondent then brought a civil action, seeking to have the statute declared unconstitutional since it placed him in imminent danger of prosecution. A heterosexual couple who were also plaintiffs in the trial court were dismissed for want of standing since they were not in any danger of injury from enforcement of the statute.

The Constitution, said the Supreme Court, does not "extend a fundamental right to homosexuals to engage in acts of consensual sodomy." The Court could see no constitutional reason to invalidate the sodomy laws of some 25 states. Compare People v. Onofre (N.Y.Ct.App.1980), where the New York court of appeals invalidated a statute that imposed a penalty for sodomy between unmarried adults but not married adults. No showing was made how the claimed statutory purpose of preserving the family was served by regulation of this type of sexual behavior only between unmarried persons.

Civil Benefits. Nor can single sex partners marry in most jurisdictions, even where there is an equal rights amendment. Singer v. Hara (Wn.App. 1974). The Washington court of appeals said the prohibition applies equally to male and female couples. The classification is therefore not based on sex, so the equal rights amendment is not invoked.

A few legislative bodies and courts have extended to single sex couples some civil benefits enjoyed by marital couples, including the right to civil registration as domestic partners. See Whorton v. Dillingham (Cal.App.1988). New York includes single sex couples in its application of a rent control statute. Braschi v. Stahl Associates Co. (N.Y. Ct.App.1989). The same court ruled that a lesbian cannot seek visitation rights to the child of her former partner because state law limits such rights to blood relatives. Alison D. v. Virginia M. (N.Y. Ct.App.1991).

Employment. The rights of homosexuals frequently arise in an employment setting. Homosexual preference, in absence of evidence of practice, was sufficient to support discharge of a teacher for immoral conduct in Gaylord v. Tacoma School District No. 10 (Wn.S.Ct.1977). A dissenting justice insisted that severe and far reaching consequences should not be drawn "from the admission of a status, which may be no more than a state of mind." Similarly, a high school counselor was fired after telling colleagues she had a lover. Rowland v. Mad River Local School District (6th Cir. 1984). Accord, Endsley v. Naes (D.Kan.1987). Contra, Gay Law Students Ass'n v. Pacific Telephone and Telegraph Co. (Cal.S.Ct.1979).

Military Security. In a narrow decision, the U.S. Army was ordered to allow a gay serviceman to reenlist on grounds of equitable estoppel. The serviceman had indicated his homosexuality on preinduction medical papers. The army accepted him anyway and accepted his reenlistment on several occasions. Watkins v. United States Army (9th Cir.1989).

The same circuit court ruled that homosexuals do not constitute a suspect or quasi-suspect class entitled to heightened scrutiny under the equal protection component of the Fifth Amendment.

High Tech. Gays v. Defense Industrial Security Clearance Office (9th Cir.1990). The suit challenged a Department of Defense policy of expanded investigation into the backgrounds of all gay and lesbian applicants for secret and top secret security clearances. The court said the DOD policy is rationally related to the government's legitimate interest in protecting national secrets.

CHAPTER 11

EDUCATION AND SPORTS

11.01 Single Sex Schools and Rules

The constitutional right of women to education is generally analyzed as a right of equal protection under the Fourteenth Amendment. States can prohibit single sex schools under their constitutions or statutes, but few have done so. Public educational facilities are exempt from operation of some state public accommodations laws.

Rational Basis Test. The Supreme Court has on several occasions addressed the constitutionality of de jure single sex schools, twice on challenge of males. In 1971, the same year as Reed v. Reed (S.Ct.1971), the Court upheld without opinion a district court ruling that male plaintiffs can be barred from a public college for women. Williams v. McNair (D.S.C.1970). The district court applied the rational basis test and said the equal protection clause does not require identity of treatment; flexibility and diversity in education, when not tainted with discriminatory overtones, may be desirable and beneficial.

Academic High Schools. The Court divided four to four on constitutionality of single sex academic public high schools, thus upholding exclusion of a

144

female plaintiff from an academic school for boys in Philadelphia, on grounds that she had the choice to attend a similar girls' academic high school. Vorchheimer v. School District of Philadelphia (3d Cir.1976). Subsequent female plaintiffs successfully challenged their exclusion from the same school, relying in part on the state equal rights amendment. The decision, which was not appealed, was not subject to collateral attack by other students. See Newberg by Newberg v. Board of Public Education (Pa.Super.1984).

Nor may a public academic school set lower admission standards for boys than for girls. There is no proof that a balance of the sexes furthers the goal of better academic education. Berkelman v. San Francisco Unified School District (9th Cir. 1974).

Gender Standard. In a third Supreme Court case, a male student successfully challenged a state's refusal to enroll him as a matriculated student in a public professional nursing school for women. Mississippi University for Women v. Hogan (S.Ct.1982). Under the narrow facts of the case, males were allowed to audit classes and participate in labs, but were denied matriculation status and degrees.

Justice O'Connor, writing for the Court, said the statute was not exempt from the gender standard because it discriminates against males rather than females. The laudatory state goal of enhancing women's professional employment is inapplicable to the nursing profession, where women already constitute a 98% majority. Exclusion of males "tends to perpetuate the stereotyped view of nursing as an exclusively woman's job." Nor does denying men a diploma after they complete all required work by attending classes insulate women from male competition in the classroom.

11.02 Sports

Perspectives. Active participation of males in competitive sports has long been recognized by the women's movement as a significant factor in shaping personalities and cultural expectations of males and females. Other women, not particularly concerned about sociological questions, simply want greater sports opportunities than have traditionally been available.

Numerous female plaintiffs have challenged the constitutionality of single sex sports teams sponsored by public schools and by private groups such as little league baseball and football. Courts usually find athletic associations engage in state action where they establish rules for public school interscholastic sports competition. Darrin v. Gould (Wn.S.Ct.1975).

Common Schools. Generally, public schools are not constitutionally required to provide interscholastic sporting activities. However, if they do, comparable sports opportunities must be made available to both sexes.

Most jurisdictions do not require that the opportunities be identical. The Fourteenth Amendment does not demand that boys be allowed to play on a girls' volleyball team when there is no boys' team because boys' physical difference would be detrimental to girls' participation in the sport. Clark v. Arizona Interscholastic Ass'n (9th Cir.1982). Similarly, a girl has no constitutional right to compete for a boys' basketball team under claim that the girls' team is not up to her level of competition. O'Connor v. Board of Education (7th Cir.1981). A gender based basketball program at the elementary level in Michigan Department of Civil Rights v. Waterford Tp. Department satisfied the constitution under the gender standard as well as the state civil rights act.

Darrin v. Gould (Wn.S.Ct.1975), relying on the state equal rights amendment, let females play in interscholastic football games. The court said there was no showing that the sisters were unable to compete with boys and that they could be protected from physical injury by appropriate equipment.

Establishing state action in athletic activities that are not directly involved with public schools has been more difficult. Use of public playing fields invoked the Fourteenth Amendment in Fortin v. Darlington Little League, Inc. (1st Cir.1975), but not in Magill v. Avonworth Baseball Conference (3d Cir.1975).

Universities. Denial of equal sporting activities for women at community colleges, four year colleges and universities has been long standing and pervasive. Female students and coaches successfully challenged a public university for numerous sex based discrepancies in its sports program. Male students had better locker rooms, better equipment and more scholarships, and were assigned the most desirable practice hours. Coaches had more perquisites, including complimentary cars and better travel accommodations. Blair v. Washington State University (Wn.S.Ct.1987). The trial judge, evaluating the program under Washington's anti-discrimination law and equal rights amendment, found for the plaintiffs on most claims. However, the trial court erred in excluding football when calculating equitable distribution of state dollars for women's sports and scholarships. The state supreme court wryly noted that the state ERA does not have an exclusion for football. Sports programs can utilize any non-state revenues they generate for their exclusive benefit.

Similar shortcomings of sports opportunities for female students were raised in Haffer v. Temple University (E.D.Pa.1987) which was ultimately settled by consent decree. Student plaintiffs in *Haffer* relied on constitutional rights under the Fourteenth Amendment, the Pennsylvania equal rights amendment, and statutory rights under Title IX of the Education Amendments of 1972.

CHAPTER 12

DOMESTIC PARTNERS

*The charge that the Equal Rights Amendment is
an evil device to destroy marriage and the family is
preposterous unless one is willing to assume that
marriage and family life depend upon the relationship of dominance and subservience*

Judge Shirley M. Hufstedler (1979)

12.01. Marital Partners

Under the English common law which shaped
United States jurisprudence in its formative years,
married women were subject to their husbands in
all matters: economic, civil and personal. Many of
these disabilities have been removed, but marriage
remains a civil contract unlike any other. The
rights, duties and obligations of the contract are
provided by the statutory and common laws of the
state, not by the parties joined in wedlock. Washington Statewide Organization of Stepparents v.
Smith (Wn.S.Ct.1975).

The extent to which sex bias is embedded in
domestic relations law is evidenced by the numerous constitutional challenges to statute and case
law governing the marital relationship. Areas
which have been litigated on grounds of sex dis-

crimination include domicile and names, discussed in Chapter 9, intrafamily and third party tort and contract claims, property and financial rights, divorce and dissolution, child custody and support.

A. FAMILY MEMBER LAWSUITS

The past decade has been marked in many states by abrogation or strict limitation to the common law doctrines of intraspousal and intrafamily tort immunity, which bar actions between family members for injuries to person or property. The challenge to the doctrines frequently arises when an insurance company disputes coverage for claims arising from intrafamily incidents. An example is St. Paul Fire & Marine Insurance Co. v. Molloy (Md.App.1980), where the company unsuccessfully argued that it was not obligated to pay a wife's share of property which was destroyed by the husband's alleged arson.

To compensate for the abrogation of intrafamily immunity, some insurance companies are writing husband/wife liability exclusions into their policies, such as the clause in the auto policy at issue in Mutual of Enumclaw Ins. Co. v. Wiscomb (Wn.S. Ct.1982). The court ruled the clause invalid on grounds that exclusion of a whole class of innocent people for no purpose is against public policy.

In related cases, Missouri rejected claims of spousal immunity in both negligence and intentional torts. The court said it was not creating a new right, but recognizing an overdue one. See

S.A.V. v. K.G.V. (Mo.S.Ct.1986) where a wife sued her husband for contraction of herpes; and Townsend v. Townsend (Mo.S.Ct.1986), where a husband shot his wife in the back. The court said it is difficult to see how suits based in tort would destroy domestic tranquility, while property and contract actions, long allowed, do not. Accord, Price v. Price (Tex.Ct.1987).

Parental immunity was disallowed and punitive damages of $100,000 awarded to an 11 year old girl sexually abused by her stepfather. The award is appropriate as punishment for the tortfeasor and deterrence for others. Laurie Marie M. v. Jeffrey T.M. (N.Y.App.Div. 2d Dept.1990). Similarly, parental tort immunity does not block a wrongful death action against a stepfather who intentionally killed plaintiff's mother. Luna v. Clayton (Tenn.S. Ct.1983). Maryland, which abandoned intraspousal immunity in 1983, retains parent-child immunity. Frye v. Frye (Md.S.Ct.1986).

Oregon retains both intraspousal and intrafamily immunity, finding a father is not liable in tort for the death of his two children from drunk driving. Winn v. Gilroy (Or.S.Ct.1984). The court listed concerns of fraud or collusion; "family exchequer"—why move money from one family pocket into another?; domestic tranquility, parental discipline and family sovereignty. The concurring opinion in *Winn* summarizes case law on parental immunity.

Foster children encounter state immunity obstacles. State licensed foster parents have qualified immunity for bodily harm allegedly suffered by children because of inadequate food and medical care. Eugene D. v. Karman (6th Cir.1989). Similarly, for sexual abuse of foster children. Doe v. Bobbitt (7th Cir.1989).

B. THIRD PARTY LAWSUITS

Liability between marital partners and third parties is a frequent subject of litigation. Legal issues arise concerning liability of one spouse to a third party because of tort or contract obligations incurred by the other spouse, or of liability of a third party to one spouse because of tort injuries the third party caused to the other spouse.

At common law, the husband was ordinarily liable for any torts to third parties committed by the wife in his presence, since he was responsible for her behavior, and also for any contractual obligations she incurred for necessaries with third party creditors. The wife was not responsible for necessaries or tort liabilities incurred by the husband.

Necessaries

The common law rule insulating the wife against suit for necessaries contracted for by the husband has been challenged by hapless creditors with increasing frequency as a violation of the equal protection clause. A constitutional challenge to the necessaries rule results in one of three positions: the doctrine is extended to creditors of the husband as well as to those of the wife; the doctrine is abolished altogether so that creditors can sue neither the husband nor the wife for necessary debts incurred by the other; or the doctrine is still viable.

Legal history of the necessaries doctrine is summarized in Sillery v. Fagan and Fagan (N.J.Dist.Ct. 1972), which extended the rule. Some states require that the assets of the primary spouse be exhausted first. Jersey Shore Medical Center–Fitkin Hospital v. Baum's Estate (N.J.S.Ct.1980). Maryland abolished the necessaries doctrine entirely, saying that a policy change so fundamental as extending the doctrine should be determined by the legislature. Condore v. Prince George's County (Md.S.Ct.1981).

Wisconsin has reaffirmed the doctrine of necessaries that limits responsibility to the husband for necessary expenses incurred by the wife. Sharpe Furniture, Inc. v. Buckstaff (Wis.S.Ct.1980). The heart of the common law rule is a concern for the support and sustenance of the family; this rule retains a viable role in modern society and is served by the necessaries doctrine.

Spouses in community property states are liable to pay income taxes on community income earned by the other spouse even when they exercise no control over the money. United States v. Mitchell (S.Ct.1971).

Tort Obligations

Prior to challenge in deElche v. Jacobsen (Wn.S. Ct.1980), a tortfeasor's interest in community property was exempt from the tortfeasor's separate tort liability in Washington, a community property state. The husband had been sued for damages in a civil action for rape and had no separate property with which to satisfy the judgment because he and his wife had executed an agreement that all of their property was community. Overruling precedent, the court said the judiciary abdicates its own function when it refuses to reconsider an unsatisfactory legal rule that was created by the judiciary.

Common law recognizes an action known as loss of consortium under which a husband can sue a third party for loss of his wife's society. Consortium includes company, cooperation and sexual relations, and is not to be confused with the injury or death to the wife which gives rise to the consortium suit. Common law did not allow a wife a comparable suit for loss of consortium of her husband.

Most states today extend to the wife the right to sue for loss of a husband's consortium. See American Export Lines, Inc. v. Alvez (S.Ct.1980).

C. PROPERTY AND FINANCIAL RIGHTS

Property and financial rights of married couples depend upon whether they live in one of the 42 common law or one of the eight community property states. In community property states, each spouse has legal ownership in one half the earnings of the other spouse. This ownership until recently was of little concrete value to a wife in so far as the husband exercised legal control over both the personal and real community property and could sell, mortgage, or otherwise dispose and encumber it without her consent. In response to the women's movement, community property states have given wives powers of management over the community property.

The Supreme Court unanimously ruled unconstitutional a statute commonly called a "head and master" law under which the husband has unilateral right to dispose of property jointly owned with his wife in Kirchberg v. Feenstra. Mr. Feenstra had executed a mortgage on the family home without his wife's knowledge as security for prepayment of legal fees to defend an incest charge.

D. DISSOLUTION AND DIVORCE

The husband's legal liability during the 19th century for his wife's torts and crimes gave him the legal right "to use such a degree of force as is necessary to make the wife behave herself and know her place". Indeed, circumstances could arise "which will mitigate, excuse, and so far justify the husband in striking the wife * * * so as not to give her a right * * * to be divorced." Joyner v. Joyner (N.C.1862). Incredibly, these laws remained in effect for years.

Husbands no longer have a legal right to beat their wives for real or imagined offenses, and women can seek divorce on the same grounds as men. All states have some form of no fault divorce.

As has been seen, terms of the marital contract are largely determined by the state. The relationship between the partners upon legal separation, dissolution, and divorce arises from a new contract similarly imposed by the state.

Where there are minor children, the legal resolution must address both their physical custody and financial support. Where there are no minor children, the interests of the spouses in property accumulated during the marriage including business, good will, pension rights, and the capacity of the spouses to support themselves remain to be addressed.

Property. In common law states property division is made traditionally on the basis of legal title, although most states temper the harshness of this rule with principles of equity and constructive trust. In community property states, property settlement varies, first as to establishing what property qualifies as community so that each spouse has legal title to one half of it, and second, as to appropriate treatment of property classified as separate. In some contexts, equal protection issues are raised. In others, the issue is limited to statutory construction.

A presumption that the husband is owner of household goods possessed and used by both spouses is not unusual. This presumption was set aside as incompatible with the Pennsylvania equal rights amendment. DiFlorido v. DiFlorido. The court recognized the value of the work contributed by the homemaker to the marriage and said household property will be presumed to be held jointly by the entireties.

Although bankruptcy proceedings do not discharge alimony and child support payments, property settlements can be discharged. In many divorce settlements, the marital home is the only property of real value. A former husband claimed the homestead exemption in a bankruptcy proceeding to avoid a judicial lien on the marital home held by his former spouse as security for her property award under the divorce. The Supreme Court unanimously rejected this avenue of escape from a property settlement in Farrey v. Sanderfoot (S.Ct. 1991).

1. Prenuptial Contracts

Before marriage, some prospective brides and grooms enter into antenuptial or prenuptial agreements that seek to identify each party's legal interest in the other's property upon death or divorce. Less frequently, similar postnuptial contracts are made during marriage. These contracts, recognized in every state, are given the same presumption of legality as any other duly executed contract. Eckstein v. Eckstein (N.Y.App.Div.2d Dept. 1987). Most states require the contracts to be in writing; certainly a written document is preferable.

There are pitfalls. A showing of fraud, duress, mistake or unconscionably changed circumstances is usually required to upset a prenuptial agreement. Scherer v. Scherer (Ga.S.Ct.1982). An agreement will not necessarily be set aside solely because one party does not fully understand the terms, Simeone v. Simeone (Pa.S.Ct.1990) or one party fails to make a full disclosure of assets, Daniel v. Daniel (Tex.App.1989), or the agreement is not fair, Chiles v. Chiles (Tex.App.1989). A contract must have been unconscionable when made to be set aside under the standard established in the Uniform Premarital Agreement Act, adopted with minor variations in many states.

Some courts demonstrate a reluctance to enforce contracts that specifically anticipate divorce. These jurisdictions, like Kentucky, may require full disclosure of assets for judicial enforcement. Edwardson v. Edwardson (Ky.S.Ct.1990).

In general, the contract must be entered into long enough before the marriage to have some objectivity. Matter of Marriage of Norris (Or.App. 1981) set aside a contract signed shortly before the ceremony.

Where the agreement seeks to settle child custody and support questions, the courts feel free to modify the agreement since the children were not party to it.

Separation Agreements. The Supreme Court established in 1836 that adequate consideration will support enforcement of a separation agreement. Wallingsford v. Allen (S.Ct.1836). The white male plaintiff claimed that the black female defendant and her two young children belonged to him upon death of his wife, from whom he had long been separated. The defendant claimed freedom for herself and her children under a deed of manumission from the wife before her death. The Court ruled the manumission valid. The wife, a feme sole because of the separation, was able to enter into a valid contract. Her relinquishment of any claim to alimony was the consideration for which she received the defendant and other property to the total value of $900, which was approximately the amount of the dowry she had brought to the marriage.

Release of claims clauses need to be carefully drafted. A separation agreement under which a woman released her former husband from all claims arising or growing out of the marital relationship was later barred from suing him in tort for transmitting to her a veneral disease which required her to have a hysterectomy. Overberg v. Lusby (6th Cir.1990).

2. Alimony

An Alabama statute placing alimony obligations only upon the husband denies men equal protection of the laws. Orr v. Orr (S.Ct.1979). The

Supreme Court applied the gender standard and found the dual state objectives of providing financial resources for needy wives, and of compensating wives for discrimination that has left them unprepared to enter the workplace, could be served as well by a gender neutral statute.

In ruling a gender based alimony statute a violation of the Pennsylvania equal rights amendment, the state supreme court said, "the thrust of the Equal Rights Amendment is to insure equality of rights under the law and to eliminate sex as a basis for distinction. The sex of citizens of this Commonwealth is no longer a permissible factor in the determination of their legal rights and legal responsibilities." Henderson v. Henderson (Pa.S. Ct.1974).

As a matter of law, many jurisdictions hold that the obligation of a former spouse to pay alimony terminates when the dependent former spouse remarries even when the alimony was awarded for an indefinite term, and did not provide for termination on remarriage. Dunaway v. Dunaway (Ohio S.Ct.1990).

3. Retirement Benefits

Government Pensions. The right of divorced women to share in federal pensions accrued by their husbands during marriage is a question of Congressional intent.

The Uniformed Services Former Spouses Protection Act (USFSPA) provides that military pensions are marital property subject to division upon divorce like any other pension. In re Marriage of Howell (Iowa S.Ct.1989). However, the USFSPA excludes from treatment as disposable property any military retirement pay which the veteran elects to waive in lieu of receiving disability benefits. Mansell v. Mansell (S.Ct.1989). Railroad pensions are federally preempted from state community property division, subject only to child support and alimony obligations. Hisquierdo v. Hisquierdo (S.Ct.1979).

The supremacy clause also bars a state court from requiring a serviceman to keep insurance issued pursuant to the Servicemen's Group Life Insurance Act in force in favor of the divorced couple's children. The clear intent of Congress is to allow the serviceman the right to change the beneficiary. Ridgway v. Ridgway (S.Ct.1981). *Hisquierdo* and *Ridgway* may also bar distribution of a share in benefits accrued under social security if the parties were married less than ten years, at which time the SSA allows participation from specifically designated funds. Distribution of non-designated funds was disallowed in Matter of Marriage of Swan (Or.App.1986) on the basis of the anti-assignment clause in the Social Security Act. Distribution was allowed in Elliott v. Elliott (Minn. S.Ct.1978).

Private Pensions. Pensions falling under the provisions of the federal Employment Retirement Income Security Act (ERISA) do not have federal contributions. Thus state distribution practices are not preempted by ERISA. Stone v. Stone (9th Cir.1980).

4. Professional Degrees and Good Will

The right of a divorced wife to share in the financial value of professional degrees to which she contributed and the good will and potential future earnings of the husband's on-going profession have been the subject of considerable litigation with mixed results. A New York trial court summarized case law regarding professional degrees in O'Brien v. O'Brien (N.Y.S.Ct.1982). Some jurisdictions reject division. A sole practitioner's law practice had no "goodwill" value for the purpose of dividing his marital property on divorce. Travis v. Travis (Okl.S.Ct.1990). Some allow for reimbursement of the non-professional spouse's financial contribution. Mahoney v. Mahoney (N.J.S.Ct.1982). *O'Brien* adopted the third view: that the professional degrees and licenses are property, can be presently valued, and equitably distributed. The court said "it is unfair to deny her a share of this asset [medical degree and license] which would not exist but for her efforts." Factors to consider are length of marriage, amount of community funds expended, amount the community would have earned had both spouses been employed, and lost employment and educational opportunities of the supporting spouse. In the Marriage of Washburn, In the Marriage of Gillette (Wn.S.Ct.1984).

E. CHILD CUSTODY AND SUPPORT

Among the most difficult questions faced in divorce proceedings are determinations of child custody and support.

1. Custody

Under early divorce law, husbands were custodians of the children. Early in the twentieth century, "tender years" statutes were enacted under which the mother was usually awarded custody of young children. The tender years doctrine has been eliminated in some states by statute and in others by judicial decree as discriminating against men in violation of state or federal constitutions. Devine v. Devine (Ala.S.Ct.1981). But see Arends v. Arends (Utah S.Ct.1974), where the court said the father's attack on the statutory maternal presumption "might have some merit * * * if the father was equally gifted in lactation as the mother."

Race may not be a factor in determining child custody. The Supreme Court overturned on equal protection grounds a family court decree denying custody of her white child to a white woman who married a black man. Palmore v. Sidoti (S.Ct. 1984).

Potential harmful effect on the moral development of the children is the focus of some statutes. A woman lost custody of her three teenage daughters because she lived with a man to whom she was not married. Open cohabitation is disregard for the law that "instructs her children by example" that they too may ignore the law. Jarrett v. Jarrett (Ill.S.Ct.1979). Similarly Parrillo v. Parrillo (R.I.S.Ct.1989), where a woman unsuccessfully appealed a court order threatening her with jail if she permitted a male friend to spend the night at her house while her young children were present.

In contrast, neither financial inability to provide necessities, nor a less than ideal home environment, nor failure of the mother's male partner to take care of the children, is sufficient to remove the children from the mother's custody. In re Jack (Cal.App.1980). In re Marriage of Tresnak (Iowa S.Ct.1980) overturned a judgment denying custody of 9 and 11 year old children to a divorced mother attending law school because she would be too busy to give them care and attention.

Preference for a partner of the same sex is not sufficient ground to deny custody to a mother. Bezio v. Patenaude (Mass.S.Ct.1980). Nor is change in circumstances of the noncustodial parent sufficient to support removal of custody from lesbian mothers. Isaacson v. Isaacson and Schuster v. Schuster (Wn.S.Ct.1978).

Gender based statutes to determine child custody have generally been found unconstitutional under state equal rights amendments. People ex rel. Elmore v. Elmore (Ill.App.1977) and McAndrew v. McAndrew (Md.App.1978). The uniform marriage and divorce act adopts the best interests of the child standard, looking to stability and continuity of environment.

Joint Custody. Joint custody, with parents sharing major decisions such as choice of school and religious training, is an option in most jurisdictions. A lack of cooperation or evidence of physical abuse between the parents will defeat joint custody. Hardin v. Hardin (Ky.App.1986).

Embryo custody reached the courts in Davis v. Davis (Tenn.App.1990). The court said that seven frozen embryos should remain undisturbed and in the joint custody of the divorced husband and wife who have equal voice in their disposition.

Custody Forum. The Uniform Child Custody Jurisdiction Act and the Parental Kidnapping Prevention Act (PKPA) attempt to insulate children from parental tugs-of-war which arise when parents seek to invoke competing forums to settle custody disputes. However, the PKPA does not create an implied cause of action in federal court to determine which of two conflicting state custody decrees is valid. Thompson v. Thompson (S.Ct. 1988).

Termination of Rights. Parental rights are terminated voluntarily through formal adoption by other parties and involuntarily through state proceedings, primarily on grounds of abuse, abandonment and neglect.

The Supreme Court has ruled that involuntary termination of parental rights by the state requires clear and convincing proof because social workers are adversaries of the parents. Santosky v. Kramer (S.Ct.1982). But a statute providing for termination of parental rights is not unconstitutionally vague in that the terms "plan" and "adequately" are not further defined. In re Hanks (Del.S.Ct. 1989).

Indian Adoption. Adoption of Indian children is governed by the Indian Child Welfare Act, which provides exclusive jurisdiction in Indian courts for adoption proceedings for children residing or domiciled on the reservation. State courts lack power to enter a decree even though the children were born off the reservation and were voluntarily surrendered for adoption. Mississippi Band of Choctaw Indians v. Holyfield (S.Ct.1989).

2. Support

If mothers have been granted the pleasures and burdens of day to day child care, fathers have been burdened with monthly support payments. It is easier to stop payment of monthly support than to stop taking care of the children. Application of federal legislation seeking to enhance collection of child support is complex. For discussion, see Ainsworth v. Ainsworth (Vt.S.Ct.1990), where the noncustodial parent was supporting stepchildren in a second marriage. The legislation includes provisions for wage withholding, interception of tax refunds, liens against real estate and personalty, and interstate enforcement. States are required to adopt strict child-support guidelines to be implemented only in absence of a negotiated settlement.

A section 1983 action by a group of Ohio parents against Ohio state officials for their alleged failure to fulfill Title IV D of the Social Security Act, which provides child support enforcement services nationwide, was rejected in Carelli v. Howser (6th Cir.1991). Accord, Wehunt v. Ledbetter (11th Cir. 1989).

Parents can be held in civil contempt of court and jailed for failing to pay court ordered child support that they cannot prove they are unable to pay. Hicks v. Feiock (S.Ct.1988).

Support obligations in states with equal rights amendments are generally imposed on both parents. The custodial parent, however, is not always required to make an equal financial contribution. Pennsylvania, for example, recognizes the financial value of the homemaker services provided by the custodial parent. Commonwealth ex rel. Wasiolek v. Wasiolek (Pa.Super.1977). Nor does the state equal rights amendment require that a pregnant mother work in order to contribute to child support. In re Marriage of Trask (Colo.App.1978).

After reviewing cases in other jurisdictions, a New Mexico court ruled that denial of visitation rights by the custodial parent should be a defense to a support enforcement suit in "extreme cases." Williams v. Williams (N.M.S.Ct.1989).

3. Surrogacy

A new area of family law addresses issues arising from artificial insemination and surrogate motherhood. Artificial insemination refers to fertilization within the mother's body without sexual intercourse. Embryo transfer refers to fertilization outside of the mother's body. Various parental combinations of sperm and egg are possible, each posing different legal relationships. A gestating woman can be either a biological or non-biological mother. Legal rights of the gestational mother, whether biological or non-biological, the biological non-gestational mother, the father and the child are all implicated.

Statutes either ban surrogacy or severely restrict it, prohibiting payment outside of medical and related expenses, and pre-birth contracts that the surrogate mother cannot revoke. In absence of statute, courts generally find the contracts not legally enforceable, and determine custody under the "best interests of the child" standard. A California family court granted custody of a child to its biological parents, holding that the non-biological gestational mother was similar to a foster parent with no parental rights.

Baby M was awarded to the biological father and his wife, who formally adopted her. The biological surrogate mother was granted visitation rights. In the Matter of Baby M. (N.J.S.Ct.1988).

Sperm Donors. Most states have legislation providing for paternity of children born of artificial insemination. A husband generally is entitled to adopt children born to his wife through artificial insemination of sperm from a third party donor to divest the sperm donor of any rights he might have with regard to the children. Welborn v. Doe (Va. App.1990). However, such a statute is unconstitutional applied to a donor who can prove he donated his sperm only after the woman agreed that his parental rights would be preserved. McIntyre v. Crouch (Or.S.Ct.1989).

Where an unmarried woman knows the donor of the semen, the man is entitled to visitation rights and is responsible for support; the "man cannot be considered to be less a father" because he is not married to the mother. C.M. v. C.C. (N.J.Super. 1977). Nor can the sperm donor and mother agree to release the father of financial responsibility. The right to support and visitation are rights of the child and not of the parents. Ernest P. v. Superior Court (Cal.App.1980).

12.02 Nonmarital Partners

Developing case law seeks to unravel property and child custody disputes arising from termination of longterm relationships. Nonmarital partners generally cannot qualify as common law married couples because they have expressly rejected marital union and hold themselves to be not married. But upon separation they too turn to the courts for whatever law can be found or fashioned to effect a fair distribution of property accumulated during the relationship, and a fair recognition of the parenting rights and obligations of both parents to any children born of the union.

A. CHILDREN

Rights of Unwed Fathers

Custody. Custody of the natural child was wholly outside the father's control in most states prior to Stanley v. Illinois (S.Ct.1972). At issue in *Stanley* was a state law that presumed an unwed mother is a fit custodial parent and presumed an unwed father is not. *Stanley* established that an unwed father who has lived with his children in a family relationship is entitled to a hearing upon death of the children's mother to determine his parental fitness before the children are taken from his custody. He has a fundamental right as a natural father not to be treated differently than a natural mother.

Adoption. The rights of a natural father who lacks the strong parental ties demonstrated by *Stanley* are less clear. The issue often arises when third parties or the mother's husband want to adopt the child and the natural father claims his own parental rights. The Rehnquist Court has retreated from Caban v. Mohammed (S.Ct.1979), which ruled unconstitutional a statute that denied an unwed father equal rights with an unwed mother to block the adoption of a natural child.

An unwed father can be stripped of his parental rights even when he is a fit parent and has actively sought custody of the child for a long period, where the court determines that termination is in child's best interest. In re Baby Girl M. (Cal.App.1987). The claims of the unwed father were not as strong in Lehr v. Robertson (S.Ct.1983). A father who has not registered with the putative father registry, has never supported and has rarely seen his child does not have an absolute right to notice and hearing before the child is adopted.

Paternity. Nor does a putative father have a constitutionally protected right to prove paternity of a child born to a woman married to another man. A state statute that conclusively presumes the husband is the father satisfies the rational basis test. The Court said the gender standard is not required where men are the disadvantaged class, and strict scrutiny is not required because non-wed fathers do not have parental rights "imbedded" in tradition. Nor are the child's filial rights violated. Michael H. v. Gerald D. (S.Ct. 1989). After *Michael H.*, putative fathers rallied enough support in the California legislature to repeal the absolute legal presumption of a husband's paternity.

Rights of Natural Children. Under the uniform parentage act, the parent-child relationship extends equally to every child and to every parent, regardless of marital status of the parents. The mother and father are equally entitled to custody and equally obligated for support. A natural mother frequently is compelled to invoke a natural father's support obligations by instituting a paternity action. The Supreme Court has unanimously agreed that a state cannot impose a statutory limit of six years after the child's birth to such actions.

Clark v. Jetter (S.Ct.1988). Nor can an unwed father escape support obligations on grounds the woman deceived him by falsely claiming she was on contraceptives. Her actions in no way impeded his use of contraceptives. In re Pamela (Fla.1982).

Should men deny paternity, they can be compelled to take paternity tests upon proof that they had sexual intercourse with the child's mother at the approximate time of conception. Such tests are not an unconstitutional invasion of privacy or improper search and seizure, or interference with right of religion. The state has a compelling interest in determining parentage, and the rights of the children prevail over the rights of the father. State v. Meacham (Wn.S.Ct.1980).

The state child support formula with standard of living adjustment is properly applied to unwed fathers to determine support needs of a natural child whose parents lived together too briefly to establish a manner or standard of living. Shuba v. Division (Del.Ct.1989).

For Supreme Court treatment of inheritance rights of natural children, see Trimble v. Gordon (S.Ct.1977), allowing inheritance, and Lalli v. Lalli (S.Ct.1978), disallowing inheritance. A sex based inheritance statute was ruled unconstitutional under the Massachusetts equal rights amendment in Lowell v. Kowalski (Mass.S.Ct.1980). Illinois, also an ERA state, said natural children lack standing to challenge such a statute. In re Karas' Estate (Ill.S.Ct.1975).

B. PROPERTY

A generation ago, unmarried domestic partners were treated as living in an illegal, immoral relationship. While the judgment of immorality has considerably diminished, legal consequences remain. Law refuses to enforce illegal contracts; courts leave the parties where it finds them. As a consequence, an unwed partner holding legal title to any property jointly acquired during the union is secure against claims from the other. The law assumes the parties intended the title to be where it in fact is. Creasman v. Boyle (Wn.S.Ct.1948).

Courts seek to temper this harsh rule where confronted with a long term, stable relationship by finding facts to support a contract, partnership, joint venture or trust, or at the minimum, to compensate for value of non-sexual services rendered. A standard that looks to the "seriousness" of the relationship and assumes that the parties intended to treat one another fairly has been adopted by Washington state. Matter of Marriage of Lindsey (Wn.S.Ct.1984), overruling *Creasman.* Similarly, In re Estate of Eriksen (Minn.S.Ct.1983).

But compare Marvin v. Marvin (Cal.S.Ct.1976), which disallowed recovery on grounds of equity and fairness; a former partner's need and defendant's ability to pay are not sufficient basis for an award either in law or equity. Illinois reiterated the "legal title controls" principle in Hewitt v. Hewitt (Ill.App.1979), saying that public policy disfavors mutually enforceable property rights between unmarried persons. In *Hewitt,* the couple had three children and the woman worked while the man went to school.

CHAPTER 13

EMPLOYMENT RELATED BENEFITS

13.01 The Homemaker

The homemaker/housewife does work recognized to be of high social and economic value. Nonetheless, work done within the home is not covered by the Old Age Survivors and Disability Insurance Act, commonly known as the Social Security Act. The homemaker consequently has no security at any time as a result of her own labors. Unless she is fortunate enough to have independent income, she is totally dependent upon her husband or welfare for sustenance, although financial problems may not appear until divorce or the death of her husband. Conversely, should the homemaker die, her husband and children have no social security to cover the considerable value of her homemaking services.

A woman who is dependent upon her husband's public and private retirement and pension benefits is concerned about spousal benefits while her husband is alive, and survivor's benefits if she survives him. Joint benefits for the retired couple are available under both public and private programs, but mandatory survivor's benefits are not common under either. Where survivor's benefits are available, under some programs, the surviving widower, as protected employee, continues to receive the same pension as was paid to the couple; the surviving dependent widow often receives only half.

Pensions payable by the private employer of her husband may be of no value to the homemaker widow. Some plans provide for benefits only for employees who reach a given age, usually 55. If the husband dies before the specified age, even if he has worked more than 30 years, his widow will receive no pension. Even when her husband is in employment covered by social security, if he dies or they are divorced before she is 60, with no minor children, she may be faced with supporting herself with no marketable skills other than domestic work in a competitive marketplace that favors younger women.

Exclusion of the homemaker from social security protection represents a continuing legislative policy judgment grounded in unexamined assumptions regarding the work performed by women in the home. Because this work is excluded from covered employment, homemakers have no standing to challenge the Social Security Act for underinclusiveness. The Court has acknowledged the difficulty of a member of an excluded class to challenge a statute for its underinclusiveness. Orr v. Orr.

13.02 Constitutional Challenges

A. GENDER SPECIFIC CLASSIFICATION

1. Social Security

In view of this historical background, it is understandable that the most significant cases challenging constitutionality of gender based classifications in the Social Security Act have been brought by men. Numerous gender based classifications in the Social Security Act have been ruled unconstitutional.

Analytic Differences. In addressing these constitutional challenges, the Court has had difficulty deciding whether the discrimination is directed to men or women. This analytic problem has been compounded because the Justices disagree whether discrimination against men should be subjected to the same scrutiny as discrimination against women. If the discrimination is defined as occurring against men, one position of the Court holds that only the rational basis test should apply. Thus, deciding whether the discrimination is directed to men or women is a critical threshold question. As a practical matter, both women and men are subject to discrimination. The primary discrimination is against women because had the wife not been working in covered employment, her spouse would have no benefits at all arising from her employment.

An example is Weinberger v. Wiesenfeld (S.Ct. 1975). The facts were analyzed variously as dis-

crimination against women, against the family, or
against children. Despite the differences in analysis, the Justices were in unanimous agreement that
a Social Security Act provision that awarded benefits to a widow but not to a widower with children
under eighteen was unconstitutional. Contempla-
tion of a widower charged with care of an infant
son brought into sharp focus the assumption that
only women take care of children.

Similarly, denial of benefits to divorced males
and proof of financial dependency for surviving
males were ruled unconstitutional in Oliver v. Califano (N.D.Cal.1977) and Califano v. Goldfarb (S.Ct.
1977).

The emphasis of *Wiesenfeld* and *Goldfarb* on
cultural assumptions also controlled in Califano v.
Westcott (S.Ct.1979). A provision that awarded
benefits under Aid to Families with Dependent
Children (AFDC) when the father but not the wife,
was unemployed, was struck as an instance of the
"baggage of sexual stereotypes that presumes the
father has the primary responsibility to provide a
home and its essentials."

Remedial Purpose. When the classification that
disadvantages men is viewed as a conscious attempt to remedy the economic disadvantages of
women arising from undercompensated work in
the employment market, the Court is likely to
uphold the provision. Califano v. Webster.

Although explicit gender based discriminations
in the social security program have been eliminat-

ed by judicial decisions, more subtle discrimination against women employees remains by virtue of the structure of the system. Women who work part time or have interrupted work histories because of child or elder care commitments are penalized because social security benefits are linked to regularity of employment.

2. Workers' Compensation

The gender standard was appropriate in analysis of a workers' compensation statute which provided payment to a widow upon the work related death of her husband, but denied such recovery to a widower unless he proved dependence upon his wife's earnings. Wengler v. Druggists Mutual Insurance Co. (S.Ct.1980).

The Court applied the mid-level scrutiny of *Craig* and stated that the statute was offensive because it "discriminates against both men and women."

It does not follow that death benefit payments will be made to the surviving husband. The California supreme court struck a similar statute rather than extend the death payment to the widower, leaving to the legislature whether to compensate both sexes or neither for the work related death of a spouse. Arp v. Workers' Compensation Appeals Board.

B. GENDER NEUTRAL CLASSIFICATION

Articulation of the gender standard of review did not resolve what constitutes gender based classification. This question is significant because a classification that is not gender based will be subjected to the rational basis test. A disparate impact against one sex is not sufficient to constitute a gender based classification. Personnel Administrator of Massachusetts v. Feeney. Nor is a classification necessarily gender based if it applies only to men or to women. The classification must disadvantage one sex compared to the other before the gender standard is the appropriate tool for analysis.

Unwed Mothers. A classification between wed and unwed mothers is not gender based. An unwed mother unsuccessfully challenged a provision in the Social Security Act that restricted "mother's insurance benefits" to widows and divorced wives of wage earners. Califano v. Boles (S.Ct.1979). The Court said it was reasonable for Congress to conclude that an unwed mother is less likely to have been financially dependent upon the wage earner than if they had been married.

Needy Parents. Classification between needy parents in the fifty states and needy parents in a territory is also not a gender based classification. A lower level of reimbursement provided to Puerto Rican recipients under Aid to Families with Dependent Children does not violate the Fifth Amendment's equal protection guarantee so long as there is a rational basis for doing so. One relevant factor, said the Court, is that greater benefits could disrupt the Puerto Rican economy. Harris v. Rosario (S.Ct.1980).

State Salaries. In the cases just discussed, gender neutral classifications invoked the deferential rational basis test, and the challenged statutes survived. In a state court ruling, the reverse has occurred. An economic based gender neutral classification that would have survived the rational basis test has been elevated to constitutional protection on analogy to Congressional legislation that prohibits payment of different salaries to men and women doing the same work.

A New York state civil service salary schedule for county judges provided a $1,000 wage differential between salaries of judges in neighboring counties. The court ruled that district judges in different counties have an equal protection right to wage parity. Weissman v. Evans (N.Y.S.Ct.App.Div. 1981). The holding is of interest because it overrides on constitutional grounds disparity in wage scales for equal work on a sex neutral basis.

Most statutes challenged in this section were prima facie gender based, and were analyzed under the gender standard of review. Gender neutral statutes were analyzed under the rational basis test.

The standard of review to determine the constitutionality of de facto and de jure sex based preferential policies is the focus of the next chapter.

CHAPTER 14

PREFERENTIAL PROGRAMS

14.01 Gender Neutral: Veterans' Preference

Affirmative action programs to aid a special class of persons were not born in the civil rights movement of the 60s. Preferential programs for veterans have been around for more than a hundred years. Many of these programs provide veterans with a lifetime absolute preference for civil service positions.

The constitutionality of a lifetime, absolute veterans' preference statute was challenged in Personnel Administrator of Massachusetts v. Feeney (S.Ct.1979). The female plaintiff, a long time civil servant, had been passed over for promotion in favor of less qualified males on several occasions because of the veterans' preference. The Court rejected her argument that the statute's admitted disparate impact against women constituted discrimination against women in violation of the Fourteenth Amendment.

Classification by veterans is gender neutral because the class of non-veterans includes many males, and the class of veterans a few females. The statute was valid because it rationally served the state goal of assisting veterans in their return to civilian life.

To establish unconstitutional discrimination under a gender neutral statute, the plaintiff must demonstrate that the legislature adopted the challenged provision "because of" its admitted discriminatory impact against women. An adverse impact is not actionable when it is an unavoidable companion to a non-discriminatory motive. Accord, Keyes v. Secretary of the Navy (1st Cir.1988).

Justice Marshall criticized the rule of Washington v. Davis (S.Ct.1976), now adopted in *Feeney*, that requires persons alleging discrimination under the Fourteenth Amendment to prove invidious intent in addition to disparate impact. He wrote, "An approach based on motivation creates the risk that officials will be able to adopt policies that are the products of discriminatory intent so long as they sufficiently mask their motives through the use of subtlety and illusion." Rather, the "common-law foreseeability presumption" should apply, under which a showing that a gender neutral policy will foreseeably have a disproportionate effect would be sufficient to support a holding of unconstitutionality.

A veterans' preference program is a form of affirmative action. The *Feeney* Court dismissed inquiry into state needs for the most highly competent civil servants available. The question of comparable qualifications is raised, however, for affirmative action programs which give preference to minorities and women. The tension of this inconsistency is unresolved.

14.02 Gender Specific: Female Preference

Perspectives. The constitutionality of governmental preferential treatment for minorities was addressed in University of California Regents v. Bakke (S.Ct.1978). Primarily because affirmative action programs generally cover both minorities and women, the reasoning of *Bakke* and its progeny has been extended to cases challenging affirmative action for women.

The circumstances between minorities and women are not identical. Race is a specifically protected class under the Fourteenth Amendment; sex has constitutional protection only through the judicially created gender standard. Pervasive discriminatory treatment of blacks exploded into a civil war, resulting in the Fourteenth Amendment, whose promise of equal rights has not yet been realized by blacks. Women, beleaguering their voting male acquaintances and husbands, particularly those in Congress and state legislatures, secured the right to vote through constitutional amendment, although other civil rights did not automatically follow.

Most significantly, minorities number about 15 percent of the national population; women just over 50 percent.

Because affirmative action programs seek positive results through action rather than verbal espousal of abstract theories of equality, they generate potential claims of reverse discrimination by any person displaced because of affirmative action on behalf of another.

Racial Preference. In *Bakke,* a white male challenged as unconstitutional his rejection to University of California Medical School because of a preferential program for minorities. The case implicated both the Fourteenth Amendment and Title VI of the Civil Rights Act of 1964, which prohibits race discrimination under federally funded educational programs.

Justice Powell's controlling opinion straddled two pluralities. He said that the Constitution permits consideration of race in setting a goal to increase minority representation, but the Constitution does not allow setting a guaranteed numerical quota. Justices Brennan, White, Marshall and Blackmun agreed that affirmative action goals for minorities did not offend the Fourteenth Amendment, and argued that numerical goals were acceptable too. They also agreed that strict scrutiny should not be applied to affirmative action programs that disadvantage white males because they are not a member of a traditionally disadvantaged class. Nor should the rational basis test be applied. Because there is a "significant risk" that racial classifications established for ostensibly benign purposes can be misused, causing effects not unlike those created by invidious classifications, the rational basis test should be set aside in favor of the standard developed in gender based discrimination cases. With this standard, any remedial statute would require justification by an important and articulated purpose.

Justices Stevens, Stewart, Rehnquist and Chief Justice Burger said the case did not present a constitutional issue at all. The language of Title VI absolutely prohibits consideration of race in the admission process. Thus there was no need to address the constitutional legitimacy of the affirmative action program or to tangle with distinctions between quotas and goals.

Female Preference. Because classification by sex is not specifically prohibited by the Fourteenth Amendment, there is less ground for constitutional challenge to affirmative action programs for women. The Supreme Court upheld the promotion of a woman over a marginally more qualified male in Johnson v. Transportation Agency, Santa Clara County (S.Ct.1987), the first affirmative action program directly involving women to reach the Court. The parties in *Johnson* did not raise any constitutional issues. The Court focused on the program's compliance with Title VII and found it consistent with the earlier Title VII affirmative action program upheld in United Steelworkers of America v. Weber (S.Ct.1979).

Chief Justice Rehnquist and Justices Scalia and White, dissenting in *Johnson,* argue that Title VII affirmative action programs violate the Fourteenth Amendment as well as the express language of

Title VII. Justice Rehnquist rejects an affirmative action employment program that disadvantages males although he has repeatedly argued for a single standard of review, and said that males are not entitled to special deference in other areas. See Frontiero v. Richardson (S.Ct.1973), Craig v. Boren (S.Ct.1976) and Michael M. v. Superior Court of Sonoma Co. (S.Ct.1981).

Constitutional concerns are central to Justice Scalia in assessing Title VII affirmative action programs. At a minimum, Justice Scalia views any affirmative action program unconstitutional that seeks to overcome societal attitudes that have caused workplace imbalance rather than to overcome the negative effect of an employer's own past discriminatory behavior. He claims the *Johnson* decision "practically compel[s]" employers, "through the operation of the legal system," to engage in "intentional race- and sex-based discrimination."

Preferential programs restricted to Indians of federally recognized tribes have withstood challenge from non-Indians on grounds the classification is not racial, but political, arising from the unique Congressional obligation to Indians. Morton v. Mancari (S.Ct.1974).

14.03 Unconstitutional Affirmative Action

The changing composition of the Court under Reagan and Bush appointments has left the future

of state and municipal affirmative action programs
in considerable doubt.

Minority Set–Asides. The Court ruled unconstitutional a 30% municipal set-aside program for
minority businesses in City of Richmond v. J.A.
Croson Co. (S.Ct.1989). The Court settled on evaluating affirmative action programs by strict scrutiny, rather than the intermediate standard favored
by Justice Brennan, and found the program constitutionally flawed. Numerous cities have programs
similar to that struck in *Croson.*

Set-aside programs that are narrowly tailored
will satisfy the *Croson* strict scrutiny requirements
for racial preference and the "mid-level" scrutiny
for gender preference. Coral Construction Co. v.
King County (W.D.Wash.1989). See also Harrison
& Burrowes Bridge Constructors, Inc. v. Cuomo
(N.D.N.Y.1990). The *Croson* Court left undisturbed
Fullilove v. Klutznick (S.Ct.1980), which upheld a
Congressional mandate of 10 per cent minority
set-aside for federal funds provided to local public
works projects.

Consent Decrees. In Martin v. Wilks (S.Ct.1989)
the Supreme Court unsettled twenty-five years of
affirmative action programs promulgated through
court-approved consent decrees. White males in
Martin who were not party to litigation initiated in
1974 and subsequently settled by consent decree
have a constitutional right to collaterally attack
the affirmative action program established pursuant to the decree at any time. Chief Justice Rehn-

quist, writing for the *Martin* Court in 1989, said "A judgment or decree among parties to a lawsuit resolves issues as among them, but it does not conclude the rights of strangers to those proceedings."

Seniority Programs. The same year, the same Court ruled that women who are negatively impacted by an employer's seniority program must challenge it within the statutory period following adoption of the program, or they are time barred from suit. The cause of action arises immediately, not when the women are adversely affected. Lorance v. AT & T Technologies, Inc. (S.Ct.1989). Justice Scalia, who voted in *Martin* to upset the consent decree, wrote in *Lorance* that "[a]llowing a facially neutral system to be challenged * * * many years after its adoption would disrupt" legitimate interests of other employees who benefited from the changes. Justice Marshall noted in dissent that the *Lorance* ruling would apply to seniority systems that intentionally discriminate against women, as well as those that do not.

Layoffs and Promotions. Nonminority school teachers successfully challenged a layoff program negotiated by their union that extended preferential protection to later-hired minorities as violating the Fourteenth Amendment. Wygant v. Jackson Board of Education (S.Ct.1986).

However, where an affirmative action promotion program is based on a compelling government interest to eradicate effects of past egregious exclusion of minorities from all positions, the program satisfies constitutional requirements. United States v. Paradise (S.Ct.1987).

* * *

Part III has traced the development of sex discrimination law under both the common law and state and federal constitutions. Federal and state remedial legislation prohibiting discrimination in employment, education and credit by both public and private entities is addressed in Part IV.

PART IV

REMEDIAL LEGISLATION
AND CASE DEVELOPMENT

*Decisions about the welfare of future children
must be left to the parents who conceive, bear,
support and raise them rather than to the employers who hire those parents*

Justice Blackmun, International Union, UAW v.
Johnson Controls, Inc. (S.Ct.1991)

CHAPTER 15

EMPLOYMENT

15.01 Perspectives

Federal action to remedy sex discrimination includes legislation concerning employment, education and finance. State and local governments have enacted statutes that parallel and in some cases exceed federal protections.

The most important federal legislation directed toward elimination of sex discrimination is in employment. This legislation addresses a social phenomenon of profound significance since World War II: movement of women into the paid work force. Presently, 50,000,000 women are working outside the home; they constitute more than two fifths of all workers. An estimated nine out of ten women are employed outside the home at some time in their lives, averaging 28 years of paid employment compared to 38 years for men.

The working woman is faced with job segregation in service work, trades and professions. In the private business sector particularly she receives lower medical, disability and pension benefits, or none at all. Federal social security computations maximize benefits to high paying positions and continuous full time employment. Working women have limited access to higher paying positions and frequently fail to satisfy the employment conditions for maximum social security benefits. Working mothers hold two jobs because the homemaking chores remain predominantly theirs.

A. WOMEN IN THE WORKPLACE

Most women work because they need the money to support themselves and their families. Whether a woman is single or married, her average paycheck is less than two-thirds that of a man who is doing work of comparable value. The more an occupation is dominated by women, the less it pays.

An employed woman who is head of a household supports her family on less than half the wages earned by a similarly situated male. Working women comprise more than half of the minimum wage employees. Those with preschool children or aged parents have the added responsibility of finding and paying for adequate day care. The minority woman is in the lowest position of all, with the highest unemployment rate, the most servient of employment and the lowest wages.

Employment pension and insurance programs have traditionally disadvantaged women. Working women must largely rely on working past retirement age, social security, spousal benefits, personal savings or welfare for their senior years.

The market place has traditionally governed job opportunities and pay scales for both women and men under the common law "at will" employment doctrine. Employers and unions alike could exclude women altogether, or discriminate against them at will in all employment matters—hiring, placement, promotion, salaries, layoff, seniority, insurance and retirement benefits.

This is no longer true. Expectations of fair treatment in employment have led to erosion of the common law doctrine that an employer can terminate any employee for a bad reason, or for no reason at all. Employees who are not protected by federal and state legislation prohibiting discrimination in employment may have a remedy under common law that was non-existent a generation ago.

"At–Will" Exceptions. In most jurisdictions, an employer's insulation from liability for an at-will firing has been eroded by exceptions. Many states allow recovery for breach of an implied contract. Existence of an implied contract is a fact question for the jury. It may arise from company practices or representations in an employee manual, Greinader v. Diebold Inc. (S.D.Ohio 1990), Woolley v. Hoffmann–La Roche, Inc. (N.J.S.Ct.1985), and/or from long term employment, Morriss v. Coleman Co. (Kan.S.Ct.1987).

Other states allow recovery in tort, arising from public policy considerations, or under an implied covenant of good faith and fair dealing.

Sexual Harassment. Case law exceptions to common law at-will employment were examined in a discharge alleging sexual bias in Wagenseller v.

Scottsdale Memorial Hospital (Ariz.S.Ct.1985). The Arizona Supreme Court overruled earlier law and recognized a public policy exception to discharge at will in the case of an emergency room nurse, who allegedly was terminated because she refused to "moon" on a rafting trip, an activity in violation of the Arizona Indecent Exposures Act. Accord, Chamberlin v. 101 Realty, Inc. (1st Cir. 1990).

Conversely, a worker who persistently harasses female co-workers and is discharged because of it does not have a right to reinstatement for alleged failure of the employer to follow notice provisions of a union contract. To compel the employer to follow the union contract would prevent it from carrying out its legal duty to eliminate sexual harassment in employment. Newsday, Inc., v. Long Island Typographical Union No. 915, AFL–CIO (2d Cir.1990).

A claim that a state employment discrimination statute preempts common law remedies for sexual misconduct in employment was rejected in Helmick v. Cincinnati Word Processing, Inc. (Ohio S.Ct.1989). Existing common law remedies are extinguished only by express statutory enactment or by necessary implication. Common law remedies survive where they supplement the limited statutory coverage. Accord, Peralta Community College District v. Fair Employment & Housing Com'n (Cal.S.Ct.1990). Employees need not exhaust ad-

ministrative remedies before seeking judicial relief
for nonstatutory causes of action.

Dismissals grounded in economic reasons, usually presented as a reduction in force, may cloak
dismissals that are arguably discriminatory. They
are, however, seldom basis for recovery. Clutter-
ham v. Coachmen Industries, Inc. (Cal.App.1985).

B. FEDERAL LEGISLATION

A major step toward employment equity for
women was the Equal Pay Act of 1963 which
requires employers to pay the same salaries to
women and men for substantially equal work.

The following year, the Civil Rights Act of 1964
was adopted. But shortly before the final vote in
the House of Representatives, an amendment adding sex as a protected class was presented in an
apparent attempt to defeat passage of the bill.
The amendment was approved virtually without
debate. To assure compatibility with the Equal
Pay Act, the Senate added the Bennett amendment
providing that any defenses authorized by the EPA
also apply to Title VII.

Civil rights statutes passed by Congress following
the Civil War expressed in gender neutral language, ostensibly enacted to provide remedies for
race discrimination, provide remedies for sex discrimination as well.

The National Labor Relations Act subjects unions to the judicially created obligation of fairly

representing all employees in the bargaining unit. Motor Coach Employees v. Lockridge. The Federal Employees Parttime Employment Act promotes permanent parttime employment opportunities at all grade levels of federal government, and the Age Discrimination in Employment Act protects individuals over age 40 from discrimination because of age.

Other federal legislation includes the Equal Credit Opportunity Act and Title VIII of the Fair Housing Act, which prohibits discrimination on the basis of sex in selling or renting a "dwelling". Seasonal dwellings fall under the act. United States v. Columbus Country Club (3d Cir.1990).

So long as a constitutional issue is not involved, Congress is free to overturn the Supreme Court's interpretation of federal statutes, and has done so in several instances regarding sex discrimination. See Grove City College v. Bell (S.Ct.1984), negated by the Civil Rights Restoration Act of 1987; General Electric Co. v. Gilbert (S.Ct.1976), negated by the Pregnancy Discrimination Act of 1978; McCarty v. McCarty (S.Ct.1981), negated by the Uniformed Services Former Spouses Protection Act.

Federal steps to eliminate discrimination include executive orders, initiated by President Roosevelt during World War II to prohibit discrimination on account of race, creed, color and national origin, and extended by President Johnson in 1967 to include sex. The executive order prohibits recipients of government contracts from employment

discrimination, and provides for affirmative action
to eliminate the effects of past discrimination. Because instituted by the executive, the protections
afforded by executive orders are subject to discon-
tinuance or nonenforcement by the executive.

C. STATE AND LOCAL ACTS

Many state and local governments have legislation and executive orders prohibiting employment
discrimination on account of sex and occasionally
marital status and sexual preference. Some states
prohibit sex discrimination in education, insurance, credit and housing. Public accommodation
statutes have supported sex discrimination claims
in widely diverse instances, from single sex business clubs to free clothing alteration policies.
State statutes providing for family leave and child
care offer affirmative aid to working parents.

When federal statutes are eroded by judicial
interpretation or lack of enforcement, state statutory remedies against discrimination in both the
private and public sector become increasingly significant. This is tempered by the principle followed in some jurisdictions that standards and
methodology of the federal statutes should be followed for cases brought under parallel state laws,
including the elements that comprise a prima facie
case and the corresponding transfer of the burden
of proof. McCullar v. Human Rights Commission
(Ill.App.1987). Compare Shannon v. Pay 'N Save
Corp. (Wn.2d 1985), allowing a jury trial under the

state anti-discrimination statute and retaining the burden of proof for an affirmative defense on defendant.

Both state and federal statutes are designed to stop present discrimination, prevent future discrimination, and provide indemnification for injured parties. Federal statutes provide that state investigation will precede federal where there is concurrent jurisdiction. The enforcement agencies are charged to pursue compliance through conference and conciliation. Should this fail, statutes provide for judicial action by the administrative agency, and case law provides a private cause of action for aggrieved individuals.

Burgeoning case law defines the scope of the statutes and requirements for a prima facie case and affirmative defense. Procedural litigation common to the several statutes includes whether aggrieved individuals are limited to statutory administrative remedies, and if not, whether they are required to exhaust administrative remedies before commencing private action. They need not, where exhaustion of remedies is futile. Clayton v. Auto Workers (S.Ct.1981). Similarly, in absence of clear congressional intent, Patsy v. Board of Regents of the State of Florida (S.Ct.1982).

15.02 Equal Pay Act

A policy statement of the Equal Pay Act states that discrimination in wages on the basis of sex constitutes an unfair method of competition.

The Equal Pay Act prohibits an employer from paying employees in an establishment at a lesser rate than that at which he pays "employees of the opposite sex" where the work is "equal", the performance requires "equal skill, effort and responsibility" and is performed under "similar working conditions." Included in the protection against discrimination are employment related payments such as overtime, uniforms and travel. Recovery is limited by four affirmative defenses.

The plaintiff must establish that he or she is doing the same tasks as an employee of the other sex, that the work is substantially equal as to skill, effort and responsibility, is performed in the same establishment under the same working conditions, and that the other employee is being compensated at a higher rate. Upon this showing, the burden shifts to the defendant to establish that the pay differential is permissible because it falls under one of the four affirmative defenses.

Because the Equal Pay Act is part of the Fair Labor Standards Act, businesses exempt from the FLSA are also exempt from the EPA. There is no numerical requirement for number of employees; two are enough, provided one is male and the other female, and a connection with interstate commerce is established.

A. PLAINTIFF'S CASE

1. Establishing the Comparison

The Equal Pay Act addresses only one form of employment discrimination: pay discrepancy between men and women. Because it requires plaintiff to establish that an employer pays one sex higher wages than the other sex for substantially equal work, the initial problem is to find men's and women's work assignments that can be compared. The EPA does not prohibit sex segregated employment. Assignment of women or men exclusively to different departments or shifts can conceal wage discrepancies that are exposed when men and women in the same department do assignments side by side. See Waters v. Turner, Wood & Smith Ins. Agency, Inc. (11th Cir.1989). Where no male employee is available for comparison, there is no violation of the act, even though the employer might pay a man a higher wage for doing the same work. Rinkel v. Associated Pipeline Contractors, Inc.

Similar Working Conditions. Requirement under the EPA that the men and women must be employed under "similar working conditions" was interpreted by the Supreme Court in Corning Glass Works v. Brennan. The employer claimed that the night shift constitutes different working conditions, which therefore justifies salary differential between men and women. The Court said that although a night shift could constitute different working conditions, the company did not treat it as different in its own classifications. Rather, the night differential arose "simply because men would not work at the low rates paid women inspectors, and it reflected a job market in which Corning could pay women less than men for the same work."

Partial Pay Equalization. In an attempt to cure the violation of the EPA, Corning Glass integrated some women into the higher nighttime male positions and equalized the rate of all new employees, male and female. The company did not adjust the pay of senior employed women on the day shift. The Court rejected this partial equalization of salary as insufficient to accommodate the EPA, saying that Congress enacted the statute recognizing the weaker bargaining position of many women and believing that discrimination in wage rates represented unfair employer exploitation of this source of cheap labor.

Sex Segregated Departments. Where a single employer has separate units under the same roof, courts have not been sympathetic to arguments that sex segregated departments cannot be compared or that the variance between them necessarily precludes a finding that the work is substantially equal. Brennan v. City Stores, Inc.

Establishment. Early interpretation of "establishment" under the FLSA limited the meaning to a single physical location. The recent trend has been to allow suits where control is centralized and employees move freely between the separate facilities.　Marshall v. Maintenance Services, Inc. Where discrimination was proved in three of 66 stores in a discount chain, an injunction against any of the stores was upheld.　Brennan v. J.M. Fields, Inc.

Policy Making Exempt Employees.　Payment of lower wages to female magistrates than to male magistrates doing the same work violates the EPA. EEOC v. North Carolina (W.D.N.C.1979).　The state argued that magistrates were not employees within the meaning of the EPA because the Fair Labor Standards Act exempts from coverage employees of public agencies who "serve on a policy making level."　Looking to the legislative history of a parallel exemption in Title VII, the court reasoned that Congress could not have intended to exempt officials with the limited duties performed by magistrates although they are vested with a portion of the state's sovereign power.

Successive Employment.　Nor will a claim be defeated because the employees work sequentially rather than contemporaneously.　A female plaintiff prevailed in comparing her final wages with the markedly higher starting wages of her male successor who took on no additional duties.　Pearce v. Wichita County.

2.　Equal Work

Application of the Equal Pay Act where the work performed by the men and women is not identical was established in Shultz v. Wheaton

Glass Co. (3d Cir.1970). The circuit court said the Equal Pay Act requires only that the work be substantially equal. Any claimed additional duties must be substantiated by facts, and must constitute more than a nominal amount of the employee's time, particularly where the pay differential is substantial. Any other interpretation would create "too wide a door through which the content of the Act would disappear."

Additional Duties. The employer in *Wheaton–Glass* claimed that a ten percent pay premium for men was justified because "male selector-packers" did sixteen additional unskilled tasks, usually performed by "snap up boys", when the boys were not available. The employer made no showing that all or even any of the men performed these tasks, nor that the "female inspector-packers" were incapable of performing them. Further, the additional work did not justify a ten percent differential in pay, since the snap-up boys received only 2 cents an hour more than the women selector-packers. Similarly, for comparison of work assignments of airline pursers and stewardesses, now known, thanks to Title VII, as flight attendants. Laffey v. Northwest Airlines, Inc. (D.C.Cir.1976).

Different Titles. Nor can dissimilar labels justify pay differentials where women and men perform substantially equal work. This subterfuge was disallowed for different laboratory titles in Hodgson v. Miller Brewing Co. (7th Cir.1972), and different officer titles in Morgado v. Birmingham–Jefferson County Civil Defense Corps (11th Cir.1983).

Skill, Effort and Responsibility. The elements of effort, skill and responsibility were addressed in Pearce v. Wichita County. The female plaintiff had 20 years experience in a hospital credit office and served as credit manager for more than four years before her discharge. A male with no prior hospital credit experience was hired for the position with a different title at a starting salary of $300 more per month; in six months, he was earning more than twice as much.

The court applied the standards for effort, skill and responsibility provided in the EPA regulations. Effort is concerned "with the measurement of the physical or mental exertion needed for the performance of a job," and responsibility is concerned "with the degree of accountability required in the performance of the job, with emphasis on the importance of the job obligation." Since no change was made in the actual duties required of female plaintiff and her male successor, both effort and responsibility remained the same; difference in job titles is not controlling. The element of skill "includes consideration of such factors as experience, training, education, and ability." Plaintiff had far more experience and an equal amount of ability and education. Since working conditions were similar, plaintiff met her initial burden of proof.

Coaching a women's basketball team requires substantially equal skill, effort and responsibility as coaching of a men's team, and payment of salary to a female coach at only half the rate of a male coach violates the EPA. Alleged increased responsibility and work for the larger boys' teams was offset by additional assistants provided to male coaches. The court noted that subsequent pay raises may provide an inference that an employee was underpaid because of her sex. Burkey v. Marshall County Board of Education.

Work performed by female practical nurses and male orderlies has been compared in a number of cases. Trial court findings that tasks assigned the female practical nurses require as much skill as those assigned to the orderlies and that additional duties assigned to both groups involved substantially equal responsibility were not clearly erroneous. Hodgson v. Brookhaven General Hospital. Contra, see Marshall v. St. John Valley Sec. Home (1st Cir.1977).

Greater Physical Effort. A difference in physical effort required is frequently claimed to support higher compensation to men. Comparisons of work done by "janitors" and "custodians" with that done by "cleaning ladies" and "maids" has had mixed results. The respective male and female tasks were found equal for EPA purposes in EEOC v. Rhode Island (D.R.I.1982). Contra, where heavy cleaners, all male, exerted greater effort than light cleaners, all female. Usery v. Columbia University (2d Cir.1977). Assigning greater value to physical efforts expended by males for approximately 4% of the time did not warrant a pay differential in Hodgson v. Daisy Manufacturing Co. (8th Cir.1971). The women had higher production quotas, and continued to expend mental effort while the men did unskilled tasks.

Male Plaintiffs. The Equal Pay Act is gender neutral, and protects men as well as women from discrepancy in pay. Male bartenders working the day shift and earning 30 to 60 cents per hour less than female barmaids working the night shift established a claim in Hodgson v. Pet, Inc.

Whether men in primarily female occupations have standing to sue for their depressed wages arising from discrimination against women co-workers is less clear. Peters v. City of Shreveport denied recovery to such male plaintiffs for past wages because this was not the type of sex discrimination contemplated by the statute. Similarly, Spaulding v. University of Washington (9th Cir. 1984). A cognizable claim by female faculty members does not thereby allow the male faculty members "to bootstrap their job grievances" into a federal sex discrimination claim, quoting Ruffin v. County of Los Angeles (9th Cir.1979). Compare Allen v. American Home Foods, Inc. (N.D.Ind. 1986), where male plaintiffs had standing under Title VII to assert their injury suffered when the employer closed a facility staffed primarily by females.

B. AFFIRMATIVE DEFENSES

The plaintiff who has established a prima facie case under the Equal Pay Act will prevail unless the defendant can justify the discrepancy under one of four affirmative statutory defenses, merit, production, seniority, or any other factor other than sex. Case law clarifying the first three affirmative defenses is sparse, largely because they are more difficult to establish than the fourth defense. By analogy to a Title VII case, when the employer's legitimate affirmative defense for a pay differential is accompanied by a discriminatory motive, the employer must prove by a preponderance of the evidence that the same pay discrepancy would have existed without the discriminatory element. See Hopkins v. Price Waterhouse.

1. Merit, Production, Seniority

Legislative history of the merit, production and seniority defenses is reviewed in EEOC v. Aetna Insurance Co.

Pay differentials based upon production and seniority are fairly straightforward. What constitutes a merit system is less clear. A salary differential is not a bona fide merit system where it is not based on how well different employees perform equal work. Classification of custodial employees into heavy and light cleaning categories did not justify a merit pay differential in favor of male heavy cleaning custodians where the city knew that both groups did substantially the same work.

National Organization for Women v. Chicago. Where difference in performance is established, a merit pay differential is justified. Herman v. Roosevelt Federal Savings and Loan Association. Competency examinations relative to the position justify pay differential for employees who pass them as a valid merit system. But where an employer has "unbridled discretion" to exempt employees from a merit system, examinations are irrelevant. Gosa v. Bryce Hospital (11th Cir.1986).

2. Factor Other Than Sex

The fourth affirmative defense, "any other factor other than sex", is a typical residual clause. These clauses are routinely included in legal documents to serve as an escape hatch for the person faced with potential liability. The EPA "factor other than sex" is aptly described by the Supreme Court in *Corning Glass* as a "general 'catch-all' ". It "embraces an almost limitless number of factors, so long as they do not involve sex." Fallon v. Illinois (7th Cir.1989).

Unlike the merit, seniority and production defenses, "any other factor other than sex" does not have distinct parameters. Employers find it more viable because it is easily framed in gender neutral terms and courts are more likely to accept it as justifying a pay differential. Decisions repeatedly reject acceptance of market wages and the willingness of women to work at lower wages as factors other than sex. To do so would undercut the purpose of the EPA. See *Corning Glass* and Hodgson v. Brookhaven General Hospital (5th Cir.1972). However, the element of market wages is integral to some factors other than sex that courts have accepted as justification for pay differentials.

Employers have defeated Equal Pay Act claims by arguing successfully that a factor other than sex includes prior wages, temporary wages, transferee wages, trainee wages, red circled wages, profitability, subjective criteria, state statutes and even the sex of third parties. The factor other than sex can be independent of both the position and the business. The list of legitimate factors other than sex is limited only by the ingenuity of the employer and the resistence of courts to erosion of congressional purpose in enacting the Equal Pay Act.

Red Circled Wages. The Supreme Court in *Corning Glass* placed the obligation squarely on the employer to prove that any "factor other than sex" was indeed other than sex, and not a pretext. The Court accordingly rejected red circling of higher wages for presently employed males as a justification for pay differential for the same work even though "phrased in terms of a neutral factor other than sex".

But red circling has been accepted under circumstances similar to *Corning.* The male employee in *Gosa* retained his "much higher" wages when temporarily transferred to work with the female plaintiff, who trained him for the new job. They worked together and performed the same functions for two years. The court rejected the employer's claimed merit pay justification, but accepted the higher wages as red circled. "It is clear," said the court, "that red-circling is a valid employment practice constituting a factor other than sex." Similarly, for temporary reassignment of a camera-man, Campbell v. Von Hoffman Press, Inc. (8th Cir.1980); and reassignment of a faculty member, Covington v. Southern Illinois University (7th Cir. 1987).

But compare Glenn v. General Motors Corporation (11th Cir.1988), which rejected transfer from a higher paying position as a factor other than sex, as well as market wages and prior salary. New Jersey has also ruled that discrepancies in pay for male and female employees doing substantially equal work are not justified on the basis that the positions are lateral, short term transfers. Grigoletti v. Ortho Pharmaceutical Corp. (N.J.S.Ct.1990).

Subjective Criteria. The first three affirmative defenses can be objectively determined. Subjective reasons offered for wage discrepancies are subsumed as a factor other than sex. Evaluation of a "personal interview" and "whether a current employee had personal knowledge of the applicant's ability" justified pay differential in starting salaries in Ebert v. Lamar Truck Plaza (10th Cir.1989). The employer did not need to prove that the "past experience" factor was part of an existing bona fide "merit system", or that "personal knowledge" justification was not sex based. Both "articulated" explanations are suspect as falling under the warning of *Corning Glass* not to allow factors phrased in sex-neutral terms to perpetuate "an illegal practice of paying women less than men for equal work," the precise circumstance the EPA was enacted to eradicate.

Similarly, a female casualty underwriter unsuccessfully claimed violation of the EPA when a newly employed casualty writer received a higher salary. EEOC v. Aetna Insurance Co. (4th Cir. 1980). *Aetna,* like *Gosa,* rejected the employer's merit pay justification. It accepted instead the subjective anticipation of value to the company of the new employees as a factor other than sex, noting that subjectivity is inevitable in employment decisions.

A different result was reached in a class action instituted by the EEOC affecting 3000 women employees which challenged an insurance company practice that based starting salaries of sales agents on prior pay. After ten years of litigation, a settlement was reached in which the women were to receive $5,000,000 in back pay.

Third Parties. Schools have successfully argued that pay differentials between male and female coaches are justified by a sex-identified factor other than sex, viz., the sex of the teams they coach. McCullar v. Human Rights Commission (Ill.App. 1987). The Seventh Circuit in EEOC v. Madison Community Unit School Dist. said the exception means a factor other than the employee's sex.

Thus the sex of the teams coached is a factor other than sex and can be taken into account in determining whether the male and female coaches do equal work.

This argument utilizes an affirmative defense (a factor other than sex) to defeat an essential element of plaintiffs' prima facie case (equal work), which must be proved before an affirmative defense can be asserted. The analytic difficulty posed by "sex of the team" defense exposes the power of the "factor other than sex" to emasculate Congressional purpose in enacting the Equal Pay Act.

Profitability. A related circumstance occurs where women are restricted to female customers in clothing stores or health clubs.

Higher wages for men in retail sales for work that is established as equal in skill, effort, and responsibility, has been justified by higher profitability. That saleswomen selling women's clothing must sell 40 to 50 percent more items to generate the same dollar volume of sales as did salesmen in the men's department was not regarded as significant in Hodgson v. Robert Hall Clothes, Inc. The court also accepted the trial court's finding that segregated personnel in clothing sales was permissible as a business necessity. Therefore, because of a classification by sex, women could not compete for the better paying jobs. Compare Bence v. Detroit Health Corp. (6th Cir.1983) where payment of lower commissions to women managers who sold only to women customers violated the Equal Pay Act.

Although the EPA does not require sex integration in employment, it is questionable for profitability to constitute an affirmative defense where the difference in profit can be traced to a sex based employee classification. If the production of the employees is not equal, an affirmative statutory defense is already available under measurement by production. To allow profitability as a "factor other than sex" eliminates distinction between production and profitability, the very distinction that the statute seeks to establish in its requirement that pay must be equal for work that is equal in effort.

Training Programs. Bonafide training programs under which trainees receive a higher wage when assigned to lower paying work while they acquire broad experience are valid justification for pay differentials. However, informal, unwritten programs where employees are hired without knowledge that they are trainees and rotation depends not on sequence but personnel needs, will generally fail as an affirmative defense. Shultz v. First Victoria National Bank. Where women are systematically excluded from the training programs, a premium payment to males is not within the defense. Hodgson v. Security National Bank. It does not follow that women must be admitted to the training program. Rather than extend the training program to women, it could be terminated or modified.

Head–of–Household. Male teachers in a church operated school received a head of family salary supplement that was not provided to female heads of household. The school failed to establish that this was a factor other than sex, or that school and church related tasks were distinguishable. Nor could it claim First Amendment exemption for lay workers. Dole v. Shenandoah Baptist Church (4th Cir.1990).

State Statutes. A gender neutral state statute setting salaries for fire communications officers (FCOs, predominantly male) but not for police communications officers (PCOs, predominantly female) was accepted by the fifth circuit as a valid factor other than sex in Peters v. Shreveport, for paying the FCOs markedly higher wages than the PCOs. The trial court had the better of the argument. It rejected the statute as a factor other than sex, noting that nothing in the statute prevented the city from raising the salaries of the PCOs to those of the FCOs. The city had, in fact, matched police personnel salaries to the mandated fire personnel salaries in every department except communications. The trial court ruled that "compliance with state law is not an exception to the mandate of equal pay for equal work under the Equal Pay Act." Where the factor of sex is implicated in payment of lower wages to women, the decision is not "based on" a factor "other than sex".

Shreveport does not address whether the statute is preempted by the Equal Pay Act if it does in fact authorize cities to establish different pay scales for men and women.   See also Fallon v. Illinois (7th Cir.1989), where a statute requiring that wartime veterans be hired to serve as veterans service officers was accepted as a factor other than sex.   To effect the statute, the state adopted a policy of hiring males as officers and females as associates. The *Fallon* court, relying on Covington v. Southern Illinois University (7th Cir.1987), said that the factor other than sex need not be related to the requirements of the particular position in question, nor to the business.

Impact of Bennett Amendment.   The Bennett Amendment to Title VII provides that pay differentials between men and women are not unlawful under Title VII if such differentiation "is authorized by" one of the four affirmative defenses of the Equal Pay Act.   Washington County v. Gunther (S.Ct.1981).   By linking Title VII to the Equal Pay Act, the Bennett Amendment has effected a substantive change in some jurisdictions in the allocation of proof in Equal Pay Act cases.   As a consequence, the congressionally intended objective proof standards of an Equal Pay Act case, with the defendant squarely responsible for the burden of proof when pleading an affirmative defense, is displaced by Title VII jurisprudence, under which the defendant pleading a gender neutral affirmative defense has only a burden of articulation but not of proof. *Shreveport* is an example.

15.03 Title VII

A. THE STATUTE

The most important legislation to eliminate gender based discrimination in employment is Title VII of the Civil Rights Act of 1964 (42 U.S.C. § 2000(e)). Efforts to add sex as a protected class to earlier titles in the Civil Rights Act of 1964 were consistently defeated. The amendment adding sex was introduced just two days before approval of Title VII by Representative Howard Smith of Virginia. Smith had vigorously opposed passage of the Civil Rights Act, and was accused by some of wishing to sabotage its passage by proposing an amendment adding sex as a protected class, which the House had previously consistently rejected. A further amendment which would have added the word "solely" to modify "sex", was defeated. "Presumably, Congress foresaw the debilitating effect such a limitation might have upon the sex discrimination amendment." *Willingham* v. *Macon Telegraph Publishing Co.* (5th 1975). Because of the late addition of "sex" to Title VII, evidence of legislative purpose for its passage is scant. This explains in part why courts rely heavily on legislative history supporting prohibition against race discrimination to determine the scope of protection from sex discrimination afforded employees and applicants for employment. Protected classes other than sex are race, color, religion and national origin.

1. Prohibitions

The statute provides that employers must not fail to or refuse to hire, or discharge, or otherwise to discriminate against any individual with respect to compensation, terms, conditions, or privileges of employment because of such individual's sex (§ 703(a)(1)). The employer is further forbidden to classify applicants or employees in any way that would tend to deprive any individual of employment opportunities because of such individual's sex. (§ 703(a)(2)).

As interpreted, the language covers the employment relationship from prehiring advertisement to postemployment references, encompassing events in between: interviewing, hiring, placement, promotions, wages, benefits, working conditions, working atmosphere, seniority, transfer, reassignment, layoff and discharge.

2. Employers and Employees

The act reaches an employer, as defined, and any labor organization or employment agency dealing with such an employer. Inclusion of labor organizations and employment agencies insures that elimination of discrimination against minorities and women in employment is not frustrated by discriminatory action on the part of these entities. Nor can the statute be frustrated by advertisements that classify by sex; advertisements for em-

ployees must be gender neutral. Pittsburgh Press
v. Pittsburgh Com'n Human Relations (1973).

   The power of Congress to regulate commerce is
the constitutional basis for Title VII. Any employer engaged in an industry affecting commerce with
at least fifteen employees for at least twenty weeks
a year, unless expressly excluded, is subject to the
prohibitions of the act. A company with fewer
than fifteen employees that is the alter ego of
other interests of its owner may also be an employer within the meaning of Title VII. Spray v.
Kellos–Sims Crane Rental, Inc. (S.D.Ga.1981).
Part-time employees are to be computed in the
fifteen required employees. Thurber v. Jack Reil-
ly's, Inc. (1st Cir.1983). The employer may be an
individual, or a business entity such as a partnership, corporation, trust, association, or union.
Where the right to be considered for partnership
status is part of the employment contract, the
partnership is an employer within the meaning of
Title VII. Nor does application of Title VII infringe the constitutional rights of expression or
association of the partners. Hishon v. King &
Spalding (S.Ct.1984). A Title VII pay claim can be
brought to challenge different wages paid to men
and women working in different schools for the
same employer. Bartelt v. Berlitz School of Lan-
guages (9th Cir.1983). However, a private association can set its own membership rules without
violating Title VII where members are not in an
employer-employee relationship and the club has

only three employees. Graves v. Women's Professional Rodeo Association, Inc. (8th Cir.1990).

The application of Title VII between the partners themselves is less clear. See Wheeler v. Hurdman (10th Cir.1987) where plaintiff unsuccessfully challenged her expulsion from a partnership. Since 1972 state and local governments and educational institutions have been included.

Excluded employers are Congress, Indian tribes, and bona fide private tax-exempt membership clubs. However, foreign firms operating in the United States are included, treaty provisions to the contrary notwithstanding. Avigliano v. Sumitomo Shoji America, Inc. (S.Ct.1981). Title VII does not protect United States citizens working for United States firms in foreign countries under the Court's interpretation in EEOC v. Arabian American Oil Co. (S.Ct.1991). These contracts, however, may be subject to laws of the host country, treaties and international law. Aliens employed in the United States, including undocumented aliens, are covered. EEOC v. Tortilleria La Mejor (E.D.Cal.1991).

Exemption of religious groups from operation of Title VII does not violate the establishment clause of the Constitution, even though the exemption extends to hiring of members of their faith for non-religious, secular employment. Corporation of Presiding Bishop of Church of Latter Day Saints v. Amos (S.Ct.1987). However, a public school district's accommodation of religious students' requirement of male rather than female bus drivers violates both the establishment clause and Title VII. Bollenbach v. Board of Educ. of Monroe–Woodbury Cent. School Dist. (S.D.N.Y.1987).

An exemption of particular significance for women provides that Title VII is not to be construed to repeal or modify any law, federal, state, territorial or local, which grants special rights or preference for veterans.

The act protects any "individual" from discrimination. An independent contractor is not an individual protected by the act. However, description of the individual in the employment contract as an independent contractor will not control. Spirides v. Reinhardt.

3. Prima Facie Case

The operative clauses of Title VII have two key terms regarding plaintiff's statement of a prima facie case. The threshold question is whether the challenged behavior of the employer occurred "because of * * * sex" (§ 703(a)). If not because of sex, the behavior is not actionable as sex discrimination under Title VII.

Stated conversely, employers who treat or classify employees because of their sex are open to a charge of unlawful discrimination unless they can establish a statutory or judicially created affirmative defense. The definitions and relationship of "because of" and "sex" determine what constitutes prohibited discrimination.

a.   Meaning of "Sex"

Males

Title VII protects men against sex discrimination as well as women.   Men cannot, for example, be excluded as applicants for employment as flight attendants.   Diaz v. Pan American World Airways, Inc.   As under the Equal Pay Act, males who are paid depressed wages allegedly resulting from sex discrimination against female co-workers generally lack standing under Title VII to protest the wages. Patee v. Pacific Northwest Bell Tel. Co. (9th Cir. 1986).   Compare Allen v. American Home Foods, Inc. (N.D.Ind.1986), where males had standing to challenge a plant closure which closure was allegedly based on discrimination aimed at women employees.   Where qualifications of applicants or employees are equal, neither sex is a protected class; the statute is neutral.   Texas Department of Community Affairs v. Burdine.

Pregnancy

Whether pregnancy constitutes a sex based classification under Title VII was addressed in General Electric Co. v. Gilbert (S.Ct.1976).   At issue was an employment disability insurance program excluding pregnancy benefits similar to that ruled constitutional under the Fourteenth Amendment in Geduldig v. Aiello (S.Ct.1974).   Following the precedent of *Geduldig,* the Court ruled the program valid because pregnancy is not a sex based classification in that the class of nonpregnant persons includes men; exclusion of pregnancy from a disability benefits plan "is not a gender-based discrimination at all."

Justice Brennan, dissenting, was not persuaded. He insisted, "[T]he Court's assumption that General Electric engaged in a gender-neutral risk-assignment process is purely fanciful." Justice Stevens said simply, pregnancy is gender based, Title VII prohibits classification by sex, and the employer did not establish an affirmative defense.

Pregnancy Discrimination Act

Congress did not agree with the Court that pregnancy based classification is not gender based and enacted the Pregnancy Discrimination Act of 1978. Under the PDA and implementing guidelines it is a prima facie violation of Title VII for an employer to refuse to hire a pregnant woman, to terminate her employment or to compel her to take maternity leave. Reinstatement rights, including those for accumulated seniority, are protected. The employer must treat pregnancy in the same manner as any other temporary disability. Both written policies and unwritten practices are covered.

Spouses. Pregnancy related expenses of spouses of male employees cannot be excluded if disability expenses are provided for spouses of female employees. Newport News Shipbuilding and Dry Dock Co. v. EEOC (S.Ct.1983).

Abortion. The act does not require that employers fund abortions other than to save the life of the mother, but the companies may not discriminate in regard to leave policy or medical complications arising from the abortion. However, the employer may provide abortion benefits unilaterally or negotiate abortion benefits in bargaining agreements.

Sexual Behavior

Whether the meaning of "sex" is limited to a neutral concept of gender, or whether it also includes the sex act and related behavior depends upon whether the activity of the employer or of the applicant/employee is at issue. Because efforts to amend Title VII to include sexual preference have been unsuccessful, courts have repeatedly rejected sex discrimination claims by applicants/employees who are homosexuals. DeSantis v. Pacific Telephone and Telegraph Co. Nor are transsexuals protected, even where the plaintiff had previously been employed in the same position. Ulane v. Eastern Airlines, Inc. (7th Cir.1984). Similarly, for effeminacy, Smith v. Liberty Mutual Insurance Co. (5th Cir.1978), or transvestism, Sommers v. Budget Marketing, Inc. (8th Cir.1982). But see Valdes v. Lumbermen's Mutual Casualty Co. (S.D.Fla.1980), where the court suggested that an employer who refused to hire gay women but hired gay men would be subject to the act.

Early cases similarly treated sexual harassment of employees by employers as outside the scope of protection. Present law recognizes a cause of action for sexual harassment, including homosexual harassment, in an employment setting.

b. *"Because of"*

Alleged discrimination that occurs "because of" reasons other than sex is not prohibited. Thus to state a prima facie case, the plaintiff must establish a link between sex and the alleged discrimination. Gender specific rules and practices are distinguished from gender neutral rules and practices in establishing the link. When an employer classification is explicitly gender based, whether in written policy or unwritten practice, the "because of" factor is easily established. The assumption is that a facial classification by sex must be serving a purpose based upon sex.

Where employer classification is prima facie gender neutral, the plaintiff must establish on other grounds that the discrimination occurred "because of" sex. In this circumstance, "disparate treatment" and "disparate impact" theories, have evolved, each with distinct elements required to constitute a prima facie case.

A third distinct theory is developing when de facto classification by sex, accompanied by depressed wages, is a consequence of intangible market and cultural career expectations of both employer and employees. Examples of comparable worth or pay equity claims are nursing and clerical careers, both dominated by women. This theory may also be called "disparate representation." The contours of a prima facie case and defenses under a disparate representation theory are not yet established.

Results of litigation to achieve pay equity have been largely indirect. Women have had more success through legislation, clearly influenced by litigation, strikes and contract negotiation.

4. Defenses

Several affirmative defenses to charges of sex discrimination are available to the employer. The defenses of legitimate, nondiscriminatory reason for disparate treatment claims, and of business necessity for disparate impact claims, are judicially created. In addition, the defendant has several statutory defenses. The most significant are the bona fide occupational qualification (BFOQ § 703(e)) and the Bennett Amendment (§ 703(h)), which links Title VII compensation claims to the four affirmative defenses of the Equal Pay Act. Other statutory defenses include ability testing, or bona fide seniority or merit systems.

5. Remedies

Title VII authorizes broad equitable relief, monetary as well as injunctive. The court may enjoin prohibited behavior, and concurrently "order such affirmative action as may be appropriate." Such action includes, but is not limited to, "reinstatement or hiring of employees, with or without backpay * * * or any other equitable relief as the court deems appropriate" (§ 706(g)).

B. THEORIES OF RECOVERY

1. Disparate Treatment

Where there is neither a facial gender classification nor a disproportionate impact upon one sex by a neutral policy or practice of the employer, the "because of * * * sex" element is difficult to establish. Cases of intentional sex discrimination are called "disparate treatment" claims; because of sex, the individual is treated disparately in a specific employment setting.

The ultimate factor at issue is intent to discriminate, thus proof of discriminatory intent or motive is required. The evidence to prove motive or intent need not be direct, but may be inferred from differences in treatment. International Brotherhood of Teamsters v. United States.

The Supreme Court set out the basic allocation of burdens and order of presentation of proof in a single plaintiff disparate treatment claim alleging racial discrimination in hiring. McDonnell Douglas Corp. v. Green. The framework established in *McDonnell Douglas* has been refined and extended, with modifications, to promotion, discharge, compensation and retaliation. Accord, as to promotions, United States Postal Service v. Aikens (S.Ct.1983). Claims of disparate treatment because of sex as well as of race are subject to the *McDonnell* allocation of burdens.

A finding of intentional discrimination by an employer is a question of fact, to be determined at trial, and will be overturned on appeal only if "clearly erroneous". The Court clarified the clearly erroneous standard in Anderson v. City of Bessemer City (S.Ct.1985), where the Court reinstated a judgment in favor of a woman who was rejected for a position as recreation director.

Failure of plaintiffs in a class action suit to establish disparate impact from a neutral employment practice does not bar individual plaintiffs from proceeding under a disparate treatment theory of intentional discrimination. Cooper v. Federal Reserve Bank of Richmond (S.Ct.1984).

Disparate treatment analysis is concerned with intentional discrimination, not "subconscious attitudes". To police subconscious attitudes and prejudices is not the intent of the law. Jackson v. Harvard University (1st Cir.1990).

a. Burdens and Presentations of Proof

To establish a prima facie case under the criteria of *McDonnell* in a private, nonclass disparate treatment action, the plaintiff must show (1) that she is a member of the class protected by the statute; (2) that the employer was seeking applicants for a position; (3) that she was qualified for the position; (4) that she applied for the position; (5) that although qualified, she was rejected, and (6) that the employer continued to seek applicants with plaintiff's qualifications. The circumstances under which she was rejected give rise to an inference of unlawful discrimination. Texas Dept. of Community Affairs v. Burdine (S.Ct.1981).

Upon establishing a prima facie case by a preponderance of the evidence, the burden shifts to the defendant to "articulate some legitimate, nondiscriminatory reason for the employee's rejection." Should the defendant carry this burden, the plaintiff must have an opportunity to prove, again by a preponderance of the evidence, that the legitimate reasons offered by the defendant were not its true reasons, but were a pretext for discrimination. Thus the final evidentiary burden is upon the complainant to establish factual proof of subjective intent of the employer to discriminate.

b. Prima Facie Case

An example of facts sufficient to establish a prima facie case of discrimination in promotion is Fitzgerald v. Sirloin Stockade, Inc.

Evidence supported findings that plaintiff was discriminated against by being paid less than men for equal work and responsibility; by being denied opportunities for advancement in a rapidly growing firm, by appointment of less qualified males to positions for which she applied, and for being retaliated against upon filing a discrimination claim.

Minimum Qualifications. To state a prima facie case, plaintiff need show only the minimum necessary qualifications to do the job. Davis v. Weidner (7th Cir.1979).

Employees seeking promotion to higher level jobs are not required to establish that they are relatively more qualified than other applicants. Hawkins v. Anheuser–Busch, Inc. (8th Cir.1983). Nor, to state a prima facie case, need applicants demonstrate that they possess subjective qualifications the employer may require for the job. Jayasinghe v. Bethlehem Steel Corp. (7th Cir.1985).

Minority Women. A black woman applied and was rejected for vacancies which were filled by white females or black males. The trial court said she did not establish a prima facie case because she was not discriminated on the basis of race, since black males were hired, nor on the basis of sex, since white females were hired. Jefferies v. Harris County Community Action Association. The appellate court reversed, refusing to condone an interpretation of race "or" sex to leave black women without a viable remedy.

Unwed Mothers. A plaintiff's claim that she was discharged because she was an unwed mother was rejected because she failed to show that male employees who fathered children out of wedlock would be treated differently. A dissenting judge said that pregnancy cannot be equated with the condition of an "expectant parent" in a male, and termination of employment because of pregnancy has a disparate and invidious impact upon women. Grayson v. The Wickes Corp. Conversely, a cause of action was stated when plaintiff was demoted from executive secretary to clerk for an out of wedlock pregnancy. Jacobs v. Martin Sweets Co.

Constructive Discharge. A claim of sex discrimination under constructive discharge for participating in equal employment opportunity programs is supported where a number of "aggravating factors" are present, including long term discrimination, futile attempts at relief from this discrimination, and failure to be promoted despite favorable performance ratings and substantial supervisory experience. Female plaintiff resigned when a person without supervisory experience was appointed to the position she sought. Clark v. Marsh.

Summer Employment. The fourth prong of the *McDonnell* test—that the employer must continue to seek applicants after rejecting plaintiff—was set aside where plaintiff sought summer employment. Each factor of the test does not necessarily apply in different factual settings, and evidence supported a finding that the defendant's reliance on an adverse job reference was pretextual. King v. New Hampshire Department of Resources.

Academic Employment

A claim that plaintiffs in an academic setting must carry a heavier burden of proof in the interests of academic freedom was rejected in Kunda v. Muhlenberg College (3d Cir.1980). To help establish discriminatory intent in denial of academic tenure, plaintiffs may compel discovery of personnel documents, including confidential peer review

files. First Amendment rights of academic freedom are not violated. University of Pennsylvania
v. EEOC (S.Ct.1990).

Compare Jackson v. Harvard University (1st Cir.
1990) which upheld the trial court's finding that a
female faculty member's failure to get sufficient
affirmative faculty votes was a legitimate non-discriminatory reason for denying her tenure. The
university had initially offered as its articulated
reason that plaintiff had not met written criteria
for tenure, and changed its reason after faculty
votes were shielded from discovery by academic
privilege.

Testimony that a university denigrates the study
of women's issues is relevant to establishing a
prima facie case of sex discrimination. Lynn v.
Regents of University of California. The university denied tenure for a female faculty member on
the basis that women's studies is not a substantial
topic for academic scholarship. The court rejected
argument by the university that the discrimination
was not based on sex because a man who concen-
trated on women's issues would have received the
same treatment. When plaintiffs establish that
decisions regarding academic employment are rooted in concepts which reflect discriminatory attitudes relating to sex, however subtly, courts are
obligated to provide the relief afforded by Title VII.

Statistical Evidence

Statistical evidence, without presentation of specific instances of intentional discrimination, is suf-

ficient to support a prima facie case of discrimination in an individual action as well as a class action. Davis v. Califano. Discriminatory intent can be inferred from substantial disparity between numbers of male and female employees and rates of promotion as between male and female employees. Plaintiff need demonstrate only minimum objective qualifications necessary for promotion since defendant, who has better access to such information, may present any specific evidence regarding qualifications in rebuttal.

A district court was reversed for discounting statistical evidence of sex discrimination in higher paying jobs on the ground that the evidence did not account for differences in career interest between male and female employees. EEOC v. General Telephone Co. (9th Cir.1989).

A prima facie disparate treatment case can be established without a showing of specific instances of overt discrimination by establishing that the percentage of female employees is less than the number of females in the applicable labor pool. United States v. Fairfax County. Conversely, statistical data alone did not suffice to establish a prima facie case of disparate treatment in Hudson v. International Business Machines Corp.

c. *Affirmative Defense*

Articulation of Legitimate Reason

To rebut a prima facie disparate treatment case, the employer must "articulate" some legitimate, nondiscriminatory reason for the discriminatory action under McDonnell Douglas v. Green.

The meaning of "articulate" and the evidence required for defendant to establish a legitimate nondiscriminatory reason to rebut a prima facie case were clarified by the Supreme Court in Texas Department of Community Affairs v. Burdine. The plaintiff in *Burdine* alleged sex discrimination in the defendant's failure to promote her. It was unclear whether the defendant's obligation to articulate some legitimate nondiscriminatory reason required him to prove that he was in fact motivated by the reason that he articulated. *Burdine* removed this uncertainty, stating that the defendant "need not persuade the court that it was actually motivated by the proffered reasons." When the defendant clearly explains the nondiscriminatory reasons for his actions, the evidentiary burden shifts to the plaintiff to show that the articulated, nondiscriminatory reason is merely a pretext.

Mixed Motive

The standard and allocation of proof to determine causation where an employer has both legitimate and discriminatory motives for an employment decision was settled by the Supreme Court in Price Waterhouse v. Hopkins (S.Ct.1989).

The Court rejected the "but for" test as reaching the absurd result that neither of two factors was a "cause" unless it can be shown that one, or both of them, were "but for" causes. The Court commented, "We need not leave our commensense at the doorstep when we interpret" Title VII. When the plaintiff demonstrates that an employment decision was influenced by impermissible sex bias, an employer who pleads a "mixed motive" justification must establish by a preponderance of the evidence that the same employment decision would have been made on the basis of the nondiscriminatory factors. On remand, the judge was unable to separate the permissible from impermissible motive, and the employer declined the opportunity to add to the record. The court accordingly resolved the doubt against the employer. Price Waterhouse was ordered to make plaintiff Ann Hopkins a partner, an appropriate remedy, and to compensate her $371,000 in back pay.

Qualifications. The *Burdine* Court established that the employer need not claim that the person hired was more qualified than the complainant. To do so "would require the employer to show that the plaintiff's objective qualifications were inferior to those of the person selected." Absent such comparative evidence, a court would in effect conclude that the employer has discriminated.

The employer has discretion to choose among equally qualified male and female candidates, provided the decision is not based upon unlawful criteria.

Management Prerogatives. The *Burdine* Court reiterated that Title VII was not intended "to diminish traditional management prerogatives."

United Steelworkers of America v. Weber. Nor
does Title VII demand that an employer give preferential treatment to women or restructure his
employment practices to "maximize the number of
* * * women hired," citing Furnco Const. Corp. v.
Waters. Statistical evidence submitted by the employer of nondiscriminatory hiring has relevance
in negating an inference of discriminatory motive,
but will not control in that Title VII prohibits
discrimination against even a single person. Cross
v. United States Postal Service.

d. Burden of Intent: Pretext

Where the defendant articulates a legitimate,
nondiscriminatory reason, the plaintiff has an opportunity to prove that the reason articulated is a
pretext. The *Burdine* Court suggests that pretext
may be established "either directly by persuading
the court that a discriminatory reason more likely
motivated the employer or indirectly by showing
that the employer's proffered explanation is un-
worthy of credence."

A partnership claimed that plaintiff was offered
a family law assignment rather than a litigation
assignment because she lacked the analytical skills
needed to handle complex legal issues. The court
found this to be pretext, noting that the plaintiff
was negatively evaluated for being too involved
with women's issues. Ezold v. Wolf, Block, Schorr
& Solis–Cohen (E.D.Pa.1990).

Personality. Defendant claimed that the plaintiff was not hired because of personality requirements of the position. Assuming this to be a legitimate requirement, which the court disclaimed deciding, when the interviewer has no established guidelines, the unavoidable subjective nature of the interview supports a ruling that the reason articulated was pretextual. Subjective selection processes provide a ready mechanism for discrimination. Johnson v. Uncle Ben's, Inc.

The subjective element of personality takes a different perspective where an employer argues that plaintiff was not promoted because she was narrow minded and difficult to work with. This articulation of a legitimate, nondiscriminatory reason was sufficient to rebut plaintiff's prima facie case, but plaintiff was entitled to show that the reason was a pretext. Evidence supported the conclusion that complainant worked well with a variety of people. An atmosphere of discrimination, suggested in part by statistics, was relevant on the issue of pretext. Sweeney v. Board of Trustees of Keene State College. A school district's claim that males had superior qualifications in leadership, ability and stability was found as pretext in Willis v. Watson Chapel School District (8th Cir.1990), where plaintiff school teacher had applied eight times for promotion to an administrative position. But see Holden v. Commission Against Discrimination (1st Cir.1982), where a public information officer failed to establish that her discharge for alleged incompetency was pretextual.

Qualifications. Lack of proper qualifications is a legitimate reason frequently given to rebut a prima facie disparate treatment case. Evidence to establish that the reason is a pretext is various. Where plaintiff demonstrated higher scores and more extensive background in special education than the male selectee, the court found pretext and ordered defendant to appoint plaintiff to the first vacancy occurring in its work force in the salary range and responsibility level at which she applied and was passed over. Sherkow v. State of Wisconsin. Reliance on a state law was rejected as pretext where the law did not apply to the woman seeking employment and it was unlikely that defendant was unaware of this. Kamberos v. GTE Automatic Electric, Inc.

However, financial constraints, low enrollment and oversupply of teachers in the plaintiff's field are legitimate, nondiscriminatory, nonpretextual reasons for her dismissal. Davis v. Weidner.

e. Sexual Harassment

Early cases rejected sexual harassment claims as not constituting an element of employment, but rather a manifestation of the "personal proclivity" of the harassing individual. Corne v. Bausch & Lomb, Inc. Lower courts subsequently allowed recovery where the harassment was intentional and plaintiff suffered some tangible financial loss, such as discharge or non-promotion. The Supreme Court unanimously and unequivocally established that sexual harassment which creates a hostile or abusive work environment is actionable under Title VII even where there is no tangible financial detriment. Meritor Savings Bank v. Vinson (S.Ct. 1986). Nor is an employee's "voluntary" acquiescence a defense when the employee fears dismissal if she does not comply. The test of employer liability is whether the advances were "welcome".

A written sexual harassment policy and established grievance procedure do not insulate the employer. He may be held liable on agency principles for actions of supervisors and managers, as well as for his own. Five of the *Meritor* justices said that the employer may introduce evidence of plaintiff's "provocative clothing or language" for inquiry into whether the advances were welcome.

EEOC guidelines define sexual harassment as unwelcome sexual advances, requests for sexual favors, and other verbal or physical conduct of a sexual nature, occurring under any of three conditions: when submission is either explicitly or implicitly a term or condition of employment; when submission or rejection of the conduct is the basis for employment decisions affecting the individual, or when the conduct has either the purpose or effect of substantially interfering with the individual's work performance or creating an intimidating, hostile or offensive working environment. The employer will be liable if he knows or should have known of the harassing conduct, although "immediate and appropriate corrective action" will rebut liability.

An injunction enjoining defendant from future gender discrimination and ordering it to establish procedures to avoid future incidents of sexual harassment are justified where the defendant tolerates repeated harassment of a single supervising employee. United States (EEOC) v. Gurnee Inn Corp. (7th Cir.1990).

Reasonable Woman. A "reasonable woman" standard is appropriate to determine whether harassing conduct is sufficiently severe or pervasive to create a hostile working environment. Ellison v. Brady (9th Cir.1991). The trial court dismissed "love" letters which plaintiff received from a co-worker, coupled with persistent requests for dates, as "trivial". The Ninth Circuit disagreed. Men and women have different perspectives. Because women are disproportionately victims of rape and sexual assault, women have a stronger incentive to be concerned about sexual behavior.

Workplace conduct can be established as unlawful even when the harassers do not realize it because Title VII is not a fault-based tort scheme. To avoid liability, employers may have to educate and sensitize their workforce to eliminate conduct which a reasonable victim would consider hostile.

An employer who discharges an employee who harasses female co-workers is protected from suit by the discharged employee because of strong public policy to eliminate sex discrimination in the workplace. Newsday, Inc. v. Long Island Typographical Union No. 915, AFL–CIO (2d Cir.1990).

Pornography. Pornographic pictures of nude and partly nude women decorating the workplace walls can create a hostile, and therefore discriminatory, working environment. Robinson v. Jacksonville Shipyards (M.D.Fla.1991). The court's decision described 30 pornographic pictures which were displayed at the shipyard, including one of a nude woman bending over with her genitals exposed. The company had previously adopted a sexual harassment policy, but the court found it had no effect on eliminating the sexually hostile environment.

Similar pictures of nude and scantily dressed women, accompanied by frequent vulgar comments about women, sometimes addressed to plaintiff, did not establish a hostile working environment in Rabidue v. Osceola Refining Co. (6th Cir.1986). The *Rabidue* trial court said that Title VII was not intended to cover "rough-hewn and vulgar" workplace language, nor "to bring about a magical transformation in the social mores of American workers." Accord, Ebert v. Lamar Truck Plaza (10th Cir.1989), where instances of foul language and unwelcome touching were found to be "sparse" and "not pervasive".

A hostile work environment may be actionable under state law. See Henderson v. Pennwalt Corp. (Wn.App.1985). State actions in assault and battery or infliction of emotional distress may allow recovery for monetary damages, which is not authorized under current provisions of Title VII.

Verbal harassment of a white male was not actionable in Young v. City of Houston (5th Cir. 1990). The city articulated several nonpretextual nondiscriminatory reasons for the firing.

The employer will be liable for constructive discharge if he has actual knowledge of the harassment and prevents the employee from relating her complaints to him. Levendos v. Stern Entertainment, Inc. (3d Cir.1990). Constructive discharge was rejected in Ezold v. Wolf, Block, Schorr & Solis–Cohen (E.D.Pa.1990).

Co-workers. The Minnesota fair employment statute includes a prohibition against sexual harassment by co-workers. The state supreme court upheld an action against the employer because it failed to take "timely and appropriate action" to stop harassment by fellow employees. The court looked to Title VII and EEOC guidelines in its opinion. Continental Can Co. v. Minnesota. An employee can also sue when she is subjected to a workplace environment where commonly recognized sexual involvement of co-workers leads to their promotions and benefits. Broderick v. Ruder (D.C.Cir.1988).

Provocative Uniforms. An employer may impose reasonable grooming and dress requirements, even where different requirements are set for male and female employees, but he does not have unfettered discretion to require employees to wear revealing and sexually provocative uniforms that subject the employee to sexual harassment. Such a requirement constitutes sex discrimination. EEOC v. Sage Realty Corp.

Single Sex Harassment. Termination of employment of a male employee allegedly because of rejection of sexual advances by his male supervisor constitutes a cause of action under Title VII. Wright v. Methodist Youth Services, Inc. The court said that the demand made on the employee was one that would not be made on a female employee, adding "Discrimination is sex discrimination whenever sex is for no legitimate reason a substantial factor in the discrimination."

As noted earlier, actions arising from sexual harassment may limit the common law doctrine of employment at will. Monge v. Beebe Rubber Co. (N.H.S.Ct.1974). Sexual harassment claims have also been upheld under the Fourteenth Amendment and 42 U.S.C. § 1983, Bohen v. City of East Chicago (7th Cir.1986), and under the Racketeer Influenced and Corrupt Organizations Act in Hunt v. Weatherbee (D.Mass.1986).

f. Retaliation

Title VII prohibits retaliation against any person who has participated in making a charge of discrimination or opposed practices made unlawful by the act (§ 704(a)). Information to a prospective employer that female plaintiff had filed a discrimination suit after leaving defendant's employ was ruled a violation of the act even though the plaintiff was no longer an employee. Rutherford v. American Bank of Commerce. Accord, where defendant manufacturer refused to give female plaintiff a letter of reference and allegedly disseminated disparaging and untrue remarks to prospective employers. Pantchenko v. C.B. Dolge Co.

Female plaintiffs' claims of retaliatory discharge because they complained of sex discrimination were supported in Vierra v. Rhode Island Municipal Police Academy (R.I.S.Ct.1988). Similarly, for a male plaintiff, see Sumner v. United States Postal Service (2d Cir.1990). Plaintiff did not need to prove the merit of his objection, but only that he believed it in good faith.

An action for damages under 42 U.S.C. § 1985(c) was not allowed to a male who charged that he was dismissed because he supported equal employment claims of women employees. Great American Federal Savings & Loan Association v. Novotny. The Court said that § 1985(c) could not be used as a remedy for an alleged discriminatory act which is properly adjudicated under Title VII procedures.

2. Disparate Impact

a. Burdens and Presentation of Proof

Discrimination under the theory of disparate impact occurs when a facially gender neutral rule or practice of the employer has a disproportionate effect on one sex. This sometimes occurs when a sex based rule, legitimate before passage of Title

VII, is replaced by a gender neutral rule that nonetheless perpetuates the prior discrimination. A disparate impact case is grounded primarily in § 703(a)(2) which prohibits segregation or classification by sex. The fact of disparate impact suggests that sex, a prohibited classification in the absence of a bona fide occupational qualification, was in fact the motivating factor for the neutral rule or practice.

The Supreme Court set forth a successful disparate impact action as one which "involve[s] employment practices that are facially neutral in their treatment of different groups but that in fact fall more harshly on one group than another and cannot be justified by business necessity." International Brotherhood of Teamsters v. United States (S.Ct.1977).

In alleging business necessity, a judicially created defense, employers must establish that the neutral rule is reasonably necessary to avoid undermining the essence of the business operation. Diaz v. Pan American World Airways, Inc. If the defendant successfully establishes a business necessity defense, the plaintiff must have an opportunity to rebut by showing that alternative legitimate means will achieve the same business purpose, or that the alleged business necessity is a pretext.

Disparate impact jurisprudence developed through examination of neutral, objective employer practices such as standardized tests and weight and height restrictions. In Watson v. Fort Worth

Bank and Trust (S.Ct.1988), the Supreme Court
included employer practices of a subjective or discretionary nature in disparate impact analysis.
Supervisors exercised subjective judgment in discretionary promotion decisions, arising from acquaintance with the candidates seeking promotion
and the nature of the jobs to be filled. Fort Worth
Bank argued such practices should be analyzed
under a disparate treatment theory because subjective business practices would "be so difficult to
defend under disparate impact analysis that employers would be forced to adopt numerical quotas
in order to avoid liability."

Justice O'Connor, for a plurality, dismissed this
concern, saying that *Griggs* "should not be interpreted as implying that the ultimate burden of
proof can be shifted to the defendant." On the
contrary, the ultimate burden in a disparate impact case "remains with the plaintiff at all times."
This was disputed by Justice Blackmun, concurring
in the judgment, who said that, beginning with
Griggs, disparate impact cases shifted the burden
of proof, not just of production, to the defendant to
establish that the employment practice is a business necessity.

Wards Cove Packing Co. v. Atonio (S.Ct.1989)
clarified and endorsed the proof allocation of *Watson,* further eroding the distinction between a disparate treatment and a disparate impact case
while purporting to follow *Griggs.* Congress has
the option of amending Title VII if the *Wat-*

son/Wards Cove interpretation of § 703(a)(2) proof requirements does not comport with congressional intent.

b. Prima Facie Case

(1) Intent Not Required. A major distinction between cases brought under the disparate treatment and the disparate impact theories is that intent is not required to sustain a disparate impact case. Facially neutral employment practices may violate Title VII without evidence of the employer's subjective intent to discriminate. The individual aggrieved under the disparate impact theory has not had discrimination directed particularly at her or him. Rather, the discrimination flows to the class, either male or female. The discrimination against the specific individual is derivative from membership in the class.

The principal case for disparate impact theory arose in a race discrimination setting. Griggs v. Duke Power Co. Prior to passage of Title VII, defendant in *Griggs* openly discriminated on the basis of race in job assignments. After passage of Title VII, a neutral rule was adopted requiring all applicants for certain desirable jobs to have a high school diploma and to pass two written tests. A markedly higher percentage of blacks than whites did not possess high school diplomas and also failed to pass the tests.

The Supreme Court, stressing that Title VII looks to consequences of employment practices, ruled that discriminatory impact of a neutral rule against blacks as a class is sufficient to establish a prima facie Title VII case. *Wards Cove* reaffirmed the principle established in *Griggs* that "[G]ood intent or absence of discriminatory intent does not redeem employment procedures or testing mechanisms that operate as 'built-in headwinds' for minority groups." Thus, plaintiffs need not prove discriminatory motive. That the employer has "intentionally" (§ 706(g)) engaged in the prohibited behavior means only that the behavior was not accidental. United States v. Fairfax County.

(2) Statistical Evidence. Most disparate impact sex discrimination cases are brought by women, often as a class action. The plaintiffs' initial task is to produce statistics that will establish a prima facie case of disproportionate effect on one sex by operation of a neutral rule or practice. Numerous cases have addressed what statistics are appropriate for establishing a prima facie disparate impact case. *Wards Cove* established that statistical evidence showing a high percentage of nonwhite workers in the employer's cannery jobs and low percentage of such workers in noncannery positions does not establish a prima facie case of disparate impact.

The proper basis generally is a comparison between the racial composition of qualified persons in the labor market and persons holding at-issue jobs. The employer produced evidence that minorities were over-represented in the cannery because the hiring was done by a minority union. The cannery workers argued that nepotism and rehiring policies, coupled with the separate hiring channel for cannery workers, were neutral rules with a disparate impact on minority workers.

The Third Circuit applied *Wards Cove* standards to Green v. USX Corp. (3d Cir.1989). The court said that *Wards Cove* does not rule out other types of statistical evidence, nor invalidate use of applicant flow data comparison with the final hire rate to establish a disparate impact from employer's neutral interviewing practices. The employer did not present any evidence of non-discriminatory evaluation, nor sufficient evidence to support its claim that many black applicants voluntarily withdrew from the hiring process.

Statistics are generally reliable only when based on a sufficiently large sample to be fairly representative.

A nepotism rule that affected only five couples was too small to be statistically significant. Harper v. Trans World Airlines, Inc.

Gross statistical disparities can be shown in a proper case, but they have little probative value when special qualifications are required to fill particular jobs. City of Richmond v. J.A. Croson Co. (S.Ct.1989).

The most readily available statistics are those which compare the employer's work force to the general population, half men and half women. This comparison does not recognize that a lower percentage of women may be in the local work force compared to men.

Applicant Flow. EEOC regulations provide for consideration of the selection rate of the employer. The proportion of women who apply and are hired for any position is compared to the proportion of men who apply and are hired. Women are adversely impacted when women applicants are hired at a rate less than ⅘ that of male applicants who are hired. *Wards Cove* suggests that applicant flow data are highly relevant evidence of an employer's labor market. Reliance on applicant flow can be misleading as evidence of discrimination since traditional job stereotyping may inhibit women or men from applying for a particular job although they have the qualifications and capacity to perform it.

Qualified Applicant Pool. A more realistic statistic compares the actual hiring rate as between women and men to the potential applicant pool comprised of women and men in the local work force who are basically qualified for the job in question. This pool should have geographic dimensions marked by ready access to the employer's place of business. See EEOC v. High Top Coal Co. (E.D.Tenn.1980), upholding on-site hiring of coal miners. If a marked discrepancy exists between men and women qualified and men and women hired, disparate impact is indicated even though the ⅘ rule of actual applicant flow is satisfied. Geographic origin of persons actually hired may be a statistic of particular significance for skilled or professional occupations.

Source of Statistics. Data to support an alleged discrimination claim can be secured from an employer under a Supreme Court ruling that allows the federal government to secure information from an employer being investigated and then to share the information with the charging employee. EEOC v. Associated Dry Goods Corp. That the employer is doing business under an affirmative action plan approved by the secretary of labor does not bar the EEOC from bringing suit alleging sex discrimination in salaries and sex segregated job classifications solely on the basis of information in the affirmative action plan. EEOC v. Keco Industries, Inc.

(3) Neutral Rules and Practices. Among the neutral rules and practices of the employer that impact women disproportionately are height and weight requirements, advanced educational degrees, and marital and parental status.

A prima facie case of sex discrimination can arise under use of neutral height and weight requirements. Dothard v. Rawlinson (S.Ct.1977). In *Dothard,* persons under 5′2″ and less than 120 pounds were ineligible for jobs as correction counselors in the Alabama prison system. Similar restrictions are common for police officers and state troopers.

An employer's prohibition against hiring flight attendants who are married or have children has a disparate impact against women, and the airline may not protect itself from sex discrimination charges by hiring a few men and applying the neutral rule to male applicants as well as female. Sandler v. Eastern Airlines, Inc.

A practice of recruiting faculty by word of mouth rather than by advertising was at issue in Presseisen v. Swarthmore College. The court ruled that such behavior in itself is not a violation of Title VII unless the resultant hiring was illegal.

c. *Defenses*

(1) Refined Statistics. Defendant is entitled to rebut a prima facie case by use of more refined, accurate and valid statistics. Movement for Opportunity and Equality v. General Motors Corp.

(2) Business Necessity. Burden of production requirements for the judicially created business necessity defense are realigning in the wake of *Watson* and *Wards Cove,* generally in favor of the employer. Should Congress overturn these interpretations of Title VII, pre-existing case law will be revitalized.

The neutral employment practice which operates to exclude the class protected by Title VII does not satisfy the business necessity requirement if the practice is not related to job performance. When no relation is demonstrated, the persons discriminated against because of its operation are entitled to equitable relief within the discretion of the court to make them whole. Franks v. Bowman Transportation Co., Inc.

Physical Requirements. Allegation that patrol police officers must be at least 5′8″ tall because a taller officer meets less resistance, gains more respect and has a better vantage point for crowd control was rejected in Horace v. City of Pontiac. Defendant failed to show that the height requirement effectively carried out the alleged purpose, and plaintiff showed that other less restrictive selection devices would also serve the employer's interest in efficient and trustworthy police officers. Similarly, defendant's minimum 5′7″ height requirement for pilots was not supported by business necessity upon evidence that persons 5′5″ could reach instruments in the cockpit and thus safely and efficiently operate the airplane. Boyd v. Ozark Air Lines, Inc. (8th Cir.1977). See also Brunet v. City of Columbus (S.D.Ohio 1986), which set aside a firefighter physical test on grounds it did not correspond to the physical demands of the job.

Compare Zamlen v. Cleveland (6th Cir.1990) where a firefighter's test measuring quantities in which men excel, such as speed and strength, but not measuring quantities in which women excel, such as endurance, does not violate VII.

Pregnancy Leave. Mandatory pregnancy leave for flight attendants has been a topic of continuing litigation. Some circuits have ruled that mandatory leave is not justified by legitimate business concerns and is not a bona fide occupational qualification. In re Pan American World Airways, Inc.,

Maternity Leave Practices & Flight Attendant
Weight Program Litigation (11th Cir.1990). Other
courts treat non-pregnancy as a bona fide occupation qualification. Because pregnancy may occasionally cause unexpected incapacity, a flight attendant must take leave as soon as pregnancy is
discovered. Condit v. United Air Lines, Inc. (4th
Cir.1977).

A requirement that a pregnant employee must
notify the employer of pregnancy upon discovery,
discontinue working on the date recommended by
her personal physician, and return to work within
60 days or when the physician gives approval, was
held a valid business practice to encourage the
employee who has fully recovered to return to her
job and assume her share of the workload. Notification of pending absence from work was also
required of men, but men were not subject to the
60 day rule. Langley v. State Farm Fire and
Casualty Co. (5th Cir.1981).

Subjective Standards. Where the neutral standards are largely subjective, a claim of business
necessity is less likely to override a statistical
showing of adverse impact in class action race
discrimination cases. James v. Stockham Valves
and Fittings Co. (5th Cir.1977). Nonetheless, a
neutral rule prohibiting hiring the spouse of a
current employee, although having a disparate impact against women, was accepted as business necessity in Yuhas v. Libbey–Owens–Ford Co. The
court accepted as plausible the assumption that it

is generally a bad idea to have both spouses working together. It is not clear how employment of husbands and wives in a large plant would undermine the essence of the business operation.

Showing of a disproportionately low number of females hired for supervisory and administrative positions in face of markedly subjective selection criteria failed to support a Title VII sex discrimination claim in Dreier v. Yanik (3d Cir.1980).

Graduate Degrees. Before enactment of Title IX in 1972 prohibiting discrimination against women in education, most professional and graduate schools had strict quotas on admission of women, sometimes as low as two percent. Nonetheless, although a woman might demonstrate mastery of subject matter in other ways, a doctorate degree may be a legitimate business necessity even though women were previously systematically excluded from doctorate programs and thus few women meet this standard. Campbell v. Ramsay.

(3) Failure to Rebut. Where the employer is unable to rebut a prima facie case, the district court has a duty to render a decree which seeks to eliminate the effects of past discrimination and bar discrimination in the future. United States v. City of Alexandria.

d. Plaintiff's Rebuttal

As in a disparate treatment case, the business necessity defense is subject to rebuttal by the plaintiff as a pretext. New York City Transit

Authority v. Beazer. However, statistical evidence of past conduct in failure to hire and promote women is insufficient to establish pretext. Peters v. Jefferson Chemical Co. This suggests that disparate impact cases have a tendency to merge into disparate treatment cases and to require proof of motive unless there is a class action.

Plaintiff may also rebut defendant's successful plea of business necessity by showing that an alternative means will achieve the same business purpose. Green v. Missouri Pacific Railroad Co.; Horace v. City of Pontiac.

3. Comparable Worth

a. *Rationale of Theory*

Disparate impact litigation under Title VII focuses on a neutral employer rule or practice that precludes individuals from employment opportunities because of sex or race with consequent under representation of that sex or race from a given occupation. Under a theory of comparable worth, discrimination may be evidenced by over representation of one sex or race in an occupation, such as nursing and domestics.

Claims under a theory of comparable worth do not raise issues of reverse discrimination or dislocate or increase competition for positions sought by white males, as does much of the litigation to date under Title VII. A comparable worth claim therefore is less disruptive of established employment patterns than either disparate treatment or disparate impact claims. It also provides enforcement for recognition of self worth for women and minorities in their chosen occupations and guarantees that essential work will be done by competent, self-secure individuals. Equal access of white males to these race and sex segregated occupations is concurrently assured under Title VII.

Statistical Proof. The initial legal issue under a theory of comparable worth is whether excess representation of one race or sex in a specific occupation has probative force of discrimination. If statistical evidence of heavy concentration of whites and males has probative force of discrimination against minorities and women, then the reverse of this picture, statistical evidence of heavy concentration of minorities and women, should have parallel probative force.

Disproportionate under representation of blacks was ruled to have probative force of intentional discrimination in Hazelwood School District v. United States. Similarly, under representation of women was accepted as prima facie indication of discriminatory motive in United States v. Fairfax County and Davis v. Califano. This concept can be extended to establish discrimination where one sex is statistically shown to be disproportionately over represented in a given occupation. Lemons v. City and County of Denver.

Market Place. Single sex and single race occupations, whether dominated by whites and males or minorities and females, reflect in part the nebulous concept of "market place." While the concept of market place cannot be identified as controlled by any one individual, yet the market place is a composite consequence of intentional individual hiring decisions of numerous employers.

Validity of use of the market place as justification for salary decisions can be challenged as circular where discrepancy in market place wages is established as grounded in race or sex stereotyping and cultural expectations. Corning Glass Works v. Brennan. The question is whether impossibility of identifying the contribution of one employer's intentional decisions should insulate reliance on market place from inquiry as to motivation for salaries in sex segregated occupations. The circumstance is similar to that of market share liability for drugs produced and marketed generically.

b.   Case Experience

Nothing in Title VII indicates Congress intended that persons discriminated against must leave their employment in order to escape the discrimination. The Supreme Court recognized this in ruling that women in sex segregated occupations are entitled under Title VII to offer proof that depressed wages are in part due to purposeful, intentional discrimination because of sex. County of Washington v. Gunther.

(1) Bennett Amendment.   Gunther addresses the operation of the Bennett amendment, which links

Title VII to the Equal Pay Act and thus impacts compensation claims made under Title VII. The reverse impact of the Bennett amendment on the Equal Pay Act was addressed earlier in this chapter. The Bennett amendment (§ 703(h)) provides that it is not unlawful under Title VII for an employer to differentiate in the payment of wages or compensation between men and women if such differentiation "is authorized by" the Equal Pay Act. The EPA requires the employer to pay equal wages to men and women doing substantially equal work in the same establishment. Four exceptions are provided: the EPA is not violated for differentiation in pay based on a merit or seniority system, quantity or quality of production, or a factor other than sex. 29 U.S.C. § 206(d)1.

In *Gunther*, female jail guards were paid $200 per month less than male guards. The women conceded that the work was not equal, but alleged that part of the discrepancy in pay was the result of intentional discrimination on account of sex. The county argued the suit was barred because the Bennett amendment incorporated the equal work requirement of the EPA into Title VII. The Supreme Court disagreed. The Bennett amendment incorporates only the four affirmative defenses into Title VII.

The Court disclaimed that it was addressing the concept of comparable worth or pay equity. Rather, female respondents are entitled to prove by direct evidence that their wages are depressed because of intentional sex discrimination by the employer in setting the wage scale for female guards, but not for male guards, at a level lower than its own survey of outside markets and the worth of the jobs warranted.

(2) Evidence of Intent. Title VII litigation attempting to prove intentional discrimination in pay discrepancies between men and women for work that is not substantially equal has generally not fared well.

State Pay Studies. Failure of a state to take compensatory steps when a wage study reveals inequity in pay between men and women for work of equal value does not of itself evidence intent to discriminate. Plaintiff's claims were rejected on both disparate impact and disparate treatment theories in American Federation of State, County and Municipal Employees v. State of Washington (9th Cir.1985), where the ninth circuit overturned the district court's finding of intentional discrimination. Similarly, plaintiffs in American Nurses' Association v. State of Illinois (7th Cir.1986), were allowed to proceed to trial on a theory of disparate treatment, but could not rely on a state pay study to prove intentional discrimination. The court noted that comparable worth is not the sort of issue that judges "should lightly assume has been given to us to resolve by Title VII or the Constitution."

Sex Segregated Departments. However, an employer discriminated against women segregated in single sex departments and intentionally underpaid the women as compared to male employees under the facts in Taylor v. Charley Brothers Co. The *Taylor* court said Title VII supports an action for intentional discrimination against a protected class, and intention may be inferred where (1) employer does not undertake evaluation of jobs between men and women; (2) employer has a pattern and practice of segregating women within a single department and of considering only women applicants for openings in this department, and (3) company officials make various discriminatory remarks.

Perpetuation of Past Discrimination. Employer in International Union of Electrical, Radio and Machine Workers v. Westinghouse Elec. Corp. had a formal job rating system. A company employment manual that pre-dated Title VII expressly stated that the rate for women's labor grades " 'do not coincide with the values on the men's scale. * * * [We] have another wage curve * * * for women *below* and not parallel with the men's curve,' " (emphasis by the IUE court). The court concluded that intentional past discrimination, as evidenced by the manual, could continue into the present and constitute a violation of Title VII.

C. STATUTORY DEFENSES

1. Seniority, Merit and Production

The statutory defenses of seniority, merit system and quantity or quality of production are a part of both Title VII and the Equal Pay Act and are similarly applied.

Considerable litigation has established broad parameters to the seniority exception. An otherwise bona fide seniority system is not illegal merely because it perpetuates past discrimination. International Brotherhood of Teamsters v. United States. The Supreme Court gave wide latitude to a definition of part time employment in ruling that an employer and union can set up a two-track seniority system providing that employees who do not work more than 45 weeks per calendar year are not permanent employees. California Brewers Association v. Bryant. Blacks complained that this seniority system discriminated against them. Because many women work part time, the decision is significant for allegations of sex discrimination.

A facially neutral seniority program that female employees allege was adopted with intent to discriminate against women triggers the statute of limitations when adopted, not when the female employees are adversely affected. Lorance v. AT & T Technologies, Inc. Justice Marshall, dissenting, said "Nothing in the text of Title VII compels" the harsh result of time-barring the plaintiffs. This case "is the latest example of how this Court, flouting the intent of Congress, has gradually diminished the application of Title VII to seniority programs."

He pointed out that Title VII exempts "bona fide" seniority programs, without regard as to whether the program discriminates via prima facie or gender neutral language.

2.   Factor Other Than Sex

The scope of the fourth defense, any "factor other than sex", in application to Title VII is unclear. Because it was incorporated from the Equal Pay Act, it can be invoked only for compensation claims.

Burden of Proof. Accommodation of the fourth affirmative defense was directly addressed in Kouba v. Allstate Insurance Co. (9th Cir.1982), where plaintiffs sued for equal pay for equal work under Title VII. *Kouba* analyzed allocations of the burden of proof arising under the affirmative defenses of the Bennett Amendment. Under conventional Title VII litigation, a shift in the burden of proof refers to the obligation of producing evidence and not to the burden of persuasion, which never shifts. Texas Department of Community Affairs v. Burdine. However, the Bennett amendment requires a different circumstance where unequal pay for equal work is established. *Gunther* stressed that the four conditions of non-liability are affirmative defenses, which result in a shift to the defendant of the burden of proof, not merely of the obligation of producing evidence. Where plaintiff establishes unequal pay for equal work, a material issue of fact is raised to the defense only. If the employer fails to proffer admissible evidence to support an affirmative defense, plaintiff is entitled to summary judgment.

However, some circuits have retreated from the EPA allocation of proof burden and allow the employer to utilize Title VII allocations of burden of persuasion. See Peters v. Shreveport. This approach is inconsistent with International Union, UAW v. Johnson Controls. In *Johnson,* the Supreme Court affirms that the allocation burden remains squarely on an employer who pleads an affirmative statutory defense to a sex-based classification. A definition by negation, "other than sex", is a sex based classification.

Public Pension Funds

Life insurance premiums are computed from actuarial tables which factor a longer life expectancy for women. Employee contributions to a pension fund based on the factor of longevity was at issue in Los Angeles Department of Water and Power v. Manhart. One female plaintiff had contributed over $18,000, while a similarly situated male would have contributed $13,000.

In striking the use of gender based tables, the Court pointed out that an actuarial distinction based entirely on sex cannot be claimed to be based on a factor other than sex. *Manhart* denied retroactive relief, distinguishing Albermarle Paper Co. v. Moody in which the Court ruled that back pay should be awarded whenever necessary to fulfill the purpose of Title VII to make injured employees whole again, as well as to eliminate unlawful practices.

The equal pension pay-in rule of *Manhart* was extended to equal pension pay-out in Arizona Governing Committee for Tax Deferred Annuity and Deferred Compensation Plans v. Norris (S.Ct.1983). Arizona did not contribute to the employee pension funds, but simply gave state employees the choice of several programs. Since all the funds relied on sex based actuarial tables, the state's plan violated Title VII. Florida v. Long (S.Ct.1988), ruled that retroactive awards for pre-Norris pensions are not required. The cases did not address gender based practices in fire, auto, life and disability insurance purchased on the open market.

3. Bona Fide Occupational Qualification

Title VII provides that an employer may discriminate on the basis of sex if sex is a "bona fide occupational qualification [BFOQ] reasonably necessary to the normal operation of that particular business * * *." The BFOQ is limited to hiring and assignment, and thus cannot be invoked as a defense to other aspects of employment covered under Title VII. A claimed BFOQ is the principal defense to a charge of sex discrimination arising under an employer practice that classifies by sex. Early cases seeking to determine the scope of the BFOQ exception were at variance, but it is now settled that the exception is narrow. Courts will not allow practices grounded in sexual stereotypes to swallow up Title VII's prohibition against sex discrimination in employment under guise of a claimed occupational qualification.

a. Single Sex Occupation Laws

When Title VII was enacted in 1964, job segregation by sex in business and industry was reinforced by state labor laws that prohibited women from working in specific occupations: bartending (recall Goesaert v. Cleary), mining, streetcar conducting and printing are typical examples.

Numerous class actions were filed after adoption of Title VII to challenge these statutes. After a period of some uncertainty, blanket exclusion of women from specific jobs by statutes authorizing job segregation, weight lifting and other physical requirements were rejected as bona fide occupational qualifications. Many women can perform the required tasks and Title VII protects their right to demonstrate individual capability to do so. Rosenfeld v. Southern Pacific Co. State law cannot conclusively presume that all women are incapable of performing certain tasks.

b. Single Sex Business Practices

Sex-Plus. Early efforts to establish a BFOQ included classification known as "sex-plus". The concept recurs under various guises. The first major Supreme Court case to address the contours of the bona fide occupational qualification rejected "sex-plus" classifications as sex discrimination in transparent disguise.　Phillips v. Martin Marietta Corp. (S.Ct.1971).　*Martin–Marietta* refused employment applications from women (classification by sex) with pre-school children (sex-plus).　The Court said the BFOQ does not permit "one hiring policy for women and another for men".

The narrow scope of a permissible BFOQ was emphatically reaffirmed when the Court unanimously rejected a fetal protection policy under which a manufacturer of batteries barred fertile women from jobs involving exposure to lead.　International Union, UAW v. Johnson Controls, Inc. (S.Ct.1991).　Justice Blackmun, writing for the Court, identified the policy as a variant of sex-plus. He said Title VII and the Pregnancy Discrimination Act "simply do not allow" a woman to be barred from a job "because of her failure to submit to sterilization."

The benign purpose of protecting unconceived offspring does not convert "fertile women" into a benign classification.　The policy is not gender neutral because it does not impact fertile men the same way it impacts fertile women.　The Pregnancy Discrimination Act, amending Title VII, clearly establishes that discrimination based on a woman's ability to become pregnant is facially sex based.

A fetal protection policy can be accommodated under Title VII, if at all, only as a bona fide occupational qualification.　The burden of establishing a BFOQ is on the employer; the burden-shifting framework of *Wards Cove* which requires a petitioner to bear the burden of persuasion on all questions does not apply to gender specific classifications.

The Court stressed that a BFOQ arises from qualifications "reasonably necessary to the normal operation" of the particular business. The terms relate to the needs of the business, not to the possible needs of a nonconceived fetus. The most telling word, said Justice Blackmun, is "occupational". The requirements consist of verifiable job-related skills and aptitudes. Capability of conceiving a fetus is not related to any skills required to make batteries. Johnson Controls' fetal protection policy does not qualify as a BFOQ.

Millions of women are benefited by the decision in *Johnson Controls*. Companies subject to Title VII cannot bar women from high paying jobs on grounds that a potential fetus could be injured by exposure in utero to teratogenic substances. Men are benefited as well in so far as the decision encourages employers to make the workplace safer for all workers. Substances adversely affecting sperm, including lead, dioxin, pesticides, radiation, solvents and alcohol, have been implicated in birth defects, either from genetic damage to the sperm or from transmission via the sperm to the egg.

Prison Guards. The conflicting constitutional rights of male and female prisoners to privacy and the statutory rights of men and women to equal job opportunities have been repeatedly addressed in the context of prison guards. Consolidation of separate actions by guards and prisoners gave a federal district court an opportunity in a case of first impression to consider jointly the competing rights of opposite sex guards and inmates in New Jersey's male and female institutions. Csizmadia v. Fauver and Allen v. Fauver (D.N.J.1990).

The guards claimed single-sex job classifications violated their rights to employment and promotional opportunities, overtime and vacation pay, under Title VII, 42 U.S.C. §§ 1981, 1983 and 1988, and the New Jersey statute against discrimination. The prisoners claimed violation of rights against invasion of privacy, unreasonable search and seizure and inhumane punishment. The court noted that prisoners' rights can be accommodated on a fact specific basis where opposite sex guards are employed.

Such employment, however, must comport with the parameters the Supreme Court established in Dothard v. Rawlinson (S.Ct.1977), where a female plaintiff sought a position as a contact guard in a male maximum security penitentiary. The bona fide occupational qualification of Title VII is to be narrowly construed. However, removal of any gender employment restrictions must consider the impact on prison security, prisoners' privacy rights, and the safety of opposite-sex officers assigned to the housing posts. A BFOQ exception was justified in *Dothard* because the prison population was estimated at 20 per cent sex offenders and the prison was characterized by "rampant violence" and a "jungle atmosphere."

Labor Room Nurses. A challenge to a hospital policy requiring female nurses in labor and delivery rooms was rejected in Backus v. Baptist Medical Center (E.D.Ark.1981). The court accepted the requirement as a bona fide occupational qualification in the interests of privacy rights and concern for sexual abuse of patients by male nurses. Justice Blackmun cited *Backus* with approval in *Johnson Controls* to answer concerns that rights of privacy could not be protected as a BFOQ.

Role Models. A woman's rights under Title VII do not include a right to be single and pregnant and employed all at the same time. A circuit court interpreted Title VII to allow dismissal of an unwed pregnant woman as arts and crafts counselor because black girls need a role model who, if unmarried, is non-pregnant; or, if pregnant, is married. Chambers v. Omaha Girls Club, Inc. (8th Cir.1987). The court said the pregnant woman has the options of abortion or marriage to retain her job. Compare Jatczak v. Ochburg (E.D.Mich.1982), where young black males were not needed as BFOQ role models at a sheltered workshop for mentally ill young adults.

Physical Capabilities. Generic exclusion of women under claims of required occupational physical capabilities is generally not a BFOQ. For railroad switchworkers, see Weeks v. Southern Bell Telephone & Telegraph Co. (5th Cir.1969); for weight lifting in excess of fifty pounds, see Rosenfeld v. Southern Pacific Co. (9th Cir.1971).

Rosenfeld prohibits exclusion of all women from positions because of generic physical capacity as a matter of law, whereas *Weeks* would allow women as a group to be excluded if substantially all women could be shown to be unable to perform the job. Physical ability tests for patrol officers with a disparate impact against women were ruled invalid because there was no showing that the exercises selected for testing were job related. Harless v. Duck.

Grooming and Dress Codes. Challenges to employer rules that set different hair grooming and dress codes for men and women have mixed results. One view regards the codes as gender neutral business regulations because they constitute "grooming in accordance with generally accepted community standards of dress and appearance." Thus short hair for males only is not a violation of Title VII. Willingham v. Macon Telegraph Publishing Co. (5th Cir.1975). Similarly, for a female attorney who was told to "tone down" her "flashy" attire, Bellissimo v. Westinghouse Electric Corp. (3d Cir.1985). Plaintiff in Wislocki–Goin v. Mears (7th Cir.1987), failed to show that the employer's dress and grooming code for employees at a juvenile facility had a disparate impact on women. Rafford v. Randle Eastern Ambulance Service, Inc. (S.D.Fla.1972), treated a prohibition against beards as discrimination between clean shaven and bearded men, not between men and women. It therefore does not discriminate on the basis of sex.

Other courts hold grooming codes that do not apply equally to men and women in violation of Title VII. For clothing, see Carroll v. Talman Federal Savings and Loan Association (7th Cir. 1979); for contact lenses and weight monitoring, see Laffey v. Northwest Airlines, Inc. (D.C.Cir. 1976).

Customer Preference. Customer preference is not a valid BFOQ. Airlines cannot require women but not men to retire on reaching a certain age, nor to resign if they marry, Sprogis v. United Air Lines, Inc. (7th Cir.1971); nor limit cabin attendents to women because of alleged customer preference, Diaz v. Pan American World Airlines (5th Cir. 1971). The *Diaz* court stressed that administrative interpretations by the enforcement agency are entitled to great deference. EEOC guidelines provide that a BFOQ should not be based on the preference of co-workers, employer, clients or customers.

c. *Equal Employment Opportunity*

Employers cannot advertise or hire for positions that are "women only" or "men only" unless sex is a BFOQ. Nor does this restriction violate First Amendment rights of free press where the state statute covers "any person" who "aids" another in an unlawful practice. Pittsburgh Press Co. v. Pittsburgh Commission on Human Relations. Since Title VII is directed to employers, employment agencies and unions, but not to employees, individuals may advertise in work wanted columns as female or male.

d. State Labor Laws

In addition to state legislation limiting or prohibiting women from working in certain occupations, gender based state labor statutes frequently provide for meal periods, rest facilities, maximum hours or premium overtime payment only for women. Such laws do not constitute bona fide occupational qualifications that the employer can invoke as defense to claims of sex discrimination. Rosenfeld v. Southern Pacific Co.

States may mandate unpaid pregnancy leave and reinstatement for women, without discriminating against men in violation of Title VII. California Federal Savings and Loan Ass'n v. Guerra (S.Ct. 1987). States have concurrent legislative power in areas where Congress has not expressed its intent to preempt state law and the state law is not incompatible with any federal law.

However, the Federal Unemployment Tax Act, which prohibits denial of compensation under state unemployment laws solely on the basis of pregnancy or pregnancy termination is not violated when a state denies unemployment benefits to a woman who requests and receives normal leave to have a baby, and is refused reinstatement three weeks after the baby's birth. Wimberly v. Labor & Industrial Relations Com'n (1987). But see McCourtney

v. Imprimis Technologies, Inc. (Minn.App.1991), which allows unemployment compensation to a woman terminated because of absences to care for a sick child.

15.04 Procedures and Remedies

The Equal Employment Opportunity Commission is charged with enforcement of the Equal Pay Act and Title VII. Section 717 of Title VII provides the exclusive remedy for employment discrimination against federal executive and civil services employees. Brown v. GSA (S.Ct.1976). States with fair employment laws have parallel enforcement agencies, often called human rights commissions. In such states, the EEOC defers action on complaints until the state agency has had opportunity to review the claims.

Aside from the obvious limitation of the EPA to wage claims, several significant differences between the EPA and Title VII will influence whether an aggrieved employee should proceed under the EPA, Title VII, or both.

Many firms have fewer than the 15 employees necessary to invoke Title VII jurisdiction. Sex based wage discrimination for substantially equal work can be addressed under the EPA in firms with only two employees, one male and one female, so long as the establishment is otherwise subject to the Fair Labor Standards Act.

A.　STATUTES OF LIMITATIONS

Under both the EPA and Title VII, payment of lower wages to one sex constitutes a continuing violation until wages are equalized or employment terminates. However, the EPA statute of limitations is more generous once the violation ceases because suit may be brought within two years of the last unequal wage payment. Jenkins v. Home Insurance Co.

Under Title VII, the period for filing claims that are not continuous violations is markedly shorter. To preserve a claim under Title VII, the aggrieved individual must file a complaint with the EEOC within 180 days of the alleged discrimination. The only exception occurs if the complaint is first filed with a state enforcement agency, in which case the complaint with the EEOC must be filed within 300 days. Filing periods for state laws vary, but cannot be less than 180 days. Failure to file within the statutory period usually bars recovery. Orahood v. Board of Trustees of University of Arkansas; Jacobs v. College of William and Mary. Claimants are advised to file personally in city, state and federal offices within 180 days of the alleged discrimination to avoid litigation on this issue.

Failure of a flight attendant to file a charge with the EEOC when she was discharged upon marriage bars her later claim for retroactive seniority upon rehiring. The formerly illegal action has no present legal consequence. United Air Lines, Inc.

v. Evans. However, flight attendants discharged for maternity were awarded retroactive competitive seniority in Zipes v. Trans World Airlines, Inc., although not all claimants had filed timely complaints. Filing a timely charge is not a jurisdictional prerequisite to suit in federal court, but like a statute of limitations, is subject to waiver, estoppel and equitable tolling.

The right of an individual to bring a private cause of action against the employer is not the same under the two statutes. An individual may initiate a private action under the EPA until two years after the discrimination ceases. She need not file with the EEOC at all. Or, the individual may file with the EEOC and let the agency investigate the complaint. If the government institutes suit, the aggrieved individual is precluded from filing a private action.

Under Title VII, the aggrieved individual cannot bring private suit unless she has first filed with the EEOC. If satisfactory settlement has not been reached in 180 days, the complainant can request a right to sue letter, upon receipt of which the complainant must commence private action within 90 days. How long the complainant may leave the matter in the hands of the EEOC without requesting a right to sue letter is unclear. See Kamberos v. GTE Automatic Electric, Inc. and Bernard v. Gulf Oil Co. (5th Cir.1979).

Federal courts do not have exclusive jurisdiction over civil actions brought under Title VII. Yellow

Freight System, Inc. v. Donnelly (S.Ct.1990). Congress did not intend to discourage state legislatures and state courts from finding remedies for employment discrimination. Nor does a state agency's award of limited damages preclude complainants from proceeding in federal court to recover make whole damages under Title VII. McNasby v. Crown Cork & Seal Co., Inc. (3d Cir.1989). The Eleventh Amendment does not bar award of a pre-judgment make whole award against a state employment referral agency. Pegues v. Mississippi State Employment Services (5th Cir.1990).

Nature of Proof. A major element of the EPA is that objective proof of unequal pay for substantially equal work is basis for judgment for the plaintiff. Elements of motive, which are judicially imposed upon both the statutory language of Title VII and the Fourteenth and Fifteenth Amendments of the Constitution, are not relevant. Objective proof suffices under the EPA to establish a prima facie case which in turn can be rebutted only by objective proof of one of the four affirmative defenses.

Jury Trial. Because the Equal Pay Act is part of the Fair Labor Standards Act, questions of fact in an EPA case may be tried by a court or a jury. Once a jury determines wilful violation, the district court lacks jurisdiction to deny an award of liquidated damages. EEOC v. City of Detroit Health Dept. (6th Cir.1990).

Circuit courts disagree whether findings of fact under an EPA claim are binding upon a Title VII claim based on the same facts. Central to the dispute is the element of intent necessary for recovery under Title VII in face of liability for compensatory damages without proof of intent under the Equal Pay Act. The EPA claim was not binding on the VII claim in Peters v. City of Shreveport (5th Cir.1987) and Fallon v. Illinois (7th Cir.1989).

Korte v. Diemer (6th Cir.1990) holds the VII claim is bound by jury determinations under the EPA claim. The *Korte* court found the distinctions between proof standards "overly technical". Conduct that a jury finds to be "based on" sex under the EPA and not motivated by nondiscriminatory reasons, cannot later be found by a district court to lack an intent to discriminate "on the basis of sex" under Title VII. The broad equitable remedies authorized under Title VII preclude a jury trial. Fitzgerald v. Sirloin Stockade, Inc. Nor can a suit for violation of Title VII be invoked under 42 U.S.C. § 1985(c). Otherwise the administrative procedure and equitable remedies provided by Title VII could be replaced with a jury trial. Great American Federal Savings and Loan Association v. Novotny.

B. REMEDIES

The Equal Pay Act specifically requires that the lower wages be raised to the higher, and fixes the amount of damages at up to double two years back pay for violation and up to double three years back pay for willful violation. Even when the employer shows good faith, the district court retains discretion to award liquidated damages. Pearce v. Wichita County.

Equitable remedies available under Title VII are extensive. They include, but are not limited to, hiring, reinstatement, assignment, transfer, retroactive seniority, front pay and back pay.

Back Pay. Under Title VII, an award for back pay may cover more than the maximum three years allowed under the EPA.

A person discriminated against under Title VII must mitigate damages by taking equivalent employment if available. An employer's liability is tolled when a claimant is offered, and rejects, the job originally sought. Ford Motor Company v. EEOC (S.Ct.1982). The employer's job offer did not include retroactive seniority, and the female plaintiffs did not want to give up the seniority rights they had earned in the job they had secured elsewhere when the employer did not hire them.

Attorney's fees can be awarded to prevailing parties who succeed on any significant claim. Texas State Teachers Assn. v. Garland Independent School Dist. (S.Ct.1989). Prevailing defendant under Title VII is entitled to fees if plaintiff's action is without foundation. Christiansburg Garment Co. v. EEOC.

Civil War Statutes. Provisions of civil rights statutes passed after the Civil War are vehicles for redress of sex discrimination. Section 1983 of 42 U.S.C. is the most widely used. It provides that "every person" who deprives "any citizen" of civil rights "under color of state law" is liable to the party injured. It is the ground for a wide array of civil rights actions in employment, Forrester v. White (S.Ct.1988); and personal injury, Thurman v. City of Torrington (D.Conn.1984). Section 1985(c) provides that any two or more persons who conspire to injure or deprive another regarding specified rights shall be liable for such injuries or deprivations. It has been used in the abortion context to prevent blockage of clinics by protesters. National Organization for Women v. Operation Rescue (4th Cir.1990). Section 1981 gives protection to black women under a guarantee that "all persons" may engage the legal system to enforce specified rights that are "enjoyed by white citizens". Patterson v. McLean Credit Union (S.Ct. 1989). However, § 1981 covers only the making of an employment contract, and not the performance of the contract, so there is no cause of action for on-the-job racial harassment. For more detailed discussion of procedures and remedies under the Equal Pay Act and Title VII, see Federal Law of Employment Discrimination in a Nutshell by Mack A. Player.

CHAPTER 16

AFFIRMATIVE ACTION

16.01 Perspectives

The word sex refers to members of both sexes
just as the word race refers to members of all
races. Although civil rights statutes and executive
orders were not drafted to protect whites against
blacks or males against females, affirmative action
programs that seek to increase minority and female representation in the workplace raise concerns of reverse discrimination. The Rehnquist
Court has been increasingly sympathetic to challenges by whites who allege affirmative action programs invade their constitutional rights.

The term "affirmative action" has several different meanings, not always distinguished, relating
progressively from neutral advertising to insure
equal employment opportunity, to mandated active
recruitment and preferential hiring where needed
to correct an imbalance between white and minority, or male and female employees.

Equal employment law for women is linked with
that for racial minorities. The facts are not altogether similar: women most notably are not a
minority, and white women have not experienced
many of the deprivations suffered upon minority

women and men. However, white women, like all minorities, are under represented in higher paying, more desirable employment positions.

Under utilization of college and professionally educated white women indicates that equal educational opportunity and equal employment opportunity are not sufficient to overcome past discriminatory practices. From this perspective, affirmative action that goes beyond neutral advertising and recruitment appears a necessary complement to anti-discrimination laws to insure integration of under represented classes across the spectrum of occupations. In periods when the executive branch does not actively pursue affirmative action remedies, programs enacted through state, local and private negotiations and litigation increase in significance.

Legal Challenges

Constitutional challenges to affirmative action programs undertaken as remedies to further statutory purpose come under two contexts. First, as a matter of statutory construction, it is argued that the executive has exceeded its authority in mandating affirmative action to recipients of federal contracts and that Titles VI and VII of the Civil Rights Act of 1964 do not authorize affirmative action. Second, it is argued that the Constitution prohibits affirmative action under any statute because of the supremacy of the Fourteenth Amendment's guarantee of equal protection of the laws.

Although the parameters of permissible affirmative action are indistinct, appropriately drafted voluntary affirmative action programs and consent decrees to which all affected persons are party will be sustained. Affirmative action law seeks to establish which persons or agencies, public and private, may properly institute an affirmative action program, and what specific provisions will satisfy statutory and constitutional requirements.

16.02   Title VII

A.   NONDISCRIMINATION REQUIREMENTS

The only affirmative steps required of employers under Title VII are to insure that employment opportunities are open to all individuals without regard to sex by instituting sex neutral advertising, interviewing and testing procedures, by eliminating job qualifications grounded in sex stereotypes, and assuring that sex is not the basis for any decisions regarding hiring, discharge, compensation, terms, conditions or privileges of employment.

Title VII expressly states that "preferential treatment" is not required merely because of statistical imbalance with a group of employees compared to "the available work force." (§ 703(j)). The employer is under no obligation to hire a woman to balance the ratio between the sexes, nor to establish that the male hired is more qualified than the female not hired, nor to hire the female rather than an equally qualified male. Texas Department of Community Affairs v. Burdine.

Although affirmative action is not mandated under Title VII, neither is it prohibited. Several avenues of permissible affirmative action have developed.

B. PERMISSIBLE AFFIRMATIVE ACTION

1. Court Action

Congress expressly granted power to the courts to order "such affirmative action as may be appropriate * * *." (§ 706(g)). This includes the power to approve a consent decree. However, where adversely affected persons are not before the trial court, consent decrees involving municipal entities are subject to collateral attack. Martin v. Wilks (S.Ct.1989). Persons who are not party to litigation are not bound by it. The application of this principle to consent decrees and judgments involving Title VII affirmative action programs for private employers is unclear. A court ordered affirmative action percentage hiring quota for women and blacks to police patrol positions was upheld in United States v. City of Chicago (7th Cir.1977).

The Court interpreted an "appropriate" remedy in private affirmative action programs to include awarding of retroactive compensatory seniority even if such relief diminishes the expectations of other, arguably innocent, employees, and establishing a goal for hiring minorities where the employer or union has in the past engaged in persistent or egregious discrimination. See Franks v. Bowman Transportation Co. (S.Ct.1976) and Local 28 of

Sheet Metal Workers' International Ass'n v. Equal Employment Opportunity Commission (S.Ct.1986).

The fifth circuit in United States v. City of Miami (5th Cir.1980) elucidated the role of the trial court in approving consent decrees. Their obligation is to determine that the proposed settlement is not unlawful or against public policy, and not unreasonable. *Martin* requires that all potentially affected parties be before the court. The trial court retains jurisdiction and has power to modify or vacate the consent decree if it appears to have been unwise. The decree will not be set aside in absence of abuse of discretion.

Academic Setting. A class action by all female academic nonstudent employees at the University of Minnesota was settled by consent decree after eleven weeks of trial, "to correct previous inequities, if any, and to achieve on behalf of women full representation with respect to faculty employment at the University of Minnesota." The consent decree approved by the trial court provided for an affirmative action program, defined to mean: (1) procedures to advise women of faculty openings; (2) good faith efforts to hire qualified women in proportion to women holding the requisite advanced degree or other relevant criteria and (3) establishment of written sex neutral criteria for evaluating the qualifications of academic employees. The University was not required to hire less qualified women candidates, but where female and male candidates are approximately equally qualified, and women are under represented in the faculty, preference is to be given to the woman. Finally, goals and timetables are to be established periodically. Rajender v. University of Minnesota. A consent decree relating to academic employment is published as an appendix to the court's opinion in Lamphere v. Brown University.

2. Voluntary Action

Private Sector. Title VII does not forbid private employers and unions from voluntarily agreeing upon bona fide affirmative action plans to eliminate conspicuous racial imbalance in traditionally segregated job categories. United Steelworkers of America v. Weber.

Public Sector. Municipal entities may also voluntarily undertake affirmative action programs under Title VII "to remedy the effects of past practices and to permit attainment of an equitable representation of minorities, women and handicapped persons". Johnson v. Transportation Agency, Santa Clara County (S.Ct.1987). In *Johnson* the county sought to increase representation of women in transportation agency employment. The Supreme Court assessed the county's affirmative action program by extension of *Weber,* a Title VII private sector case, and found the county did not violate Title VII although the white male challenger was marginally more qualified. The woman promoted was fully qualified as road dispatcher, and her sex was just one factor in the employment decision.

Justice Stevens, concurring in *Johnson*, stressed the voluntary nature of the program. Nothing in Title VII, he said, imposes a duty on an employer "to determine whether his past conduct might constitute an arguable violation of Title VII" before he can voluntarily give a preference for promotion to one applicant over another. A "focus on the future" may well be "more helpful" in determining the limits of an affirmative action program.

Justice Scalia, in a dissent joined by Justice Rehnquist, would reconsider and overrule *Weber* because of its Fourteenth Amendment "ramifications". *Weber*, said Justice Scalia, "rewrote the statute it purported to construe." He also thought it strange for the Court to interpret Title VII to permit public sector action which he said is forbidden by the Constitution. The adversely impacted white males, "predominantly unknown, unaffluent, unorganized—suffer this injustice at the hands of a Court fond of thinking itself the champion of the politically impotent. I dissent." Justice White, dissenting in *Johnson*, would also overrule *Weber*.

An acceptable plan requires that it be made in good faith and in writing. It must evidence a comprehensive survey and analysis of employment needs and workforce profile in order to structure an appropriate affirmative action program. Goals, timetables, procedure for grievance, effective publication, and periodic evaluation with provision for termination upon reaching the stated goals are indicated. Carefully drafted plans address such obstacles to effective affirmative action plans as vested rights under tenure and seniority, parttime and temporary help policies, application of the program in times of business recession, and company and employee attitudes.

Executive Order. An executive order issued by the mayor authorized an affirmative action program for all city departments to insure that women and minorities are included in the final pool of candidates for appointment or promotion to municipal positions, with the ultimate goal of representation proportionate to composition of the available work force. The executive order was upheld in Maehren v. Seattle.

16.03 Mandated Programs

A. FEDERAL EXECUTIVE ORDER

The more commonly understood meaning of affirmative action is that required under Executive Order 11246, as amended by the addition of sex in EO 11375. Contractors with the federal government are required to "take affirmative action to ensure that applicants are employed * * * without regard to * * * sex * * *." Such affirmative action includes upgrading, demotion, transfer, layoff, termination, rates of pay or other forms of compensation, and selection for training, including apprenticeship.

Employers subject to the executive order are estimated to employ one of every three persons in the national work force. Three basic obligations are placed on these affirmative action employers. First, is a requirement to survey and analyze their workforce in all job categories. Second, if an imbalance is discovered in employment between men and women, the employer must establish goals and timetables to correct deficiencies. Third, the employer must document progress in achieving affirmative action goals. Affirmative action requires goals, not quotas, although numerical goals are permissible.

Judicial review of affirmative action plans developed by federal agencies under EO 11246 is available to insure that officials include mandated elements in the affirmative action plan that they formulate. Legal Aid Society v. Brennan. The court did not address constitutionality of affirmative action as to hiring and promotion preferences, saying that affirmative action as to recruitment and providing equal employment opportunity might be sufficient to remedy the labor force imbalance.

Alleged reverse discrimination under EO 11246, as well as the Fair Labor Standards Act and Title VII, was at issue in EEOC v. American Telephone and Telegraph Co. The court ruled that utilization of all segments of society in the available labor pool is a valid governmental objective and that EO 11246 is directed to this goal. This broad governmental interest is sufficient to justify relief directed at classes rather than individual victims of discrimination.

B. CONGRESSIONAL LEGISLATION

The Public Works Employment Act provides that ten percent of federal funds granted for local public works projects be used to secure services or supplies from minority owned businesses. This congressional provision for an affirmative action quota survived constitutional challenge in Fullilove v. Klutznick (S.Ct.1980). Fullilove addressed the remedial powers of Congress under section 5 of the Fourteenth Amendment. The Court judgment also found justification for the MBE program in the commerce clause and spending powers of Congress to provide for the general welfare. The Court rejected argument that Congress must be wholly colorblind in remedial contexts. Nor is it a constitutional defect that the expectations of nonminority firms may be disappointed. To cure the effects of prior discrimination, "a sharing of the burden" by innocent parties is not impermissible.

A concurring opinion by Justice Marshall applied the gender standard of review and said the statute was constitutional because remedying present effects of past discrimination is an important governmental objective and a 10 percent set aside for minorities substantially serves this purpose. The Court specifically exempted *Fullilove* from its ruling in Richmond v. J.A. Croson Co.

which struck as unconstitutional a 30 percent minority set-aside for city contracts.

A Congressional mandate for affirmative action in licensing allocations by the Federal Communications Commission was upheld in Metro Broadcasting v. FCC and Astroline Communications Co. Ltd. Partnership v. Shurberg (S.Ct.1990). The Court said the Congressional efforts to ensure "diversity of views and information on the airwaves" serve an "important governmental objective."

* * *

Equal opportunity in employment is of illusory value for all but unskilled jobs unless accompanied by equal access to education, a necessary complement to Title VII. The next chapter addresses equality of educational opportunity for women, the objective of Title IX of the Education Amendments of 1972.

CHAPTER 17

EDUCATION

17.01 Title IX

Education is traditionally the prerogative of the states. Public grade school education has been widely available for more than 100 years to both boys and girls, and secondary education since this century. Entry of women to public higher education has increased dramatically since World War II with impetus from establishment of community colleges. By 1980, the number of women enrolled in both two and four year undergraduate schools exceeded that of men. Enrollment of women in professional graduate schools in more than token numbers dates from enactment of Title IX of the Education Amendments Act of 1972.

Title IX addresses only discrimination on the basis of sex. Recall that sex was included as a protected class in a twelfth hour amendment to Title VII, the employment section of the Civil Rights Act of 1964. Sex had not been included as a protected class in Title VI, the education section of the 1964 statute. Congress belatedly enacted Title IX in 1972 to prohibit sex discrimination in federally funded educational institutions.

Title IX provides that no person shall be excluded from participation in, be denied the benefits of, or be subjected to discrimination on the basis of sex under any educational program or activity receiving federal financial assistance. 20 U.S.C. § 1681(a). Many states have parallel statutes which may set more stringent requirements for sex equity in education.

The threshold question for application of Title IX is whether the educational institution receives federal funds. If not, discrimination because of sex of the individual is not a violation of Title IX.

The Supreme Court's narrow interpretation of Title IX in Grove City College v. Bell (S.Ct.1984) was nullified by the Civil Rights Restoration Act of 1987. This statute applies Title IX to a college, university, or other postsecondary institution, "any part of which is extended Federal financial assistance."

Whether student organizations receive sufficient indirect, intangible benefits to bring them within the scope of IX is unclear. See Iron Arrow Honor Society v. Schweiker (5th Cir.1981), which was dismissed as moot after the president of Miami University barred the all male honor society from campus until it ended its discriminatory membership policy.

As with other federal legislation, regulations formulated by the administrative agency after public hearings and published in the Code of Federal Regulations (CFR), spell out the scope of Title IX.

Regulations are not the work of the legislature and in theory are not strictly law; in practice, however, regulations are given great deference. Laffey v. Northwest Airlines, Inc. Regulations foster nationwide uniformity by guiding decisions of enforcement personnel in application of the statute. Proposed revisions for Title IX regulations are directed primarily to remedies and enforcement procedures.

A. ADMISSIONS

Some schools that receive federal funding may exclude members of one sex from admission under Title IX. Most significant are pre-kindergarten through high school, private undergraduate schools, and public undergraduate schools which have been single sex since their inception. Women may also be excluded from admission to religious institutions and military schools. Other exemptions include the YWCA, YMCA, Girl Scouts, Boy Scouts, Camp Fire Girls, social sororities and fraternities. Exclusion of females or males from these groups may, however, be in violation of state public accommodation laws. See Isbister v. Boys' Club of Santa Cruz, Inc. (Cal.S.Ct.1985); Frank v. Ivy Club, Tiger Inn & Trustees of Princeton University (N.J.S.Ct.1990).

Educational entities that are expressly prohibited from excluding either men or women in admissions are vocational institutions, including vocational high schools, public undergraduate coeducational institutions, and graduate and professional institutions, which before Title IX had low quotas for women. The increase in women professional students is most marked in law and medicine, where women in some schools are almost 50 percent of the student body. Women are also enrolling in increasing numbers in doctorate programs in the physical sciences, engineering and architecture. Re-entry programs, originally designed to facilitate re-entry of women to higher education, must also be open to men.

The provision in Title IX that public colleges that have been single sex since their inception may remain single sex was unconstitutional as applied to the narrow facts of Mississippi University for Women v. Hogan (S.Ct.1982). The Supreme Court held that MUW could not constitutionally refuse to enroll a male registered nurse in its baccalaureate nursing program in that males were admitted for audit, and women constitute a majority of the nursing profession.

The Equal Education Opportunity Act of 1974 provides that "dual school systems" in which public school students are assigned solely on the basis of race, color, sex or national origin, deny the students equal protection. The fifth circuit interpreted the EEOA to require that schools which were sex segregated before racial integration was abolished must be opened to both sexes. United States v. Hinds County School Board.

B. AFTER ADMISSION

All schools, even those exempt as to admissions, must comply with Title IX curriculum requirements. Only contact sports, chorus and sex education instruction may be single sex. Sex education classes have survived First Amendment free exercise and establishment clause challenges where participation is optional. Smith v. Ricci (N.J.S.Ct.1982). Extra curricular activities, financial aid, scholarships, housing, teaching assistantships and research opportunities must be equally available. Discrimination in career counselling or because of pregnancy, marital or parental status is also prohibited.

In deference to First Amendment free speech and press concerns, federal regulations under Title IX do not provide that sex biased textbooks and films be eliminated from use. Some states require that career counseling and educational materials be free of sexist language and stereotypes.

C. INSTITUTIONAL OBLIGATIONS

The regulations place obligations upon the institutions receiving federal funds to review their academic, vocational and extra curricular offerings to insure that none foreclose participation by either women or men, and take remedy to eliminate any such exclusion or other discrimination.

In addition, recipients of federal funding are required to adopt and publish internal grievance procedures to resolve student complaints alleging discrimination prohibited by Title IX. Students are not required to utilize the internal grievance procedure but may file a complaint directly with the Department of Education, Office of Civil Rights. Each institution is required to designate a specific individual to coordinate school efforts to insure compliance with Title IX.

D. REMEDIES

Enforcement of Title IX is provided through institutional compliance review and individual complaint.

1. Compliance Review

Under compliance review, the enforcing agency selects a number of institutions receiving federal funds and conducts investigations to determine whether the recipients are complying with the statute. Schools found in noncompliance may be required to take affirmative action to remedy past discrimination. Upon failure to reach satisfactory resolution, process may be initiated leading to termination of federal assistance.

2. Complaint

An individual may invoke Title IX by making complaint within 180 days of the alleged discrimination to the Office of Civil Rights, which will investigate the complaint, and attempt voluntary reconciliation if discrimination is found. If satisfactory resolution is not reached, the OCR will issue a right to sue letter to the aggrieved individual.

Title IX remedies include an implied right for an injured individual to bring a private cause of action against a discriminating educational institution. Cannon v. University of Chicago (S.Ct.1979). Applying the analysis of Cort v. Ash (1975), the Court noted that the female surgical nurse seeking admission to medical school was a member of the class the statute was designed to help; that a private remedy was consistent with the purpose of the statute; that legislative intent to allow a private cause of action was present, and that allowing a private suit would not invade exclusive state rights. Congress did not intend that termination of funding be the sole remedy under Title IX. Compare Thompson v. Thompson (S.Ct.1988), where Justice Scalia, concurring, takes "the categorical position" that the right to bring a private cause of action "will not be implied" under federal statutes.

Plaintiff's cause of action ultimately failed because a plaintiff in a IX disparate treatment case must establish discriminatory intent. Cannon v. University of Chicago (7th Cir.1981); Cannon v. University of Health Sciences/The Chicago Medical School (7th Cir.1983); Cannon v. Loyola University of Chicago (7th Cir.1986).

Ms. Cannon challenged the university's neutral rule against admission of older students to medical school on the basis that the rule has a disproportionate impact against women in that women disrupt their education to raise a family.

Circuit courts disagree whether individuals can seek damages under Title IX or are limited to equitable relief. Pfeiffer v. Marion Center Area School District (3d Cir.1990), said IX authorizes compensatory damages. *Cannon* rejects damages, and further holds that the Eleventh Amendment forecloses legal relief against state universities. Similarly, Franklin v. Gwinnett County Public Schools. Congress enacted Title IX under spending clause powers. Remedies that might be available if enacted under the commerce clause powers, as was Title VII, are inapplicable.

A comprehensive law suit was filed in 1970 to compel government officials to enforce civil rights statutes that prohibit federal funding to organizations that discriminate against protected classes. In the course of litigation, Title IX, enacted in 1972, was included. The litigation ended in 1990 when the Circuit Court for the District of Columbia Circuit ruled that the plaintiffs could not maintain an action directly against federal government officers who are charged with monitoring and enforcing funding recipients' compliance with statutes that prohibit discrimination. Women's Equity Action League v. Cavazos (D.C.Cir.1990).

17.02   Title IX Case Experience

A. SPORTS

K through 12.   Many schools, either independently or in accord with state and local athletic association rules, limit sport teams' intermural competition to one sex.

Such teams are generally acceptable where comparable sports opportunities are made available to the opposite sex. Title IX regulations permit exclusion of girls from contact sports participation.

Title IX is permissive for participation by both sexes in contact sports under the interpretation in Yellow Springs Exempted Village School District Board v. Ohio High School Athletic Association. The school may establish separate teams, but if only one team is available, participation by both sexes is discretionary, neither required nor prohibited.

College Sports.   Actions against colleges and universities on both constitutional and Title IX grounds have successfully challenged disparate treatment for women's sports in offerings, scholarships, promotion, recruiting, scheduling, coaches' salaries, travel, equipment and facilities. A consent decree settled Haffer v. Temple University (E.D.Pa.1987), after denial of the University's motion for summary judgment. The district court found that material issues of fact were presented by plaintiffs' allegations that women had only ⅓ of the opportunity to participate in sports as did males, and that they were allocated only 20% of the athletic operating funds although women comprised 50% of the student body. There was evidence that talented and interested women student athletes would take advantage of increased sports opportunities at the University. Similar issues were successfully raised in Blair v. Washington State University, (Wn.S.Ct.1987), which was litigated under state statutory and constitutional grounds.

B. CHILD CARE

Women in higher education, particularly in community colleges, tend to be part time, older students, often with child care demands not experienced by male students.

A suit was brought under both the Fourteenth Amendment and Title IX for declaratory and injunctive relief to restrain community college defendants from maintaining an allegedly discriminatory "anti-child care" policy and requiring them to take affirmative steps to develop a child care program. The trial court's decision to dismiss for failure to state a cause of action was reversed. De La Cruz v. Tormey. An out of court settlement was reached with the three defendant community colleges agreeing to apply for state, federal and private foundation funds to establish day care centers within a specific target date.

The Education Amendments Act of 1980 for the first time allowed students who attend school less

than half time to have access to work-study assistance, a provision which is of particular benefit to
women students with children since they frequently are less than half time students.

C. EMPLOYMENT

Title IX was interpreted to prohibit discrimination in employment in educational institutions receiving federal funds in North Haven Board of
Education v. Bell (S.Ct.1982). Plaintiff, a tenured
teacher, had not been rehired after a one-year
maternity leave.

The interface of employment claims in education
under Title IX and Title VII is unclear. See Mabry v. State Board of Community Colleges and
Occupational Education (10th Cir.1987). In Mabry,
the female physical education instructor and coach
in a junior college was allegedly terminated because of reduction in workforce, resulting from
decreased enrollment. She alleged that she was
terminated on the basis of her sex and/or marital
status. Mabry did not prevail on a Title VII claim,
and was precluded from proceeding on her Title IX
claim. For litigation in education employment under Title VII, see University of Pennsylvania v.
EEOC.

D. SEXUAL HARASSMENT

Sexual harassment of students by educational
employees has been the focus of an increasing
number of actions. The suits are being challenged

with countersuits of libel, slander and defamation. Among the many educational institutions which have adopted positive programs against sexual harassment of both students and employees is the University of Wisconsin. The university took an official position that incidents of sexual harassment are demeaning to all persons involved and impair the ability of the system to perform its education functions. Institutions that develop policies prohibiting sexual harassment need to provide for effective mechanisms for complainants to seek redress while assuring due process protections for those accused of the harassment.

An action seeking to enjoin Yale University to institute a procedure for receiving and investigating complaints of sexual harassment of students was unsuccessful where complainants failed to establish deprivation of "educational" benefits upon which showing Title IX authorizes courts to provide relief. Alexander v. Yale University. The court noted that Yale had in fact instituted a grievance procedure for sexual and other forms of harassment, so "the major relief sought in this suit has already been granted."

Termination of a tenured professor who sexually harassed some of his female students was sustained in Levitt v. Univ. of Texas (5th Cir.198_).

A female employee/student in a medical school surgical residency program alleged that she was subject to sexual harassment and was ultimately dismissed without cause from the program because

she was a woman. She claimed violation of Title
VII, Title IX, and 42 U.S.C. § 1983. Lipsett v.
University of Puerto Rico (1st Cir.1988). The circuit court found Lipsett stated a prima facie case
with detailed pleadings of derogatory comments
about women as surgeons and of sexist language,
including sexist nicknames for the few women in
the program, lewd pictures and sexual proposi-
tions. Whether the sexual advances of defendant
director were unwelcome are to be considered from
the perspective of both plaintiff and defendant.

Sexual harassment of students takes place in
secondary schools as well. A female student subjected to intentional sexual intercourse by a
coach/teacher was denied damages in Franklin v.
Gwinnett County Public Schools (11th Cir.1990).
Her remedy is limited to specific performance,
which the district fulfilled by taking steps to prevent similar future misconduct. Contra, see Pfeiffer v. Marion Center Area School District (3d Cir.
1990), discussed in chapter ten, which said Title IX
supports compensatory damages as well as specific
relief.

See also Continental Casualty Co. v. Canadian
Universal Insurance Co. (1st Cir.1991), where the
University of Massachusetts sought indemnification for almost $500,000 for liability arising from
sexual harassment of eight female work-study students by the male director of a university health
program, and for eliminating the position of a staff
worker who reported the harassment.

CHAPTER 18

FINANCE AND PUBLIC ACCOMMODATIONS

18.01 Credit and Insurance

A. EQUAL CREDIT OPPORTUNITY ACT

Coverage

The federal Equal Credit Opportunity Act (15 U.S.C. § 1691) prohibits discrimination on account of sex or marital status in the granting or terms of credit. All creditors who regularly extend credit are covered by the act, including banks, small loan and finance companies, retail and department stores, credit card companies and credit unions. The act addresses approval, denial, renewal or extension of credit, and requires a creditor to tell an applicant why credit is denied. Creditors may not set different standards in determining creditworthiness for men and women.

The statute seeks to correct inequity in granting credit to single, married, divorced or widowed women as compared to similarly situated men. Several provisions are specifically directed to protecting the credit rights of married women. Creditors may not require a married woman to reapply for credit in her husband's name; refuse her credit in her name; or ask questions about family planning or fertility. Nor can creditors ask information about the spouse unless joint credit is sought, the spouse will use the credit, or the borrower is relying on the spouse's income, alimony or child support in securing the credit. A creditor may not ask marital status if a woman applies for an unsecured account except in community property states. Creditors are prohibited from discouraging applicants from applying for credit, and must release from liability any persons improperly required to co-sign.

Remedies

The objective of the ECOA is to remove barriers to women in granting of credit. The act does not automatically guarantee that women, any more than men, are entitled to credit as a matter of right. Nor does the act remove all credit obstacles occasioned by marriage. The Equal Credit Opportunity Act does not require a creditor to investigate a facially valid judgment against a female credit card applicant to ascertain whether a derogatory item on a woman's credit record is attributable to her spouse. Denard v. Michigan National Bank. Requirement of a spouse's signature violated the act in Anderson v. United Finance Co. Cancellation of a "supplementary" card holder's account upon death of the "basic" card holder violates the ECOA, which prohibits discrimination on marital status as well as sex. Miller v. American Express Co. (9th Cir.1982). However, requiring a spouse to co-sign a note when the applicant is relying on the spouse's future earnings in order to qualify for the loan, does not violate the ECOA. United States v. ITT Consumer Financial Corporation (9th Cir.1987).

B. INSURANCE

Most insurance is subject only to state regulation. Fewer than half the states have statutes prohibiting sex discrimination in insurance. Discrimination because of sex and marital status occurs in life, disability, health, casualty, business and pension insurance. Women are denied equal access to coverage, options at various stages in the duration of the policy, amount of coverage, and rates charged. Some rates discriminate against men, primarily in auto rates for young males. Women are disadvantaged compared to other male drivers in that they are charged the same rates and do far less driving.

Pennsylvania has ruled that the state equal rights amendment prohibits discrimination on the basis of sex in issuing or renewing automobile insurance. Bartholomew v. Foster (Pa.Cmwlth. 1988). The state insurance commissioner subsequently extended the ban against gender discrimination to other lines of insurance.

Congress in 1974 passed the Employees Retirement Income Security Act (ERISA) to establish minimum standards for private pension plans. Employers may provide more benefits than ERISA demands, but not fewer. Women who combine

homemaking with work outside the home are disadvantaged in that workers under 25, the years
when most women are fully employed, can be excluded from coverage, as can workers who begin
employment within five years of retirement age.
Companies may also exclude part time employees
who work less than 20 hours per week. These
exclusions are precisely the work patterns of wom-
en who are also homemakers. Another discrimination against women under ERISA is exclusion of
small professional offices, staffed largely by wom-
en, from pension fund insurance. The employees
may find, upon retirement, that the fund is fund-
less.

18.02 Public Accommodations

Federal legislation does not address sex discrimination in public accommodations. Many states
and local municipalities have statutes prohibiting
denial of access to public accommodations on the
basis of sex. Litigation under these statutes has
resulted in front doors to business organizations
and quasi-public clubs all across the country being
opened to women who formerly had to walk in the
back door, in company of a male, at limited times,
if at all. Public accommodations statutes have
survived numerous challenges on First Amendment right of privacy and association grounds.
See discussion in chapter ten.

"Ladies' Day Discounts" have not fared well under public accommodations statutes. In a broadly

worded opinion, California ruled that the statute
prohibited sex based discounts offered by many
carwashes, nightclubs and sports events. Koire v.
Metro Car Wash (Cal.S.Ct.1985). The defendants
claimed the ladies' day discounts were permissible
because they compensated for the lower wages
which women receive. Accord, Commonwealth,
Pa. Liquor Control Board v. Dobrinoff, (Pa.Cmwlth.
1984).

Chief Justice Rose Bird noted in *Koire* that "ladies night" basketball is permitted under the
Washington State public accommodations law and
the state ERA. MacLean v. First Northwest Industries (Wn.S.Ct.1981). "With all due respect," said
Justice Bird, the Washington court "succumbed to
sexual stereotyping."

The California law also applies to non-profit community organizations. Single sex clubs for boys
must admit girls. Isbister v. Boys' Club of Santa
Cruz, Inc. (Cal.S.Ct.1985). A dissenter lamented
that the decision "will strain our social fabric and
* * * strike a death knell for fraternities and sororities."

But Connecticut's public accommodation statute
does not require boy scouts to select a female troop
leader. Quinnipiac Council, Boy Scouts of America, Inc. v. Commission on Human Rights and
Opportunities (Conn.S.Ct.1987). The plaintiff in
Quinnipiac had served as cub scout den mother,
merit badge counselor, troop committee member,
and de facto scoutmaster for four years when no

males were available either as scoutmaster or assistant scoutmaster, during which time five boys became eagle scouts.

PART V

CRIMINAL LAW

The house of every one is to him as his castle and fortress, as well for his defence against injury and violence, as for his repose

Justice Stevens, Payton v. New York (1980), quoting Semayne's Case (K.B.1603)

Criminal law is the second of two major divisions into which law is normally classified. It is distinguished from civil law in that the state, acting on behalf of society, prosecutes a person who does some act which is prohibited under penalty of fine or imprisonment. Failure to fulfill a statutory duty may also be a crime.

An individual may interact with the criminal law as a defendant, a victim, or a participant in the judicial process. Criminal defendants are concerned that they receive every protection of due process of law to which they are constitutionally entitled. Women learn about the criminal justice system most frequently as victims. A relatively small proportion of the total population is criminal, but of this group, statistics indicate that men are the major perpetrators of violence against both women and men. Part V begins with an examination of the rights of women and children primarily as victims of violence. The following chapter addresses discrimination between men and women as criminal defendants.

CHAPTER 19

VICTIMS

19.01 Violence Against Women and Children

A. INCIDENCE

Physical abuse suffered by women and children is not random. It usually occurs by the hand of a male relative or acquaintance, and requires medical treatment more frequently than abuse by a stranger. It is largely unreported and therefore is not legally visible.

Spousal abuse is particularly likely to be unreported because of fear of reprisal, the private nature of family life, and an attitude on the part of both husband and wife that assault by one's husband is not a crime.

Three of four victims of intrafamily assault are women. Between spouses, the percentage is even more dramatic. The wife was victim 95 percent of the time in 655,000 reported spousal assaults. The report did not specify the extent to which the husbands who were victims had been the initial aggressors. Of all victims, the wife was least likely to respond with force.

B. CONTEMPORARY REMEDIES

Physical assault is a crime in every state; it follows that wife beating is a criminal activity nationwide. Prosecution, however, is lacking. Behavior that would be prosecuted as a crime if it occurred upon the street between strangers is not prosecuted if it occurs within the family. The traditional response of police personnel when they are called to domestic disputes is to stop the fighting and leave the parties to work out their differences by themselves.

The battered woman who gets no help from police has several choices. She can flee her home if she has a place to run to. She can submit to more abuse. Or she can defend herself against the batterer. Should she follow this latter course, and the self defense results in death to the batterer, she will likely be prosecuted for murder and become a defendant at criminal law.

Efforts to stop domestic violence have expanded through judicial, legislative, and private avenues. They address stricter enforcement of existing criminal laws, flexibility in civil remedies, and establishment of shelters for abused women and their children. Federal constitutional claims of First Amendment rights to petition for redress of grievances, and violation of Fourteenth Amendment due process and equal protection guarantees have been made on behalf of battered wives. Action can also be brought under state law, as was done in Bruno v. Codd.

In *Bruno,* twelve battered women instituted a class action for declaratory and injunctive relief alleging that the New York City police engaged in a pervasive pattern and practice of non-intervention in domestic disputes. The admitted policy of the New York City Police Department was to make arrests in all cases of reasonable cause except as between husbands and wives. The plaintiffs alleged that the police practice on non-interference violated their rights to legal protection.

In refusing to grant a motion to dismiss, the trial court said, "If the allegations of the instant complaint—buttressed by hundreds of pages of affidavit—are true, * * * wife-beating is still condoned, if not approved, by some of those charged with protecting its victims."

The suit was settled with a consent judgment which requires police to respond to every request for assistance. When the officer has reasonable cause to believe a felony has been committed, attempt at reconciliation is prohibited. The officer is to arrest the battering spouse, and follow normal procedures to locate and arrest a battering spouse who has left the premises.

Apprehension of batterers is hindered in some jurisdictions because police cannot arrest without a warrant unless they have witnessed the battering, which usually takes place before their arrival. Arrest without a warrant in one's own home was ruled a violation of the Fourth Amendment although there was reasonable cause to believe the defendant had committed a felony in Payton v. New York. *Payton* did not address the validity of a warrantless arrest in the arrestee's home where there are exigent circumstances, including risk to innocent persons, or where access was gained by the consent of an occupant.

Protective Orders. Some states provide for issuance of an order of protection to an abused spouse providing that the husband shall not assault or otherwise harass or endanger his wife or children. In some instances, the order of protection may provide that the batterer must stay away from the family home. The juvenile division of a probate court may issue such an order for the well being of a 16 year old sexually abused daughter. Kent County Dept. of Social Services v. Macomber (Mich.S.Ct.1990). A statute providing that a protection order may be issued to an abused wife before hearing testimony from both spouses was upheld against constitutional challenge in Minnesota v. Errington.

Other Remedies. A few jurisdictions have malicious harassment statutes, seeking to curb long-term harassment which sometimes erupts in injury or death to the victim. The First Amendment generally blocks criminal charges for verbal harassment alone. Civil orders prohibiting contact are generally impotent.

Other legislation is directed to controlling actions of convicted predatory sex offenders. Provisions include a civil commitment procedure allow-

ing the state to hold offenders upon their sched-
uled release from prison; increased prison sentences, and post-release registration.

19.02 Child Abuse

Child abuse is even less visible than violence
against women. It is frequently connected with
sexual exploitation. Studies suggest that children
who are physically and sexually abused repeat the
pattern when they have children of their own.
The role of law in prosecution for child abuse may
thus be critical in breaking the cycle of recurrence
for future generations as well as for the individual
child victim.

A. KNOWN ABUSERS

Most offenders of children are family members,
friends, neighbors, coaches, teachers, counselors,
day care workers, clergy. They are usually, but
not always, male. The abusers may be wittingly or
unwittingly aided by adults who fail to intercede
on the child's behalf. The abuse may be physical,
or sexual, or both. The child victims are both
male and female.

Incest. Incest is commonly defined as sexual
intercourse between persons who are related to the
whole or half blood either as parent and child or
brother and sister, including adopted children and
step children. Offenders cajole, bribe, threaten or
intimidate the child into compliance. Children
usually do not speak to anyone about the abuse,

intuitively knowing that the activity is taboo. When not reported, the sexual abuse may continue for years. Incestuous behavior usually begins at a very early age, not infrequently before age six, and instances as young as 18 months have been reported. Older brother/younger sister incest may be the most common, although father/daughter incest is more frequently prosecuted.

Principal difficulties in prosecution of sexual abuse cases are failure of children to report the abuse, and refusal of family members to believe the children if they do talk about it.

Reporting Statutes. Authorities seldom become aware of abuse by relatives or acquaintances until the child requires medical treatment. Compulsory child abuse reporting statutes for physicians, teachers and social workers who have reasonable cause to believe children are being abused seek to make these victims more visible. The Washington State Supreme Court rejected a claim by religious counselors that a reporting statute violated their First Amendment right to attend allegedly child abusive parishioners through prayer and religious counseling. Washington v. Motherwell (Wash.S.Ct. 1990).

Many jurisdictions require the testimony of the child to be corroborated by independent evidence. Even where supporting evidence is not legally required, juries are reluctant to convict an adult solely on verbal statements of the child.

A five year old female victim was a competent witness in a criminal trial for first degree statutory rape and indecent liberties in State v. Johnson. The test for competency of a child witness was listed by the court as (1) an understanding of the obligation to speak the truth; (2) mental capacity at the time of the occurrence; (3) capacity to express in words the memory of the occurrence; and (4) capacity to understand simple questions about it. Admission of the testimony is within the discretion of the trial court. The veracity of the witness is a question for the jury.

Fourth Amendment rights are implicated when social service workers enter homes to investigate reports of child abuse and to physically examine the unclothed reportedly abused child. Where the administrative agency in exigent circumstances follows an established, reasonable procedure, the Fourth is satisfied. Requiring a warrant or a probable cause standard would often leave children unprotected. E.Z. v. Coler (N.D.Ill.1985).

When authorities have reason to suspect a child is dead and "production is required as part of a non-criminal regulatory regime," a mother may be jailed indefinitely for civil contempt for failing to produce her child or to give information about the child's whereabouts. Baltimore City Dept. of Social Services v. Bouknight (S.Ct.1990).

Child Abuse Syndromes. Courts are in disagreement as to admission of testimony on the battered child syndrome, under which experts testify relative to the child's injuries. The ninth circuit granted federal habeas corpus relief to a man convicted of murdering his infant daughter because evidence of the child's previous injuries has no relevance to the defendant where the prosecution fails to establish that the defendant inflicted those injuries. McGuire v. Estelle (9th Cir.1990).

Some jurisdictions allow admission of expert testimony on the child sex abuse accommodation syndrome to help jurors understand behavior that might appear inconsistent to them with a sexual assault. Michigan v. Beckley allowed such testimony to explain why a 15 year old daughter who lived with her father delayed reporting his alleged sexual intercourse with her. (Mich.S.Ct.1990).

Corroborating evidence is not needed for a victim's testimony of prior instances of sexual abuse which satifies the requirement of clear proof. Iowa v. Jones (Iowa S.Ct.1990).

Repeated Molestation. A particularly pernicious defense is raised by "resident" child abusers who have molested children over a long period of time. The child often is unable to specify a particular time and place of the offense. Some states apply the "either/or" rule: either the prosecution must elect and prove the time and place of a specific occurrence, or else must give an unanimity instruction to the jury that they all must agree that one event is proved beyond a reasonable doubt for a conviction to hold. Washington v. Camarillo (Wn. S.Ct.1990).

California has taken a more realistic approach. Proof of particularity of time and place traditionally required for conviction of a crime is not an essential element of the offense of "continuous sexual abuse of a child". Rather, a child victim's testimony that sexual offenses occurred "Sundays after he came to live with us," "on camping trips", "in bathrooms and showers", "once or twice" a month, does not deny defendant due process. People v. Jones (Cal.S.Ct.1990).

The defendant was former navy pilot with top security clearance, a public school teacher and scout leader. The victim, his adopted son, was 9 when the offenses occurred. The resident child molester should not be immunized from substantial criminal liability merely because he has repeatedly molested his victim over an extended period of time. The court said a defendant has ample notice of the charge against him so he can prepare a defense where the alleged acts take place within a given time frame. Greater specificity goes to credibility of the victim, but is not needed to support conviction.

Confrontation. Protection of child witnesses from undue trauma in testifying face to face against their abusers runs into direct conflict with a defendant's constitutional right to confront the complaining witnesses. Several U.S. Supreme Court cases have tried to balance these rights of defendants with the state's interest in protecting children who have been victims of abuse.

A one-way screening device in the court room which blocked defendant from the view of the testifying victims violated the defendant's confrontation rights in Coy v. Iowa (S.Ct.1988). But while face to face confrontation is preferable, it is not indispensible. A six year old victim who allegedly was abused at defendant's kindergarten testified by one way video. This is acceptable where reliability of the testimony is otherwise assured: the witness is subject to cross exam, and the judge, jury and defendant can see the witness. Maryland v. Craig (S.Ct.1990). A four year old girl was physically present in the court room but was not called by the prosecution to testify in People v. White (Ill.App. 1990). Nonetheless, hearsay testimony by the girl's mother and babysitter was admissible as spontaneous declarations.

Prior Sexual Experience. The Court has established that the right of confrontation includes the right of reasonable cross examination to impeach the complaining witness. A black acquaintance rape defendant can cross examine a white female complaining witness regarding her alleged co-habitation with another black male to establish that she had a motive to lie when she claimed her intercourse with defendant was non-consensual. Olden v. Kentucky (S.Ct.1988).

Admission of such evidence is within the discretion of the trial court. Exclusion of testimony regarding victim's alleged promiscuity did not deny the defendant effective cross examination to impeach the witness. Washington v. Hudlow & Harper (Wn.S.Ct.1983). Nor does a statute requiring the accused to give the prosecution ten days notice to offer evidence of a prior sexual relationship with the alleged victim violate the defendant's confrontation rights. Michigan v. Lucas (S.Ct.1991).

Defendants frequently raise issues of prior sexual experience of young victims of abuse to challenge their credibility. A defendant charged with sodomy of his girlfriend's 10 year old niece can question the witness regarding her sexual knowledge, past lies and possible motives for lying about him. But her privacy rights block any questions about past sexual experience. Utah v. Moton (Utah S.Ct.1988). Contra, see Wisconsin v. Pulizzano (Wis.S.Ct.1990). A defendant is entitled to present evidence that the five year old complaining witness's knowledge of sexual matters may have arisen from sexual assaults prior to defendant's alleged sexual assault. Also, the trial court abused its discretion by permitting argument to the jury that the defendant was more likely to have committed the assault she was charged with because she had been sexually abused herself as a child.

Hearsay. Hearsay statements are inadmissible in part because they impinge on the confrontation clause. Conviction for lewd conduct with a minor was set aside where the child victim's out-of-court statements to a treating pediatrician lacked the "particularized guarantees of trustworthiness" required for admissibility of hearsay statements that do not fall under established exceptions to the hearsay rule. Idaho v. Wright (S.Ct.1990).

Spousal Privilege. The common law rule that one spouse cannot testify for or against another has a long-standing exception that the rule does not apply when one spouse has injured the other spouse. The exception was extended to crimes against the children of either spouse in United States v. Allery.

The teenage girl who is the victim of incest has an evidentiary problem compounded by the fact of her physical development. She is challenged with fabricating the story out of spite or vindictiveness or as an alibi for pregnancy. To protect against false charges in absence of corroborative evidence, the defendant in sex crimes is given wide latitude in cross examinations to show motive or credibility. State v. Peterson.

Fetal Homicide. Prosecution of persons who kill a viable fetus may be compromised by the operation of the common law. A man who assaulted his estranged wife and killed a viable 28–week–old fetus could not be charged with criminal homicide. Because "person" was not defined in the homicide statute, the common law, which holds the fetus is not a person, governs. Hollis v. Kentucky (Ky.S. Ct.1983).

Some states have enacted fetal homicide statutes to fill this common law hiatus. Such a statute applied to a 28 day old fetus does not violate the

14th Amendment.   Minnesota v. Merrill (Minn.S. Ct.1990). The court rejected defendant's argument that he was denied equal protection of the laws in that a woman can legally abort a non-viable fetus, saying the murdered woman did not consent to the murder of her fetus.

Drug Moms. Some child abuse is an unintentional consequence of parental action. Use of alcohol and illegal substances by pregnant women can cause their babies to suffer mild to severe neurological, mental, cardiac and respiratory defects. Fetal exposure to alcohol and other teratogenic substances is implicated in some 375,000 births each year, approximately one in 11 births nationwide. In some inner city hospitals, an estimated one in 10 babies is born drug-addicted, some of whom are afflicted with the HIV virus. These mothers may face charges of child neglect, and loss of custody or parental rights at birth. Some states have enacted statutes specifically allowing for prosecution of fetal abuse.

An early case upheld a neglect conviction of the mother of a newborn whose urine tested positive for cocaine. The court said that every human being has the legal right "to begin life unimpaired by physical or mental defects resulting from the neglect of another." Endresz v. Friedberg (N.Y.Ct. App.1969). However, the commissioner must prove neglect by a preponderance of the evidence, and must demonstrate a causal connection between the mother's conduct and the alleged harm to the child. In re Stefanel Tyesha C. & Sebastian M. (N.Y.App.Div. 1st Dept.1990).

Compare Matter of Fletcher (N.Y.Fam.Ct.1988) dismissing a neglect petition. The mother's admitted prenatal drug use and the newborn's positive toxicology report are not alone sufficient to establish the elements of child neglect. "This court sees no [legislative evidence] that New York State has seen fit to regulate a pregnant woman's body or to control her diet, medication, exercise or smoking habits on behalf of a fetus." An expectant mother, just like any other person, is protected by a constitutional right to privacy and bodily integrity which the State may not violate without showing a compelling state interest.

Several prosecutions of pregnant drug abusers have been pursued under statutes prohibiting delivery of drugs on charges of delivery via the umbilical cord. A conviction under such a count was upheld by an appellate court in Johnson v. Florida. A Michigan appeals court disallowed such charges as outside the intent of the statute, and a violation of the woman's due process rights. Michigan v. Hardy.

Pregnant substance abusers have traditionally been refused access to drug abuse programs. New York City has established a drug treatment program specifically designed for pregnant women.

B. STATUTORY RAPE

Statutory rape laws, like incest laws, are ostensibly designed to protect young females from sexual abuse. In both incest and statutory rape, by definition the consent of the victim is irrelevant. Proof of the prohibited act and the relationship or age of the victim is sufficient to sustain conviction.

The age of consent for statutory rape varies from 10 to 18. Some statutes require that the underage victim of statutory rape be of "previous chaste character". An unchaste defense will fail where the defendant was responsible for the previous loss of chastity. In re M.C.N. v. Florida (Fla.App.1987). Because juries are reluctant to convict a defendant of statutory rape where his age is close to that of the victim, newer codes set degrees of statutory rape with punishment differing as to the relative ages of the parties and the nature of the sexual involvement. A Florida trial court ruling that Florida's statutory rape law was unconstitutional on grounds that a minor who can consent to an abortion can consent to sexual intercourse was reversed on appeal. Florida v. Phillips & Williams (Fla.App. 4th Dist.1991).

Many newer codes are also gender neutral. As in incest, without corroborating evidence the testimony of the victim of statutory rape is traditionally insufficient to warrant submission of the case to the jury. United States v. Wiley. However, a conviction of forcible rape will stand on the uncorroborated testimony of a child under twelve where the child is competent to understand the nature of an oath. People v. Fuller.

Juvenile prostitution should be treated as a category of statutory rape. By definition the prostitutes are young, frequently below the age of consent. Juvenile male prostitutes often are not protected under statutory rape laws, although other criminal statutes may be applicable.

Rape of mental incompetents is generally classified as statutory rape. Institutionalized mental patients are particularly vulnerable to sexual abuse. State officials generally do not have an affirmative duty to protect citizens in their custody from injury. See Shaw by Strain v. Strackhouse (3d Cir.1990) where a profoundly retarded male patient confined to a wheelchair brought a § 1983 action against custodial personnel for failing to protect him from sexual assault by an unknown assailant. The court held professional defendants to the "professional judgment" standard and non-professionals to the "deliberate indifference" standard.

19.03 Rape

A. COMMON LAW DEFINITION

Rape at common law is defined as unlawful carnal knowledge of a woman without her consent. The law requires that the victim's testimony be corroborated by external evidence in each of the three material elements of the offense: force, or lack of consent; penetration, and identity of the assailant. People v. Linzy. Because the crime usually takes place without witnesses, corroboration is difficult to establish. Rape reform legislation limits the requirement of corroboration in some circumstances.

A key element of the crime is force, or non-consent, which must be proved by the prosecutor. The defendant will introduce evidence to establish that consent was in fact given. Words of denial are not sufficient to establish non-consent. That a woman meant "yes" when she was screaming "no" is an integral part of the law of rape. Law reflects this perspective by requiring evidence that the woman forcefully resisted the intercourse to establish that the intercourse was nonconsensual, and therefore rape.

B. PROSECUTION AND TRIAL

Rape Trauma Syndrome. Victims of rape sometimes exhibit specific behavior that a jury might find incomprehensible. The New York Court of Appeals admitted expert testimony of the rape trauma syndrome to aid jurors in understanding why a young rape victim initially refused to identify her known, armed assailant.

But expert testimony regarding "the presence, or indeed of the absence, of [rape trauma] symptoms" is not admissible where the testimony bears solely on proving that a rape has occurred. New York v. Taylor and Banks (N.Y.Ct.App.1990).

Hypnotic recall. Considerable appellate review has addressed the validity of introducing hypnotically recalled, enhanced or induced testimony. Early cases tended to treat such testimony by prosecuting witnesses the same as recollections refreshed in other legally acceptable ways, affecting its weight as evidence, but not its admissibility. Harding v. Maryland (Md.App.1968).

New York's high court examined and rejected the rationale for *Harding* in New York v. Hughes (N.Y.Ct.App.1983). In setting aside defendant's conviction for first degree rape, the court noted that no generally accepted scientific method exists for determining whether a statement made under hypnosis is "an accurate recollection, deliberate fabrication or unwitting confabulation." Hypnosis is akin to "truth serums and lie detectors, the results of which are generally excluded at trial". Similarly, Michigan v. Lee (Mich.S.Ct.1990) reversed conviction of a defendant for admission of hypnotically induced testimony relating to eye witness identification which linked the defendant to murder of an 11 year old girl.

Lie Detector Tests. Widespread prosecution practice requires women victims of rape to take lie detector tests before charges are pressed. This practice has been challenged as depriving women of due process rights in that evidence that is not admissible in trial because unreliable is accepted as sufficiently reliable to bar prosecution in the first place. Equal protection rights are invaded because only victims of rape are subject to lie detector tests to establish the credibility of their complaint. Women who fail these lie detector tests have sometimes been prosecuted for false criminal accusation.

Psychiatric Tests. Court ordered psychiatric tests for victims of sex crimes are a companion technique to the lie detector tests that operate to put a witness on trial. Psychiatric examinations are ordered almost exclusively for women. A defendant's request that a victim of sexual abuse be compelled to undergo a psychiatric examination to determine whether she was capable of fantasizing the abuse of which defendant was charged was rejected by the Iowa supreme court. The court has no constitutional, statutory nor common law authority to order such an examination. Iowa v. Gabrielson (Iowa S.Ct.1990).

Jury Instructions. Instructions to the jury in a rape case normally include three elements not required in other crimes of violence: (a) a warning regarding the vulnerability of rape prosecutions to false accusations or blackmail by the complaining witness; (b) a requirement for evidence corroborating the fact of penetration; and (c) a requirement for evidence that the victim actively resisted the aggressor. The first element is offered as justification for the second and third.

A trial court committed reversible error by refusing to give a cautionary instruction that rape is difficult to disprove but easy to charge in State v.

Smith. By contrast, after passage of the state equal rights amendment, the Pennsylvania legislature repealed the section of the criminal code requiring special instructions to the jury regarding the emotional involvement of the victim in a rape case, or the possibility that the rape did not in fact occur. The legislature regarded it as anachronistic that a sexually abused woman is a less capable witness than a male victim of a violent crime.

The difficulty of securing corroborative evidence, the fallacious inference that because a woman does not forcefully resist she has consented to the rape, plus severe penalty upon conviction, combine to make rape convictions extremely low in proportion to estimated occurrence of the crime. In one California survey, arrests were made for only sixteen percent of the forcible rapes reported; conviction rate was less than half of those arrested. Many rapes are never reported and thus are not reflected in the statistics.

C. NON–CONSENT

Non-consent is an element of the crime of rape; conversely, consent is a bar to prosecution. In crimes of violence other than rape, the focus of the prosecution is on the behavior of the defendant. In rape prosecutions, attention is focused on the victim's behavior—before, during and after the alleged rape—primarily to establish the presence or absence of consent. The requirement to establish non-consent is particularly difficult for the victim of acquaintance rape, a crime of greater proportion than official statistics disclose. The requirement of non-consent underlies the instruction to the jury that to convict the defendant they must find evidence that the victim actively resisted the aggression.

Fresh Complaint. An inference has long persisted at common law that a rape has not occurred if the victim doesn't quickly tell someone about it. Thus courts have long allowed testimony of a "fresh complaint" as an exception to the hearsay evidence rule. Because a victim of acquaintance rape is often reluctant to tell anyone of the assault, she lacks a "fresh complaint" to buttress her charge.

The New Jersey Supreme Court examined and reconfirmed the wisdom of the fresh complaint exception to the hearsay rule in companion cases. In New Jersey v. Hill (N.J.S.Ct.1990), the court said, "[N]o one contends that subtle and overt bias against women victims of rape has been eradicated." Given this continuing bias, if the fresh complaint exception were discarded, "rape victims would suffer" whenever jurors believed that women who do not complain have not been raped. "Hence, we hesitate to discard the benefit of this rule to a woman who does complain without a clearer understanding of the burdens the rule may impose on the woman who does not complain."

In New Jersey v. Bethune (N.J.S.Ct.1990) the court said that a fresh complaint made by a five year old girl in response to questioning is admissible so long as the questioning was not coercive.

1. Resistance

Early law specified that the woman must resist to her utmost for a man to be convicted of rape. This stringent view has been discarded, but the requirement of active resistance remains. Traditionally, the victim of rape is excused from active resistance only if the assaulter in fact uses deadly force or the victim objectively and reasonably fears that the aggressor will use deadly force. Absence of active resistance is treated as consent, and consent negates that the intercourse took place against her wishes. Current law is unsettled as to the degree of resistance necessary, particularly as to unarmed assault. The resistance, however, must continue until physical penetration has occurred.

Verbal Denial. Generally, verbal protests unaccompanied by physical resistance are viewed as pretext. The jury was cautioned that mere verbal protestations are insufficient in State v. Dizon. However, where there is an implied threat of injury, verbal denial is sufficient to sustain a conviction. State v. Gonzales.

Mental and Physical Disability. Statutes and modern case law override older decisions that mental inability to offer resistance because of drugs or alcohol prevents a conviction for rape. Defendants in New York v. Di Noia (N.Y.App.Div.2d Dept.

1984) appealed convictions for raping a woman who was incapacited by "a narcotic or intoxicating substance". The court affirmed their conviction even though the prosecution failed to specify and prove what substance caused the incapacitation. Testimony established that one appellant said several days before the incident that he wanted to drug the victim and "take her out and gang bang her". Motel maids testified the victim was carried out of the motel, unconscious, over the shoulder of one of a group of males. Nor did the state need to prove who administered the incapacitating substance.

Physical disability on the part of the woman, however, is not in itself sufficient to nullify the requirement of resistance. The conviction of a man accused of raping a cerebral palsy victim after he had verbally threatened her was overturned on the ground that the woman did not resist with sufficient physical force. State v. Perry. A statute defining rape as sexual intercourse "by force and against the person's will" refers to actual physical force, and does not include threats of harm of lesser magnitude than death, bodily injury, or kidnapping. State v. Colson.

Objective or Subjective. Whether the degree of resistance that the victim must use in order to establish non-consent is to be judged subjectively or objectively is at variance.

Argument that the fear experienced by the victim should be addressed from her perspective was specifically rejected in Rusk v. State. Such a position would require submission to the jury in every case where the victim testified that she consented because she was afraid. Dissenting justices in *Rusk* stated that the majority improperly invaded the province of the trial jury, giving new life to myths about the crime of rape. An objective standard from a woman's perspective was upheld in Lottie v. State. The woman must manifest her opposition through active resistance, but the jury was nonetheless properly instructed that she need offer no more resistance than her age, strength and attendant circumstances make reasonable.

Statutory Change. The court in California v. Salazar (Cal.App.1983) rejected defendant's claim that the trial court erred in failing to instruct the jury that resistance by the victim was an element of rape. The clause in the state rape statute reading "Where a person resists, but the person's resistance is overcome by force or violence", was replaced by "Where it is accomplished against a person's will by means of force or fear of immediate and unlawful bodily injury". The court observed, "[I]t is no longer necessary for a rape victim to develop corroborative evidence by resisting and thereby precipitating further physical violence."

2. Past Sexual Conduct

Interrogation by the defense seeks to establish that the woman consented to the act of rape. This is done through inquiry into the woman's past sexual behavior, both as to experience unrelated to the incident under accusation, and prior experience with the defendant. The thrust of the inquiry is twofold: to impeach the credibility of the witness and to establish that she did in fact consent in the instance at trial. Conversely, questions of the accused rapist's past sexual history cannot be raised because the defendant is protected by the constitutional right against self incrimination.

Contemporary rape shield laws limit inquiry into the past sexual behavior of the complaining witness, both as to credibility and consent. The Massachusetts shield law was interpreted to command closure of sexual assault trials during testimony of complainants who are minors and to allow the judge to close other portions of the trial. The interpretation was overturned as a violation of First, Sixth and Fourteenth Amendment rights. Globe Newspaper Co. v. Superior Court (S.Ct.1982).

Women can be convicted of rape. A female defendant who incites, sponsors and intentionally aids in the commission of the offense by male defendants is properly indictable. New York v. Merfert (N.Y.Co.Ct.1976). Some states have gender neutral rape statutes which support charges for female and single sex rape. Brooks v. Maryland (Md.App.1975).

D. MARITAL RAPE

Under common law, marital rape is a logical contradiction in terms since common law defines rape as "unlawful carnal knowledge" of a woman, and a wife is lawfully wed to her husband. Sir Matthew Hale, a seventeenth century English jurist, wrote that the husband cannot rape his wife because under the contract of marriage the wife "hath given up herself in this kind to her husband, which she cannot retract." Primarily on the authority of Hale's statement, a marital rape exemption was explicitly codified in many state statutes.

The tendency in both legislation and case law is to limit the spousal rape exemption, particularly as to couples that are living apart.

A defendant living apart from his wife under a court order of protection was convicted of forcibly raping his wife. The court agreed that the statute was unconstitutional because it applied only to males and extended its coverage to women. The court also struck the marital exemption, finding "no rational basis exists" for distinguishing between marital and nonmarital rape. Arguments about the "sanctity of marriage" and "reconciliation of spouses" cannot withstand the simplest scrutiny. New York v. Liberta (N.Y.Ct.App.1984). The New Jersey supreme court refused to imply an exception for spousal rape in a statute which was silent on the issue because the notion that the wife has consented to forceful assault is "offensive to

our valued ideals of personal liberty." New Jersey
v. Smith.

The common law spousal exception to rape has
been repealed or modified by statute in a few
states. The revised New Jersey code provides:
"No actor shall be presumed to be incapable of
committing a crime under this chapter because of
* * * marriage to the victim."

19.04   Pornography

A link between abuse of women and children
and verbal and visual images that portray their
sexual or violent exploitation has not been conclusively proved. If such a link is established, there
will be a direct clash between opposing constitutional rights: the right of freedom of speech and
press on the one hand, and on the other, the right
of women and children to be free from physical
violence against their persons.

Censorship. Some groups want prior censorship
of pornographic material and films. Others try to
contain pornography through education and boy-
cott rather than prior constraint, which has repeatedly been held unconstitutional by the Supreme Court as a violation of First Amendment
rights of free speech, press and expression.

Obscene material which falls under the standards of Miller v. California (S.Ct.1973) is not protected by the First Amendment. But a state cannot padlock bookstores and seize contents without
a judicial determination that some of the materials

sold by the stores are legally obscene. Fort Wayne Books, Inc. v. Indiana (S.Ct.1989). Nor may a city create a prior restraint on sexually oriented speech through an arbitrary licensing scheme. FW/PBS Inc., d/b/a Paris Adult Bookstore II v. Dallas (S.Ct. 1990).

Much pornography does not meet the *Miller* test for obscenity, and thus is protected speech. Some control of porn can be achieved through zoning regulations of adult theaters where the ordinance provides reasonable alternative avenues for communication of ideas. Renton v. Playtime Theatres, Inc. (S.Ct.1986).

An attempt by Indianapolis to create a statutory civil remedy for victims of pornography as a class failed as an invasion of First Amendment rights. See chapter nine re American Booksellers Association, Inc. v. Hudnut (7th Cir.1985).

Dial–A–Porn. Dial-a-porn vendors have a lucrative business. Their business is aided when the telephone company does their billing for them. But they cannot compel a telephone company to carry their messages. The 9th Circuit in Carlin Communications, Inc. v. Mountain States Tel. & Tel. Co. upheld the right of Mountain States Telephone Company, as a private business, to refuse to carry dial-a-porn on its 976 network. The refusal does not violate the telephone company's duty to offer service without discrimination under the Arizona public utility law.

A federal law banning "any obscene or indecent communication for commercial purposes" over interstate telephone lines at any time of day was unanimously overturned by the Supreme Court in Sable Communications of Cal., Inc. v. FCC (S.Ct. 1989). Only obscene, not indecent, dial-a-porn messages may be banned.

"For Adults Only". As a response, Congress enacted a new law which limits the ban on "indecent" commercial communications to those under 18. Adults wanting to use the special lines for indecent messages must pre-subscribe to the service in writing. A panel for the ninth circuit upheld federal regulations under the law. Information Providers' Coalition for Defense of the First Amendment v. FCC (9th Cir.1991). A district court in the second circuit struck the statute in American Information Enterprises, Inc. v. Thornburgh (S.D.N.Y.1990). The court said that protection of minors from indecent telephone speech is a compelling purpose, but the means selected was not the least invasive possible. A similar state statute was ruled unconstitutional in Fabulous Associates, Inc. v. Pennsylvania Public Utility Com'n (3d Cir.1990).

Most states have statutes similar to a Virginia statute prohibiting display of sexually explicit books "harmful" to juveniles "in a manner whereby juveniles may examine or peruse" them. The statute was upheld as not unconstitutionally vague in American Booksellers Association v. Virginia (4th Cir.1989).

Child Pornography. Attempts to curtail exploitation of children as porn models have had some success.

Under Stanley v. Georgia (S.Ct.1969), one has a constitutional right to possess obscene material in the privacy of one's home. But an exception is carved out for statutes which seek to "protect the victims of child pornography". Possession of child porn in one's home can be criminalized without infringing the First Amendment. Osborne v. Ohio (S.Ct.1990).

The Court reasoned that pictures of children permanently record the abuse of the victim. A ban on possession of child porn encourages destruction of the pictures. It also may protect other children since evidence indicates that lewd pictures of children are used to entice other victims into posing as models or sexual activity. Justice Brennan, dissenting, argued that the language was unconstitutionally broad, and could permit prosecution of persons who owned pictures "even of toddlers romping unclothed." The Supreme Court earlier had upheld a New York statute criminalizing the distribution of child pornography. See New York v. Ferber (S.Ct.1982) where the Court says the *Miller* tests of "community standards", "redeeming value" and "prurient interest" are not relevant to child porn.

The Federal Child Pornography Statute is not void for vagueness. Congress intended a broader term than "obscene" in prohibiting "lascivious" exhibition of genitals. Pictures mailed by defendant to an undercover sting officer showed nude prepubescent girls facing cameras with their legs apart to expose their genitals. A caption read, "Little Girls F—k too." United States v. Arvin (9th Cir.1990). Nor are defendants in child pornography prosecutions that arise from a mail order sting operation victims of "outrageous" government conduct where they voluntarily respond to the mail solicitation. United States v. Mitchell (9th Cir.1990).

19.05   Victim Remedies

A.   LEGISLATION

Increasing focus has been directed in recent years to the victim of crime. Many states and the federal government have crime victim restitution statutes. Some statutes exclude compensation to the victim who is living with the person who commits the crime, a restriction which bars compensation to battered wives and abused children.

The victims' rights statutes often require notification to victims of critical court proceedings and allow victims to make impact statements at sentencing, even in capital cases. Payne v. Tennessee (S.Ct.1991), ruled that such statements do not violate the Eighth Amendment ban on cruel and inhuman punishment. Overturning two recent cases, *Payne* reasoned that stare decisis has less import where "the basic underpinnings" in any closely decided constitutional precedent were challenged by "spirited dissents". Justice Stevens, dissenting, said such evidence sheds no light on the defendant's guilt or moral culpability, and serves no purpose but to encourage jurors to decide in favor of death rather than life on the basis of emotion rather than reason.

New York's so-called Son of Sam law was upheld against First Amendment challenge in Simon & Schuster, Inc. v. Fischetti (2d Cir.1990). The statute requires escrow of earnings from books derived from exploitation of crime to assure payment of damages which victims may recover in civil judgments. Although the statute is content based, it is narrowly drawn to serve the strong public interest in preventing criminals from profiting from their crimes while the victims are uncompensated.

B. CIVIL ACTIONS

Civil actions are proliferating against both the actor and third parties who may have had some actionable relationship between the actor and the victim. Recovery is uncertain. The lesser value generally placed on women's work is reflected in lower compensation for damages in cases involving women victims. Expert testimony for the value of homemakers' services has supported higher damages in some wrongful death cases. De Long v. Erie County (N.Y.Ct.App.1983).

Suit Against Assaulter

Civil actions against the assaulter are being litigated with increasing success. Tort actions by battered wives and children against family members for intentional torts are now possible in most jurisdictions because of abrogation of the common law intrafamily immunity doctrines, as discussed chapter twelve. Civil actions for acquaintance rape are also being successfully litigated. deElche v. Jacobsen.

Private Third Party Liability

Landlords, innkeepers, and common carriers may be liable to a victim under a theory that defendant breached a duty to protect the plaintiff from violent assault.

Landlord Liability. A landlord's failure to provide security is a breach of duty to the plaintiff who was assaulted in the hallway, a common area of the building over which the landlord retained control. Kline v. 1500 Massachusetts Ave. Apartment Corp. (D.C.Cir.1970). A man struck with a tire iron by a prostitute when he refused her advances in a hotel recovered against the hotel in Jenness v. Sheraton–Cadillac Properties, Inc. (Mich.App.1973).

A cause of action for negligence was stated where the manager of a condominium complex hired a man with a record of criminal assault to commit murder without checking his references and assigned him to maintenance, which gave him access to passkeys. He entered the victim's apartment and allegedly assaulted her. Williams v. Feather Sound, Inc.

Media Liability. Suits against the media by victims who have allegedly been injured by viewers who "copycat" media violence are generally unsuccessful on First Amendment grounds. A TV show depicting "artificial rape" with a plumber's helper of an adolescent female inspired the assault of a nine year old girl with a bottle by juvenile assailants who had viewed and discussed the film. The court said that civil liability for speech does not extend outside the law of defamation. To allow negligence actions for television broadcasting would lead to self censorship, which would "dampen the vigor and limit the variety of public debate." Olivia N. v. National Broadcasting Co., Inc. (Cal.App.1981). Similarly, a tort action will not lie against a magazine for publishing an advertisement seeking to find an ex-marine willing to take "high risk assignments," through which a murder victim's husband recruited her assassin. Publication fell within the standard of conduct established by the state's risk-utility analysis. Eimann v. Soldier of Fortune Magazine, Inc. (5th Cir.1989).

Nor will a civil suit lie against a newspaper for publishing a rape victim's name in violation of state law. The Supreme Court ruled that the statute impermissibly punished the paper for publishing truthful information acquired from official sources. Dissenters said the Court obliterated a noteworthy legal invention of the 20th century: "the tort of the publication of private facts." The Florida Star v. B.J.F. (S.Ct.1989).

Legitimate Drugs. Other actions attempt to recover damages against sellers of legitimate drugs, alcohol and guns because of injuries caused by their customers. A high proportion of injuries from domestic violence is associated with alcohol abuse. Conventional negligence law blocks liability of third party providers of alcohol on grounds the drunk actors are the independent, proximate cause of any injuries suffered at their hands. Some 34 states have enacted dramshop laws, with varying provisions, to override this rule. The Iowa statute supports a common law action against social hosts. See Clark v. Mincks (Iowa S.Ct.1985).

An award for selling a gun to a drunk who then killed his wife's lover was upheld in Viscomi v. S.S. Kresge Co., K.Mart (N.Y.App.Div. 4th Dept.1988). But compare Delahanty v. Hinckley (D.C.Cir.1990), which denied recovery to Officer Delahanty who suffered injuries when Hinckley attempted to assassinate President Reagan.

Governmental Liability

Civil suits against federal, state and local entities and personnel for injuries stemming from their actions or omissions are frequently barred by governmental immunity, as discussed in Chapter eight.

Prosecutorial and Judicial Immunity. Prosecutors are subject to civil suit for advice given to police during the investigative phase of a criminal case. Such advice is not "so intimately associated with the judicial phase of the criminal process that it qualifies for absolute immunity." Burns v. Reed (S.Ct.1991). *Burns* allowed a civil suit by a woman subjected to hypnosis by police investigators under advice from the prosecuting attorney. The police sought to elicit information under hypnosis that would indicate whether the woman suffered from a split personality and had murdered her two children. Other evidence was lacking and she had already tested negative in handwriting analysis, voice stress and lie detector tests. Compare Collins v. King County (Wn.App.1987), which extended immunity of the prosecuting attorney to the prosecuting attorney's victim assistance unit in a case where a man murdered his wife and assaulted their three children.

For judicial immunity, see Stump v. Sparkman (S.Ct.1978). Judges retain judicial immunity even if the action they take is in error, is done maliciously or in excess of authority. Judges are subject to civil liability only when they act in clear absence of all jurisdiction.

No Affirmative Duty. Even where immunity is not applicable, the Court has ruled that municipal and local authorities have no affirmative duty to protect persons who are not in state custody from violence by private third parties. This rule applies even where the public personnel are grossly negligent in carrying out their public employment. De-Shaney v. Winnebago County Dept. of Social Services (S.Ct.1989). The four year old victim in *De-Shaney* was profoundly and permanently brain damaged from beatings by his father. Social workers had repeatedly received reports and observed evidence of the abuse but failed to take action to protect the boy. The Court said that the Fourteenth Amendment's due process clause guards only against state deprivations of life, liberty or property. Concerns of federalism dictate that states should decide whether they want to shoulder affirmative responsibility in factual circumstances like *DeShaney*.

The Eighth Circuit refused to apply the rationale of *DeShaney* in Freeman v. Ferguson (8th Cir. 1990). The court said that at some point, actions of municipal authorities do create a federal constitutional duty to protect. In *Freeman*, a police chief was lax in enforcing a restraining order against a personal friend, who, unrestrained, shot to death his estranged wife and their daughter.

Deliberate Indifference. The Supreme Court has established that section 1983 liability will lie against public personnel who display "deliberate indifference" to the constitutional rights of persons with whom they come in contact. Estelle v. Gamble (S.Ct.1976). Deliberate indifference was established when a municipality failed to investigate repeated complaints that a traffic officer forced women to have sex in a cemetery across the street from the station house after arresting and detaining the women for traffic offenses which the victims denied committing. Harris v. City of Pagedale (8th Cir.1987). Accord, Wood v. Ostrander (9th Cir.1989).

A major victory for battered women was won in Thurman v. City of Torrington (D.Conn.1984). This particularly egregious section 1983 case found the Torrington police deprived Thurman of her constitutional rights under the Fourteenth Amendment in failing to protect her from her husband. The Torrington policy had an informal policy not to arrest husbands in domestic disputes. This constituted providing lesser protection to wives who were victims of domestic violence than to other victims of violence. The court applied the gender standard to this informal policy and said the sex classification was unlikely to have a "substantial" relationship to an important governmental purpose.

Several state courts have found liability under similar circumstances. For negligent release of a psychiatric patient from a state hospital who injures a foreseeable victim, see Wofford v. Eastern State Hospital (Okl.S.Ct.1990). Issuance of a protective restraining order against an abusive husband imposes a statutory duty on the police department to enforce the order. Nearing v. Weaver (Or.S.Ct.1983). Similarly, Massachusetts was responsible for sexual assaults in a locked storage closet against preadolescent boys by a public school teacher, a probationary convicted sex offender with a 22 year history of sex offenses. A.L. v. Commonwealth of Massachusetts (Mass.S.Ct.1988). Compare D.T. v. Independent School District, where sexual abuse at a summer basketball camp lacked state action. (10th Cir.1989).

CHAPTER 20

DEFENDANTS

For every victim of crime, there is a potential criminal defendant. This chapter begins with a gender profile of the criminal and the elements necessary to constitute a crime. Following are specific instances of disparate treatment between men and women under criminal law.

20.01 Gender Profile

Classifying criminal offenders by sex sharply exposes the proportion of men compared to women for number and nature of crimes committed. State and federal institution populations in 1988 numbered 627,400 inmates. Of these, 5 percent were female, and 95 percent male. Most women are convicted of white collar crimes—forgery, shoplifting and fraud. Persons convicted of crimes classified as violent constitute approximately two thirds of the prison population. Females in 1986 accounted for an estimated 1 in 15 of first time offenders incarcerated in state institutions for violent offenses.

Statistics do not reveal how many of these female inmates are battered women who ultimately killed their batterers. The low recidivist rate for

351

violent offense for females, only 1 in 50 compared
to males, suggests that women who resort to violence do so on more specific provocation than do
men. Some governors have pardoned or commuted
sentences of battered women serving terms for
killing their batterers.

Estimates of women held in jails is variable,
numbering at any given time some 9 percent of the
jail population. These women have generally been
arrested for the crimes of prostitution, alcoholism
and drug abuse.

The average woman in custody is a minority,
under 30, unemployed and single. She is also a
mother, usually with more than one child. Some
women become mothers while in custody.

20.02 Elements of Crime

Every crime has two elements. First, the specific act defined by statute as criminal must have
been committed. This is known as actus reus.
The second necessary element of crime is mens rea,
or criminal intent. An actus reus committed by an
insane person is not a crime because the requisite
state of mind is lacking. Conversely, an intent to
commit a crime without actual performance of it
also is not a crime because the requisite actus reus
is lacking. Both actus reus and mens rea must be
proved by the prosecution as necessary elements of
criminal behavior. However, the distinct requirements of these two elements sometimes disappear
in disparate treatment between men and women in

crimes involving sex. Prostitution ordinances that classify by sex or are selectively enforced are examples.

20.03 Statutory Classification

A. MARITAL RELATIONSHIP

Gender specific classification of crime stems principally from common law notions of sex roles which are incorporated into criminal statutes. Nowhere is this more apparent than in criminal law surrounding the marital relationship.

The marital community protects the husband (most often) from conviction for crime because of the spousal witness privilege. Until recently either spouse could bar testimony by the other spouse regarding crimes committed against third persons, both as to verbal communications made by the defendant spouse to the witness spouse and as to events which the witness spouse may have directly observed. Trammel v. United States limits the spousal privilege to the witness spouse, who can neither be compelled to testify nor foreclosed from testifying against the other spouse.

Common law regarded marriage as a state of coverture. A wife was under the cover, both as to protection and authority, of her husband. The resulting physical, moral and intellectual control of the husband over the wife, plus the concept of the marital partners as an indivisible unity, combined to place criminal responsibility on the husband for any crimes committed in his presence by his wife, who was presumed to be under the coercion of her husband and was therefore an unwilling participant. The Nineteenth Amendment bars the plea of coverture by women as defense to crimes committed against the federal government. United States v. Hinson. The state equal rights amendment grounded abandonment of the defense of coverture by the Pennsylvania Supreme Court in Commonwealth v. Santiago. At common law, a husband and wife could not be guilty of conspiracy with each other since they were the same legal person. This rule was rejected in United States v. Dege.

B. FEMALE

1. Status Offenses

At common law, both males and females became subject to prosecution for crime as adults at age 14. Codes establishing juvenile courts provided jurisdictional age differentials, normally setting an older age for women. These statutes have been ruled unconstitutional under equal protection challenges. Crisp v. Mayabb (10th Cir.1981). Although de jure gender based age differentials have been eliminated, de facto enforcement of status offenses, making criminal such nonspecific behavior as truancy and incorrigibility, is frequently more stringent against juvenile girls. Adult women are arrested for offenses to which men are not subject: soliciting, streetwalking, being a lewd and dissolute person. Women are frequently arrested under these statutes for harassment purposes only, the officer having no intent to prosecute.

Status offenses have been challenged on due process grounds because they fail to give fair notice of the activity that is prohibited, and, on equal protection grounds, because the vague language places too great discretionary power in the police, thus fostering selective enforcement practices. In addition, status offenses are an invasion of the right to freedom of mobility on public roads, a fundamental precept of personal liberty. Shapiro v. Thompson.

General vagrancy laws were ruled unconstitutional in Papachristou v. City of Jacksonville. Justice Douglas, writing for a unanimous Court, said "A presumption that people * * * who look suspicious to the police are to become future criminals is too precarious for a rule of law." Nonetheless, vague status offense laws are still widely enforced.

Expressive Activity. A state can ban non-obscene nude dancing even though it constitutes expressive conduct within the outer perimeters of the First Amendment. Barnes v. Glen Theatre, Inc. Chief Justice Rehnquist, writing for the Court, noted that symbolic speech is not entitled to full First Amendment protection. The substantial governmental interest in protecting societal order and morality is unrelated to the suppression of free expression, since public nudity is the evil the state seeks to prevent. State constitutions may be more protective of nude dancing. See Seattle v. Johnson (Wn.App.1990).

2. Prostitution

With the exception of a few counties exercising local option in Nevada, prostitution is illegal throughout the United States. Although language of the statutes and interpretive case law varies, prostitution can generally be defined as indiscriminate sexual intercourse for hire. However, a state can remove the requirement of exchange of money. A statute defining prostitution as "licentious sexual intercourse without consideration" does not offend the constitution. Tatzel v. State (Fla.S.Ct. 1978).

An ordinance which does not define "sexual conduct" and "sexual acts" was ruled void for vagueness in South Euclid v. Richardson (Ohio S.Ct. 1990). Compare Seattle v. Slack (Wn.S.Ct.1989), which ruled a prostitution loitering statute did not offend equal protection or due process rights.

Rarely do statutes make the customer criminally liable for seeking out a prostitute or for purchasing prostitution. Where customers are subject to prosecution, the criminal penalty is often considerably less than that set for the prostitute. Prosecution of men is minimal in states which have gender neutral prostitution statutes.

A gender neutral prostitution statute was sustained against charges of selective enforcement in People v. Superior Court of Alameda County. The police department's practice of employing more male than female decoys was justified because the enforcement effort legitimately focused on the profiteer rather than the customer of commercial vice.

Alameda also said it was not a denial of equal protection to subject prostitutes to custodial arrest while releasing their customers with written notice to appear in court, nor to quarantine the arrested prostitutes, but not the customers. Prostitutes do not ordinarily satisfy standards for release, and customers are less likely to communicate venereal diseases.

A dissenting justice wrote, "Several centuries of law enforcement history belie any claim that a 'profiteer'-directed enforcement program is an effective means of eliminating prostitution * * *." Experience with sex neutral enforcement demonstrated that "the arrest of male customers, coupled with newspaper publicity * * * resulted * * * in a 'devastating' reduction in observed levels of prostitution related offenses." He concluded that arrest of male customers in addition to female prostitutes is a singularly more effective law enforcement strategy than the approach traditionally employed by the police.

AIDS Testing. Persons charged or convicted of crimes involving sex may be subjected to technological procedures not imposed for other offenses. Some states have criminalized a defendant's actions which the individual knows may transmit the

HIV virus to another person. HIV testing has been mandated in some states for convicted prostitutes and sex offenders, and proposed for these arrestees.

A California law mandating that all convicted prostitutes be tested for the HIV virus was upheld against search and seizure, due process and equal protection claims. The state's special need to stem the spread of AIDS outweighs the prostitutes' privacy rights, which are only minimally intruded by blood tests and the restricted publication of test results. Love v. Superior Court (Cal.App.1990).

Compare Washington v. Farmer (Wn.S.Ct.1991), which ruled unconstitutional a mandatory HIV test to determine severity of the sentence for a defendant convicted of patronizing a juvenile prostitute. The outcome of the test was irrelevant to whether the defendant was infected at the time of the criminal acts for which he was convicted.

Element of Consent. The element of consent of the male customer of the prostitute invites comparison to the prosecution of men for rape. Fictitious consent is imputed to the female victim of rape if she does not offer sufficient resistance; and presence of consent is a bar to prosecution of the male because the element of mens rea is absent. It can be argued on equal protection grounds that actual consent of the male customer should therefore be a bar to prosecution of the female in a prostitution charge. It is anomalous that a male is not prosecuted for rape although the female has in fact not consented, but that a female is prosecuted for prostitution when the male has in fact consented. The doing of the act is sufficient to satisfy mens rea for the woman in a prostitution charge but is insufficient to satisfy mens rea for the male in a rape charge.

This inconsistent position of the law suggests that the alleged purposes of rape and prostitution laws are not as publicly claimed, although an inarticulate premise that would reconcile the inconsistency is at best conjectural. Inconsistent laws tend not to be enforceable. It is not to be wondered that prostitution and rape statutes have a selective, ineffective enforcement record. The movement of women to equal treatment before the law has exposed discrepancies in treatment between men and women for sex crimes. Open discussion of the discrepancies should in the long term be beneficial.

C. MALE

Aside from the male only registration for the draft, upheld in Rostker v. Goldberg, statutes that single out men for prosecution are predominately sex crimes—rape, statutory rape and incest. The decision in Michael M. v. Superior Court of Sonoma County allows states to prosecute only men for these offenses. *Rostker* and *Michael M.* are discussed in Chapter 7 under the constitutionality of single sex statutory classifications.

Where the rape statute limits the offense to penetration of a female victim's sex organ by a male's sex organ, the constitutional prohibition against ex post facto laws blocks conviction of rape for forcing a child to commit oral sodomy upon him.   McGahee v. Florida (Fla.App.1990).

A group of women wearing buttons reading "Women Against Rape" was allowed to sit a few feet from the jury box in Norris v. Risley (9th Cir.1990). On a habeas corpus petition, the Ninth Circuit set aside the defendant's conviction for rape as a denial of due process. The message of the buttons eroded the presumption of innocence, and was all the more dangerous because not subject to confrontation and cross-examination.

20.04 Substance and Procedure

A. THE TRIAL

Because most criminal defendants and justice system personnel are male, criminal law has been shaped from a male perspective. This circumstance has operated to make a fair trial less likely for women defendants, particularly those accused of violent crime.

1. Impartial Trial

Taylor v. Louisiana and its progeny, in increasing the number of women serving on juries, has removed one bar to a fair trial for women. Others, however, remain, including persistent use of male pronouns in statement of legal principles, an unconscious linguistic bias which may subtly influence lawyers, judges and juries in prosecution of women defendants.

2. Self Defense

Past experience of a female defendant with a male assailant and use of the male pronoun in jury instructions on the law of self defense were at issue in State v. Wanrow. Yvonne Wanrow was convicted of second degree murder in forcefully protecting herself and her children against an abusing male. The conviction was reversed and remanded for improper instructions to the jury on the law of self defense as it related to the defendant.

At common law, self defense is an affirmative defense which the defendant must prove by a preponderance of the evidence. South Carolina and Ohio retain this rule. See Martin v. Ohio (S.Ct. 1987). Other states require the prosecution, once a self defense plea is made, to prove that the force used was unreasonable under the circumstances. Generally, the force used to repel the attack cannot exceed the force utilized by the attacker. Thus one cannot normally use a weapon to repel an unarmed attack. In addition, the danger must be imminent, and the victim must retreat if possible to escape the assault. The extent to which prior experiences with the attacker are part of the "circumstances" may therefore be critical to establishing self defense. Particularly is this true for circumstances such as those in *Wanrow,* where the murdered man was a neighbor with a reputation of

sexual abuse of children, and where abusive husbands or boyfriends are killed by their battered
women.

In reversing Wanrow's conviction, the Washington state supreme court found two errors in the
jury instructions. The first was the limitation of
the defendant's anticipation of bodily harm to
events "at or immediately before the killing." The
jury is entitled to consider past events in determining whether the defendant had reasonable grounds
to fear severe bodily injury.

The second error was use of the male gender in
the instructions, which said that unless the defendant had reasonable grounds "to believe that *his*
person is in imminent danger of death or great
bodily harm * * * *he* had no right to repel a
threatened assault * * * by the use of a deadly
weapon * * * " (emphasis by *Wanrow* court).

The court said that persistent use of the mascu-
line gender [nine times in one sentence] leaves the
jury with the impression the objective standard to
be applied "is that applicable to an altercation
between two men." To require a 5'4" woman with
a cast on her leg and using a crutch to somehow
repel an assault by a 6'2" intoxicated man without
employing weapons in her defense "violates the
respondent's right to equal protection of the law."
The respondent was entitled to have the jury consider her actions in the light of her own percep-
tions of the situation.

Self Defense Against Rape. Whether a victim
may use deadly force and kill her attacker in order
to resist rape depends upon the state where the
rape took place. A third of the states allow deadly
force to repel a felony, and expressly list rape as a
felony which justifies resistance with deadly force.
Another third of the states allow deadly force to
repel a felony. Courts in many of these states,
perhaps gratuitiously, read the legislative mind as
not intending to include the felony of rape. See
Washington v. Castro, upholding a conviction of
manslaughter for an 18 year old male who pleaded
the killing took place to ward off a felonious rape
assault. (Wn.App.1981). Whether a victim in the
remaining states can use deadly force to repel rape
is unclear.

At issue in California v. Caudillo (Cal.S.Ct.1978)
was a statute that placed heavier sentences on
burglary, robbery or rape if "great bodily injury"
was inflicted in the course of the assault. The
California Supreme Court, acceding to legislative
intent, ruled that forcible rape is not an infliction
of "great bodily injury" where the victim did not
have "any serious impairment of physical condition or any protracted impairment of function of
any portion of her body."

Where the self defense plea is allowed, the vic-
tim/defendant must convince the jury to reject
prosecution claims that her belief of fear of rape
was unreasonable, that the danger was not imminent, and that she had no place to retreat. Texas

allows deadly force to repel kidnapping or rape. Nonetheless, a black woman who testified that she was kidnapped and gang raped by four white males failed to overcome the prosecutor's argument that she invited the assault as a prostitute. She was convicted of first degree murder. Thomas v. Texas (Tex.Crim.App.1979).

The celebrated conviction of Inez Garcia for murdering her rapist was overturned in California v. Garcia (Cal.App.1975). A second jury acquitted her on grounds that the murder was not revenge for the first rape, but in defense of the threatened second rape.

Defense Against Battering. Battered women who kill their battering husbands or boy friends traditionally have pleaded temporary insanity, and, like Julia Hoyt, often not successfully. They run the risk of being committed to a mental institution for an indeterminate time if found not guilty by reason of insanity. See Foucha v. Louisiana (La.S.Ct. 1990).

More in tune with the facts, many battered women in recent years have pleaded that they killed their partner in self defense. But battered women have met legal resistance because their circumstances do not match those of the barroom brawls that shaped Anglo–American law of self defense. An initial difficulty is to overcome judicial treatment of wife beating as a misdemeanor even though the legislature has termed it a felony. California v. Jones (Cal.App.1961).

It is well established that a homicide is not justifiable in the absence of imminent danger. A battered woman who kills her sleeping husband has little likelihood of prevailing with a self defense plea. California v. Aris (Cal.App.1989).

As *Wanrow* indicated, contemporary law is providing a more realistic standard for establishing the elements of imminence of harm and use of non-excessive force. A problem remains, however, in face of the common law principle that dictates that the victim must retreat to escape the assault. Only against a wall or at the door of his castle, his home, can the victim take a stand to protect himself with deadly force. A battered woman cannot retreat; she is already home, frequently with her back against a wall. But for her it is no castle. A prejudice persists that she has an obligation to retreat out of her house. "Why didn't she just move out?"

The battered woman, from long experience with the spiral of abuse which increases in ferocity with each assault, usually kills just before the most violent stage erupts. As a consequence, the jury may disbelieve that her fear was reasonable, or the danger imminent.

Battered Woman Syndrome. Expert testimony on the battered woman syndrome is now admitted in many jurisdictions to aid the jury in deciding if the defendant acted in self defense. Maine v. Anaya (Me.S.Ct.1981); Ohio v. Koss (Ohio S.Ct. 1990). The testimony may aid the jury in assessing the reasonableness of the defendant's belief that she was in imminent danger of death. New Jersey v. Kelly (N.J.S.Ct.1984), or understanding why the battered woman delayed reporting and did not leave the batterer. Washington v. Ciskie (Wn. S.Ct.1988). But the battered woman syndrome is not admissible to establish an alleged accidental death, nor to establish general credibility. Washington v. Hanson (Wn.App.1990).

3. Search and Seizure

Traffic Offenses. A long standing practice of the Chicago police department to subject women but not men to strip and cavity searches following arrest for minor offenses was at issue in Jane Does v. City of Chicago. Among the more than 200 plaintiffs was a woman who went to the police station to protest a ticket issued when her car was parked on a snow covered street and could not be driven. She was arrested upon complaining about the ticket and was then subjected to a routine strip search.

The plaintiffs alleged violation of Fourth Amendment rights to be free from unreasonable search and seizure, and denial of constitutional and statutory equal protection rights under the Fourteenth Amendment and the federal Revenue Sharing and Safe Street Acts in that men were not subject to search upon arrest for similar minor offenses.

Under a consent decree the city is permanently enjoined from subjecting any woman to a search procedure more invasive than that to which similarly situated men are subjected. Further, the city cannot search any individual charged with a traffic, regulatory or misdemeanor offense unless specific facts establish a reasonable belief that the individual is concealing weapons or contraband. Prior written approval must be secured and a report made of the factors justifying the search and the items uncovered as a result. A cavity search is not permitted without a search warrant and must be conducted by or under the supervision of a physician.

Without a particularized suspicion that the detainee might harm herself or be in possession of contraband, visual observation of urination by police is an unreasonable strip search. DiLoreto v. Borough of Oaklyn (D.N.J.1990). Plaintiff, a pregnant woman, was detained for suspicion of a stolen car, which proved to be not stolen. The court noted that the Second, Fourth, Fifth, Seventh, Eighth and Tenth Circuit Courts of Appeal have invalidated searches under similar circumstances. See for example Weber v. Dell (2d Cir.1986), where a woman who was arrested for falsely reporting that a gun was involved in a fracus following a wedding was subjected to a cavity search.

4. High Tech Evidence

Forensic tests on body tissues or blood are an integral part of contemporary prosecutions. This evidence can exonerate as well as convict a defendant. The Supreme Court has ruled that police do not have a constitutional duty to preserve evidence that might exonerate criminal defendants. In Arizona v. Youngblood (S.Ct.1988), the police failed to use the best available techniques to test semen samples saved from the body and clothing of the boy whom defendant was charged with sodomizing. The police also failed to save samples of the semen, so that defendant was unable to run his own tests.

DNA Prints. Legal ramifications of DNA testing are being hammered out in courts across the country. DNA stands for deoxyribonucleic acid, a chemical found in all body cells except red blood cells, and carries an individual's genetic code. Thus DNA testing can be performed on hair, skin, tissue, semen, body fluids, white blood cells and fetal tissue. First introduced in 1986, DNA testing has been performed in thousands of paternity disputes and criminal investigations. The general judicial approach is to admit the DNA testing as a reliable scientific technique accepted by the scientific community as meeting the relevant test of Frye v. United States (D.C.Cir.1923). See Caldwell v. Georgia (Ga.S.Ct.1990), Spencer v. Virginia (Va. S.Ct.1989), and Perry v. State (Ala.Crim.App.1990).

Appellate courts that have rejected DNA evidence have done so largely for limited reasons. The most controversial issue regards standards for laboratory procedures. The principal concern is the possibility of false positive identifications. In United States v. Two Bulls (8th Cir.1990) the defendant was charged with raping a 13 year old girl. Semen stains on her underwear were subjected to a DNA profiling technique. In setting aside the conviction, the eighth circuit ruled that a proper foundation for admissibility of DNA typing requires a showing of scientific acceptability, of reliable testing procedures, and of use of these reliable procedures in the case at hand.

Several states require DNA testing of convicted offenders. Law enforcement proposals call for storing DNA specimens, and placing DNA test results of convicts and of evidence collected at crime scenes into national computers. Due process and privacy issues are implicated.

5. Hypnosis

A criminal defendant has a constitutional right to testify on her own behalf. This includes the right to use her own hypnotically induced testimony under the Supreme Court's ruling in Rock v. Arkansas (S.Ct.1987). A state's legitimate interest in barring unreliable testimony does not extend to an absolute exclusion of testimony which may be reliable. The Court noted that states are not in consensus on admissibility of hypnotically induced testimony, and left open the door for less than an absolute bar.

B. SENTENCING

A tenet of criminal law sociology holds that women are more amenable to rehabilitation than are men. To adjust the period of incarceration to the time needed to rehabilitate, women have been subjected to indeterminate sentencing for periods longer than the determinate minimum terms for men. These statutes have been held unconstitutional on equal protection grounds. State v. Chambers. However, statutes that provide for more severe sentences for men escapees than for women escapees have been upheld against equal protection challenges on the basis that male escapees pose a greater threat because women are not as prone to violence as are men. Wark v. State.

The death penalty is too severe a punishment for rape of an adult woman. A death sentence was set aside by the Supreme Court as disproportionate to the crime and excessive punishment forbidden by the Eighth Amendment. Coker v. Georgia (S.Ct. 1977).

Mandatory Registration. Mandatory registration of sexual offenders upon their release from prison is not a denial of equal protection because the purpose is not to punish, but to prevent future sex offenses from occurring. People v. Adams (Ill. App.1990). Similarly, the Supreme Court has ruled that proceedings under a statute providing that individuals found "sexually dangerous" may be committed to a maximum security institution are not criminal within the meaning of the Fifth Amendment's guarantee against self-incrimination. Allen v. Illinois (S.Ct.1986).

Probation Conditions. When a state may impose conditions relating to tobacco, alcohol and drug use on a pregnant or fertile probationer is less clear. Mandatory birth control for women has been imposed as a condition of probation, without investigation of possible medical implications. California v. Pointer (Cal.App.1984) ruled that a condition of probation which prohibited defendant from conceiving a child during the probationary period was reasonable since it was related to the crime of child endangerment for which the defendant was convicted. However, any such condition must be subjected to strict scrutiny as an invasion of the fundamental right of privacy. The case was remanded because less invasive alternative means were possible in that the child endangerment resulted from the mother's feeding her family a strict macrobiotic diet.

Where a probationer consumed alcohol in violation of his probation, a trial court imposed his previously suspended sentence. The eighth circuit reversed, although noting that the Eighth Amendment is not necessarily violated whenever an addict is punished for using a drug to which he is addicted. Wickham v. Dowd (8th Cir.1990). See Robinson v. California (S.Ct.1962), which said that imprisoning a person merely because of status as an addict shocks the moral conscience of reasonable persons and inflicts cruel and inhuman punishment prohibited by the federal constitution.

C. INCARCERATION

The extent to which prison authorities may curtail fundamental rights of prisoners has been the subject of numerous lawsuits.

Mandated Treatment. The right of privacy is implicated in mandatory medical treatment. In Washington v. Harper (S.Ct.1990) the Supreme Court ruled that a state may compel a prisoner, by force, to take anti-psychotic drugs without a judicial hearing. Prisoners are not entitled to strict scrutiny analysis when their fundamental rights are invaded; the correct standard of review is the rational basis test. The state here demonstrated a rational relationship to a legitimate penological interest. By extension, a state could prohibit a pregnant prisoner from smoking or compel a pregnant prisoner to have a blood transfusion or caesarian section.

Marital Rights. Prisoners do not have an absolute right to marry. The Supreme Court upheld a Missouri statute that prohibited inmates from marrying other inmates or civilians unless the prison superintendent determined that there were "compelling" reasons for the marriage. Reasons other than birth of a child or pregnancy would generally be found not compelling. Turner v. Safley (S.Ct. 1987).

Nor do federal male prisoners have a procreative right for artificial insemination of their wives. Goodwin v. Turner (8th Cir.1990). If allowed, equal protection obligations would compel the prison to allow artificial insemination of female prisoners by their husbands, citing Madyun v. Franzen (7th Cir.1983). The *Goodwin* court said that the significant expansion of medical services to a pregnant female population and the additional financial burden of added infant care would have a significant impact on limited prison financial and personnel resources. The rational basis standard applies to prisoners' rights. The defendant is not entitled to a strict scrutiny standard for alleged denial of his wife's procreative rights. Defendant, who was serving a five year term, and his 30 year old wife were concerned about the increased risk of birth defects as a result of increasing maternal age.

New York is among the states which provide for inmate conjugal visits. The state may prohibit an inmate who tests positive for AIDS from participating in the conjugal visit program. Determination that AIDS is a communicable disease provides a rational basis for disallowing participation. In Matter of Doe v. Coughlin (N.Y.Ct.App.1987).

For accommodation of privacy rights of prisoners where guards of the opposite sex are employed, see the discussion of Csizmadia v. Fauver in chapter fifteen. Cases are determined on a fact specific basis, with attempts to balance the employment rights of guards with the privacy rights of the prisoners.

Distant Incarceration. A major discrimination against women prisoners is confinement at facilities far removed from their homes. Males generally are incarcerated closer to home. Female inmates sentenced in the District of Columbia unsuccessfully challenged their confinement in a distant federal facility. The court said the assignment substantially served the District's goal of easing crowded facilities in the District. Pitts v. Thornburgh (D.C.Cir.1989).

Female inmates were also unsuccessful in challenging their inelegibility for early release under the District of Columbia Good Time Credits Act. No women who were serving terms of over one year could qualify because they were not incarcerated in the District. The women were not deprived of equal protection rights because some male prisoners were also sent outside the District, and female prisoners sentenced for less than a year did qualify for the early release. Jackson v. Thornburgh (D.C.Cir.1990).

Sex Segregated Prisons. Constitutional challenges to sex segregated prison facilities on grounds of cruel and inhuman punishment in depriving prisoners of the normal companionship of the opposite sex and encouraging unnatural sexual relations have been rejected by the courts. Stuart v. Heard. Women challenge single sex facilities as providing less access to educational and vocational programs, recreational facilities and work/study release programs. Special programs and facilities offered only to men in a county jail system violate equal protection rights of women. Molar v. Gates.

The court left to the county whether to extend the programs to women or eliminate them for the men.

Incarcerated Mothers. Although accurate statistics are not available, most incarcerated women appear to be single mothers who are responsible for the care of their children. Incarcerated women lose physical contact with their children when they are incarcerated and may lose legal custody as well. Lassiter v. Department of Social Services. Visiting privileges are not normally subject to judicial review, and local practices vary widely, from not allowing children to visit at all to providing nursery facilities.

Inadequate Medical Care. Deliberate indifference to the medical needs of prisoners violates the Eighth Amendment. Estelle v. Gamble (S.Ct.1976). Nonetheless, the unique medical needs of pregnant prisoners are seldom adequately attended. The concern for security is overriding, and each year a considerable number of "emergency" births take place in prison. Todaro v. Ward ordered that the medical system of a women's correctional facility be improved. Facts disclosed use of a dangerous x-ray machine, inappropriate work assignments for pregnant women, and interminable delays in primary and follow-up care. A single nurse, with only one office hour per day, handled intake for 380 inmates. She averaged 15 to 20 seconds per patient. An action for damages against federal prison officials for death of a prisoner because of failure to provide adequate medical care was allowed under the Eighth Amendment in Carlson v. Green. Similarly, Cleveland–Perdue v. Brutsche (7th Cir.1989).

Sexual Assault. Assault of male prisoners by other prisoners is not uncommon. The male victim of sexual abuse is usually slight and young, often white but sometimes minority. A black prisoner satisfying this profile who had previously been subjected to abuse was bunked with a prisoner with a known violent sexual assault record, and was again a victim. An action under § 1983 granted declaratory and injunctive relief requiring prison officials to provide inmates with reasonable protection for aggressive sexual assault. Withers v. Levine. The Supreme Court upheld punitive damages to a young male first time offender against a guard and others for failing to protect him from gross sexual assault by his cellmates. Smith v. Wade (S.Ct.1983).

Appendix 1

STATES WITH EQUAL RIGHTS AMENDMENTS

State	Year Adopted	
* Wyoming	1890	) "male and
		) female
Utah	1896	) citizens"
* Hawaii	1968	
Illinois	1971	
* Pennsylvania	1971	
Virginia	1971	
* Alaska	1972	
* Colorado	1972	
* Maryland	1972	
* Texas	1972	
* Washington	1972	
* Montana	1973	
* New Mexico	1973	
* Connecticut	1974	
Louisiana	1974	
* New Hampshire	1975	
* Massachusetts	1976	
[* New Jersey	1947	"All persons"]
[Indiana	1984	"All People"]

*Ratified the Federal Equal Rights Amendment

Additional states that ratified the federal ERA are: California, Delaware, Idaho, Indiana, Iowa, Kansas, Kentucky, Maine, Michigan, Minnesota, Nebraska, North Dakota, New York, Ohio, Oregon, Rhode Island, South Dakota, Tennessee, Vermont, West Virginia and Wisconsin. Five states later voted to rescind: Idaho, Nebraska, Tennessee, South Dakota and Kentucky. Kentucky's rescission was vetoed.

Two constitutional issues regarding ratification of the Equal Rights Amendment were addressed in Idaho v. Freeman (D.Idaho, 1981). The district court ruled that rescission by individual states prior to unrescinded ratification by three-fourths of the states is constitutional, and that Congressional extension of the period for ratification was unconstitutional. Review was granted and the judgment stayed by the Supreme Court. National Organization for Women v. Idaho; Carmen v. Idaho.

The federal equal rights amendment was first introduced to Congress in 1923, and was submitted to the states for ratification in 1972.

Proposed Equal Rights Amendment

Section 1. Equality of rights under the law shall not be denied or abridged by the United States or by any State on account of sex.

Section 2. The Congress shall have the power to enforce, by appropriate legislation, the provisions of this Article.

Section 3. This Amendment shall take effect two years after the date of ratification.

Appendix 2

SUPPLEMENTARY CASE READINGS

This nutshell is appropriate for use in an undergraduate course in sex discrimination when supplemented by readings from pertinent cases. Supreme Court decisions are available in most school libraries. The following cases are suggested as supplementary readings. Citations are found in the table of cases.

Part I. Reproductive Rights

Griswold v. Connecticut, Roe v. Wade, Harris v. McRae, Webster v. Reproductive Health Services.

Part II. Historical Development

Bradwell v. Illinois, Goesaert v. Cleary, Reed v. Reed, Frontiero v. Richardson, Craig v. Boren.

Part III. Contemporary Issues

Rostker v. Goldberg, Michael M. v. Superior Court of Sonoma County, Personnel Administrator of Massachusetts v. Feeney, Santa Clara Pueblo v. Martinez, Kirchberg v. Feenstra, Mississippi University for Women v. Hogan.

Part IV. Remedial Legislation

Phillips v. Martin–Marietta Corp., Corning Glass Works v. Brennan, Dothard v. Rawlinson, County of Washington v. Gunther, Texas Department of Community Affairs v. Burdine, California Federal Savings and Loan v. Guerra, Meritor Savings Bank v. Vinson, Watson v. Fort Worth Bank and Trust Co., New York State Club Ass'n v. City of New York, Johnson v. Transportation Agency, Santa Clara County, International Union, UAW v. Johnson Controls.

Part V. Criminal Law

Washington v. Wanrow, Maine v. Anaya, Michael M. v. Superior Court of Sonoma County, New York v. Liberta, California v. Superior Court of Alameda County.

With the exception of three Supreme Court cases, Santa Clara Pueblo v. Martinez, Webster v. Reproductive Health Services and International Union, UAW v. Johnson Controls, the cases listed here are reproduced or discussed in SEX–BASED DISCRIMINATION, TEXT, CASES AND MATERIALS, 3d Ed., by Herma Hill Kay, American Casebook Series, West Publishing Co., 1988. The statutory appendix to Kay's book includes Title VII of the Civil Rights Act of 1964, as amended; Post Civil War Civil Rights Acts; The Equal Pay Act of 1963; Title IX of the Education Amendments of 1972, as amended, and Civil Rights Restoration Act of 1987.

INDEX

References are to Pages

381

MILITARY SERVICE—Cont'd
Military schools, male only, 96–97.
Women and, 49, 80, 83, 96, 103–106.

MINORITY WOMEN
Economic concerns, 180, 193.
Health, 9, 375.
Incarcerated, 352.
Military service, 104.
Native American, 123–125, 166.
Title VII, 230.

MINORS, 12, 23–24, 51, 98, 131
See also Abortion, Minors; Contraception, Minors; Criminal
    Law, Defendants, age and sex profile; Criminal Law,
    Victims; Education, First Amendment Rights, Pregnant
    students; Health Care, Teens; Incest; Prostitution, Juve-
    nile; Rape, Statutory; Sterilization.

NAMES, 54, 125–127

NATIONAL LABOR RELATIONS ACT, 196

NECESSARIES
See Marital Partners.

NONMARITAL PARTNERS
    See also Child Custody; Child Support; Single Sex Partners.
Property interests, 169, 173–174.
Unwed fathers, 168, 170–173.
Unwed mothers, 137–148, 180.

PAY EQUITY
See Title VII, Bennett Amendment; Title VII, Comparable
    Worth.

PENSIONS
See Divorce and Dissolution, Pensions and professional degrees;
    Employment, Pensions; Title VII, Pensions.

POLICE POWER, STATE, 54–55, 63–65, 110

PORNOGRAPHY, 129–131, 339–343

PRECEDENT, 18, 343

PREGNANCY
See Abortion; Caesarian Sections; Contraception; Employ-
    ment, Pregnancy; Fertility; Health Care; Medical Mal-
    practice; Product Liability; Sterlization; Title VII, Preg-
    nancy.

PRISONS AND JAILS, 351, 372–376

PRIVACY, RIGHT OF, 4, 10, 36, 69, 137–143, 355, 372

PRIVATE SECTOR
See Equal Pay Act; Public Accommodations; Title VII, all
   headings.

PRIVILEGES AND IMMUNITIES CLAUSE, 55, 57

PRODUCT LIABILITY
Contraceptives and generic drugs, 42–49.
Tort law, 38–39.
Uniform Commercial Code, 40–41.

PROSTITUTION
Customers, 100–356.
Definition, 356.
Juvenile, 328.
Sex, classification by, 100.

PUBLIC ACCOMMODATIONS, 133–136, 308–310.

RAPE
Abortion following, 20.
Civil action for, 345.
Consent as bar to, 332–337.
Definition, 328.
Evidence, corroborating, 332.
Forcible, 332, 334.
Jury instructions, 334.
Lie detector, use of, 330.
Marital and domestic partners, 338.
Rape shield laws, 337.
Resistance, 334–335.
Self defense against, 368.
Sex, classification by, 97–99.
Statutory, 97–99, 328.

RATIONAL BASIS TEST
Gender classification, with "bite", 74–87.
Statement of, 66–67.
Traditional application, 72–74, 144, 181.

REGULATIONS, 293

REMEDIES
See Affirmative Action; Civil Remedies; Domestic Violence;
   Equal Pay Act, Remedies; Title IX, Remedies; Title VII,
   Remedies.

†